# THE COMPLETE
# BRITTANY SPANIEL

When Dual Ch. Avono Happy posed for this picture, some measurements were taken of him to serve as a guide in writing the standard. Other dogs also were studied and measured before the standard was completed.

# The Complete
# Brittany Spaniel

by

Maxwell Riddle

Fourth Printing—1978
HOWELL BOOK HOUSE
730 Fifth Avenue,
New York, N.Y. 10019

# Contents

# Foreword

NO man walks alone. A book is never the work of one man alone, whether it is a technical book such as this one or a novel. The author is indebted to many people, living and dead, for their help. The following are only a few of the acknowledgements which could be made.

In preparing this book, I have had the use of three great libraries: those of the American Kennel Club and the Cleveland Public Library; and the private library of Herm David. I have had the use of the American, Canadian, and French Kennel Club stud books. A. Hamilton Rowan Jr., secretary of the American Kennel Club, gave personal help. The Canadian Kennel Club permitted me to check through the records of every Brittany Spaniel registered in Canada up to July, 1971.

I gratefully acknowledge the help given to me by Jacques R. Joubert, brother of René; Mrs. Gertrude L. Thebaud, widow of Louis A. Thebaud; and by Mme Monica Choulot, daughter of Juan Pugibet. Mrs. René Joubert and Mrs. Walter B. Kleeman also supplied valuable information and pictures. Mme Genie Rundle also helped in supplying information on the modern Brittany Spaniel in France.

Jack L. Whitworth and Donald L. Benjamin supplied valuable early information. John G. and Ellyn Lee, and Mr. and Mrs. James

Cohen also helped. So did Bill Brown and his staff at the *American Field*. I am indebted, too, to Mrs. Nicky Bissell, brilliant editor of the *American Brittany Magazine,* and to Mrs. LaReine Pittman, secretary of the Missouri regional club.

In Canada, Jack Mayer of Moncton, N.B., Bill McClure of Manotic, Ontario, and Mrs. Pat Ristau of Regina, Sask. helped.

The magazine, *Brittany Field and Bench,* which has become the *American Brittany Magazine,* has been a treasure chest of information. Jack Whitworth and the Lees supplied most of the past issues for reference.

The people who made the magazine, and who have kept its high quality, deserve both credit and thanks. They are Jack Whitworth, Dr. David Ruskin, Hugo Blasberg, Mrs. Evelyn Monte, Dr. Allen Truex, Dr. Fred Z. White, Mrs. Nicky Bissell, and others. In addition, Dr. White was the author of the *Brittany Spaniel In America.*

A special thanks goes to Señora Thelma von Thaden of the Mexican Kennel Club for her help. To others whom I may have overlooked, though not intentionally, my grateful thanks.

*Maxwell Riddle*

# A Note on Brittany
# Names and Spellings

THE names given to dogs are often complicated. Owners may misspell them in their registration applications. Importers may misspell them. Confusion sometimes results. In this book, the author has used the actual names registered, even though the dogs have been customarily known by a slightly different name.

There are two examples which may be used. The first American champion was an imported dog. In both the French and American studbooks, the dog is listed as Hasbask Guid de Charvogue. But the dog was usually known as Habask Guid de Charvogue.

Louis A. Thebaud imported Franche du Cosquerou. The dog was sent to Eudore Chevrier's kennels at Winnipeg to be used at stud. Chevrier returned him to Thebaud, who then sent him to Rene Joubert at Detroit. This dog became, under Joubert's handling, one of the most famous of all time. He impressed the entire Midwest sporting world. Everyone—Thebaud, Joubert, and all sportsmen—knew the dog as Fanche. But he was registered in the French, American, and Canadian stud books as Franche.

Many of the early dogs were registered first in the *Field Dog Stud Book*. Dr. R. C. Busteed registered a dog in that stud book as Broad

Arrow of Richmont. The dog was later registered in the American Kennel Club as Broad Archer of Richmont. As such, he became a dual champion.

In general, French breeders have used "de," which means "of" without capitalizing. Most Americans, and some Canadians, have capitalized it. However, this has not always been the case, so that no generalization can be made.

Typists may further confuse the matter by using the lower case once and the upper case the next time. Thus, Mae de Cornean is the French name and spelling. But it sometimes appears as Mae De Cornean.

"Cornouaille" is the Breton name for Cornwall. Dr. Chester Keough named his kennel MacEochaidh. It is said to be the Gaelic for Keough. The "Mac" makes it "son of."

## The Michigan State Dog

IN 1957, the Gaines Dog Research Center suggested that states should have official state dogs. Harry Miller, then director of the Research Center, argued that states had official state flowers and, many of them, official state birds. Why not a state dog? Harvey Barcus, of the *Detroit News,* thought this was a great idea. Barcus talked to state officials, and then convinced *The News* to conduct a state-wide poll. The breed which would get the most votes would then be declared the official Michigan State Dog.

Ballots were sent out over the state and Barcus, who was dog editor, also published one in *The News.* When balloting had ended, 29,245 people had thought enough of the project to vote. Of these, 6407 voted for the Brittany Spaniel. The breed led all the others by a wide margin. This was adequate testimony on the popularity of the Brittany Spaniel in Michigan, and the place it had won in the hearts of sportsmen in less than 25 years.

Detroit City Historian, George W. Stark, also was interested in the project. "There is definite evidence," he reported, "that the Brittany Spaniel was brought here by Cadillac when he founded Detroit in 1701, and began to colonize the Detroit Shore." We do not know the source of his evidence. But those wishing to believe it can claim that the Brittany Spaniel arrived in Canada and what would later become the United States with some of the first white settlers.

# 1

# The Development of
# Bird Dogs

---

THE arts of the pointing dog and the flushing spaniel were developed more than 300 years ago. These were dogs with highly developed aptitudes for using wind borne scents in locating upland game birds. There are no names in this period. We do not know how the training and hunting procedures were developed. But we can speculate upon why they arose.

During the 16th Century—the great age of discovery—a landed gentry came into being. World discovery was followed by world conquest. The treasuries of the explorer nations—England, France, Spain, and Portugal—were filled with gold.

So were the pockets of the merchants and artisans. From these two groups there came the landed gentry. They were not nobles. They were gentlemen. They had the leisure time for field sports, for hunting and fishing. This was particularly so in England.

By 1650, a wealthy middle class had sprung up. This was particularly so in England. More and more men found more and more time to fish for trout or to hunt for upland game. The passion which these men had for hunting and fishing led to a demand for authoritative texts on the subjects.

Izaak Walton is one of the most famous of all the world's authors. He wrote excellent biographies. But he lives for most of us because of *The Compleat Angler*. The first edition was published in 1653 and had 13 chapters. The fifth edition, published in 1676, had 21.

In 1674, Nicholas Cox wrote *The Gentleman's Recreation*. Cox had a remarkable understanding of dogs, and of their uses in the field. In his own time, and for a century later, Cox was as famous as Walton. The sixth edition of his book was published in 1721.

Cox included a section on partridge hunting with dogs. We quote it here because it is a classic description of the use of dogs.

"There is no Art to taking Partridges so excellent and pleasant as by the help of a Setting Dog; wherefore before we proceed to the Sport we shall give you an Account of what this Setting Dog is.

"You are to understand then, that a Setting Dog is a certain lusty Land Spaniel, taught by nature to hunt the Partridge more than any chace whatever, running the fields over with such Alacrity and Nimbleness as if there was no Limit to his Fury and Desire;

"And yet by Art under such excellent Command, that in the very height of his Career by a Hem or Sound of his Master's voice, he shall stand, or gaze about him, look in his Master's Face and observe his Directions, whether to proceed, stand still or retire:

"Nay, when he is even just upon his prey, that he may even take it up in this Mouth, yet his Obedience is so framed by Art, that presently he shall either stand still, or fall down flat on his Belly, without daring either to make any Noise or Motion till his Master comes to him, and then he will proceed in all Things to follow his Directions.

"Having a Dog thus qualified by Art and Nature, take him with you where Partridges do haunt, there cast off your Dog, and by some Word of Encouragement with which he is acquainted, engage him to range, but never too far from you.

"And see that he beat his Ground justly and even, without casting about, or flying now here, now there, which the mettle of some will do, if not corrected and reproved. And therefore when you perceive this Fault, you must presently call him in with a Hem, and so check him that he dare not do the like again for that Day, so he will range afterwards with more Temperance, ever and anon looking in his Master's face, as if he would gather from thence whether he did well or ill.

"If in your Dog's ranging you perceive him to flop on the sudden, or stand still, you must then make in to him (for without doubt he has set the partridge) and as soon as you come to him, command him to go nearer him, but if he goes not, but either lies still or stands shaking of his tail, as who would say Here they are under my nose, and withal now and then looks back, then cease from urging him further and take your circumference, walking fast with a careless Eye, looking straight before the Nose of the Dog, and thereby see how the Covey lie, whether close or straggling.

"Then commanding your dog to lie still, draw forth your Net and prick one End to the Ground and spread your net all open, and so cover as many of the Partridges as you can, which done, make in with a Noise, and spring up the Partridges, which shall no sooner rise but they will be entangled in the Net. And if you shall let go the old Cock and Hen it will not only be an act like a Gentleman, but a means to increase your pastime."

Thus, almost 300 years ago, the art of the setting spaniel was defined. Might we not almost say, the art of the Brittany Spaniel?

By implication, Cox tells us how the Setters got their name. They kept game "setting" until the hunter could come up. Cox links "setting" and "spaniel," and this is important. But he does not explain the origin of "spaniel." He is not interested in specific breeds, only in performance.

In his day, there were no stud books. The passionate interest in breed type had not yet developed. Yet even in 1670, a family of Land Spaniels existed. They probably differed greatly in type.

They were alike in having excellent scenting powers, and in using body scents carried to them by air currents. From these Land Spaniels came the Setters. And from some of them, and from other spaniels elsewhere, there arose the Brittany Spaniel.

# 2

# Origin of the Spaniel

MOST writers have given the origin of the name, spaniel, to a family of dogs which came from Spain. In this group are the English Pointer, the Setters, many of the pointing breeds of France and Italy, and those dogs we now call Spaniels. It is supposed that though these breeds developed in other countries, they are still descendants of dogs which came from Spain. Yet the problem is puzzling.

The Greeks called the Spanish Peninsula, Iberia, and its people, Iberians. After the Celtic invasions of Northern Spain in the 7th and 6th centuries B.C., the Greeks called the people, Celtiberians.

The Greeks were interested in both dogs and hunting. They do not mention hunting dogs in Iberia. Had they found such dogs there, it seems certain that they would have called them Iberian dogs. The Celts had moved across the Pyrenees, and had settled in Northern and Central Spain. They are believed to have brought several types of dogs with them. But there is no record of a Celtic dog of spaniel type.

In the 4th Century B.C., the Carthaginians conquered most of the coastal areas of Southern Spain. The Romans drove out the Carthaginians in 206 B.C. during the second Punic War. The Romans, too, were interested in hunting. But they do not mention a Carthaginian dog of spaniel type.

The two provinces seized from Carthage were *Hispania Citerior* and *Hispania Ulterior*. Hispania was the ancient Latin name for Spain. Spaniards call their country *España,* pronounced Es-pan-ya. The relationship between Hispania and España is obvious.

Questions immediately arise. Did the Carthaginians develop the spaniel family? Did the Romans, finding the dogs in their new provinces of Hispania, name them after the provinces? If not, who did? And did the Romans take the dogs into France, and later to Britain? If so, why didn't they take the dogs home to Rome?

The Velasquez Spanish Dictionary suggests that the word spaniel is derived from the French, *espagneul.* Webster's Third International Dictionary also states that spaniel is derived from the Middle French word for Spaniard, *espaignol.*

This would indicate that spaniels were taken into France, and later into Britain. If so, then there is meaning to the modern French, *epagneul,* and the various English terms, spainell, spanyell, spanyol, and finally spaniel.

The answer is not so simply reached. The earliest known reference to the spaniel is in a Welsh manuscript, dated about 300 A.D. It mentions a "native spaniel." The next reference also is from Wales. It appears in the laws of King Howell Dda, who ruled from 943 to 950. These laws list the Greyhound, Tracker, Buckhound, and Spaniel. The latter was said to be of equal value to the king's Buckhound, or to a stallion.

It is not until 1387 that spaniel appears in French. In that year, Gaston de Foix, or Gaston Phoebus, wrote his *Livre de Chasse.* Gaston de Foix lived near the Spanish border. At times he had as many as one thousand dogs. Some of them were spaniels, and Gaston said they came from Spain.

Edward C. Ash studied the paintings which illuminated the famous Gaston Phoebus manuscript. One picture showed spaniels fairly close to modern Springer Spaniel type. In another, the spaniel was clipped in Poodle fashion.

Edward, second Duke of York, based his *The Master of Game* on the *Livre de Chasse.* It was written between 1406 and 1413. He wrote that "hounds for the hawk and spaniels, for their kind, cometh from Spain, notwithstanding that there are many in other countries."

It will be seen later that some authorities have suggested that the Brittany Spaniel and the Welsh Springer Spaniel are closely related. The latter is a red and white dog.

To summarize, the preponderance of the evidence is that the spaniel

Reproduction of an 18th Century painting by Jean Baptiste Oudry, showing an early type of spaniel found in France and The Netherlands.

family gets its name from the Roman provinces of Hispania on the southern coast of the Iberian Peninsula. They were known in Wales before they were found in England, Scotland or France. It is possible that the name has no connection with Spain, and that the original spaniels were taken from Wales to Spain. There they prospered. From Spain, they then spread into France, England and Scotland.

# 3

# Origin of the Brittany Spaniel

---

$D$OG shows became popular about one hundred years ago. Most dog breeds, as we know them today, do not date before that time. The years after 1870 were those of great change. The industrial revolution was destroying the largely rural order. Isolated areas were being connected and opened up by railroads.

The need for cattle, drover, and sheep dogs was disappearing. Isolated, and even less isolated areas, had their own locally developed breeds, or strains of breeds. Suddenly, the dog fanciers of the day realized that the breeds which they admired so much were disappearing.

Dog shows helped to save these breeds. Fanciers gathered together. They studied the various strains they had developed. The best points of each strain were selected. Breed standards were set up. Stud books were established. The era of the purebred dog had begun.

The Breton peasant was not wealthy. In Brittany, as in the rest of rural France, local varieties of hunting dogs, principally setters and spaniels, had been developed. There were also the pointing breeds known as Braques. These local dogs were excellent workmen. But the fancy of the day was the English dog.

Wealthy English sportsmen brought their own beautifully trained dogs with them for the shooting season. These were sometimes Pointers, but more often English Setters and Irish Setters. A few spaniels, probably the red and white Welsh Springers, were brought in. Some of these sportsmen left their dogs with local people to await the next shooting season.

To show what happened, let us quote from John Kemp, whose *Shooting And Fishing In Lower Brittany* was published in 1859. Kemp spent years in hunting and fishing, so that he was one of the great authorities of his day.

"If, however, I had to select the brace of dogs best adapted for every kind of shooting throughout the season, I should, without hesitation, prefer a brace of well-broken spaniels; but as no dogs are more difficult to obtain, and I have just a sneaking affection for an animal with a little more dash than the aforesaid breed, I have tried the following cross with success.

"I have put a spaniel to a well-bred setter bitch, and been lucky enough to combine the ranging qualities of the latter and the hunting perseverance of the former. The French have tried this cross frequently. I lately purchased one of the produce; and I can say that few dogs perform better in the field than this one. My reason for discarding Pointers is, that they are too thin skinned for the work required in Landes for partridge shooting, and are of little use, as every one knows for cover shooting."

Kemp writes of the shooting at Callac and Mael Carhaiz in the Côtes du Nord, and at Huelgoat and Carhaix in the Finistere. But he hunted and fished in other areas as well. At the time he wrote, it had been announced that a railroad would be built from Nantes to Brest. It would make a "grand detour" around the north coast. Of Callac—a most important district in Brittany Spaniel history—he wrote:

"It is a capital district for shooting that quite rivals the preserves near Cairhaix . . . I knew most of the people in the country, and consequently had no difficulties thrown in my way by farmers and others. Strangers who have dropped in have found it the contrary, because they have managed to excite the jealousy of the natives by exhibitions of much slaughtered game, and by their general behaviour. A mild and inoffensive individual would get on well with the 'men of Callac,' jealous and sensitive though they are respecting field sports."

Kemp supplies clear and irrefutable evidence that as early as 1850,

local French sportsmen were crossing their spaniels with English Setters. They were doing so to get a dog superior to either—the dog
that eventually would be the Brittany Spaniel.

About 1910, M. Le Comte Le Conteux de Canteleu drew up a
chart of current French breeds. He lists one of them as the *Chien
de Bretagne,* the dog of Brittany. For reasons not known today, he
did not call it the *Epagneul Bretagne*—the Brittany Spaniel.

Louis De Lajarrige, who wrote the *Manuel Pratique de L'Amateur
De Chiens,* followed the Comte Le Conteux de Canteleu's chart. But
De Lajarrige relied upon the research of Ronan de Kermadec and
others. And by their day, the breed had become known officially as
the Brittany Spaniel.

In 1906, Major P. Grand-Chavin, a cavalry officer and veterinarian,
was assigned to the garrison at Pontivy. His job was to classify the
cavalry horses, and to order discarded those which he considered
unfit. He was also to search the provinces of Morbihan, Finistere,
and Côtes du Nord for suitable horses which might be purchased.

Everywhere he went, he noticed small spaniels with short tails,
or no tails. They had rather short ears for a spaniel. Their colors
were white-orange, white-liver, and white-black. Some were tri-colors.
The major reported that they had, what he called a "short gait."

It is sometimes difficult to translate words representing colors. Moreover, words for color often change in meaning from time to time.
Thus, early writers on the Brittany Spaniel used the word *marron.*
This has been translated as "maroon." To us, this is a shade of very
dark red. Modern French dictionaries translate marron as dark chestnut or mahogany. The latter is a very dark reddish brown or liver
color. Since liver and mahogany are more familiar terms to Americans,
we use these terms, instead of maroon or chestnut.

Now while the major's job was to classify horses, he seems to
have done so in a leisurely manner. This allowed him many full
days of hunting, a sport in which he was both enthusiastic and profi-
cient. Also, since he was both a horseman and a veterinarian, he
had an excellent knowledge of animal conformation and field
performance.

Major Grand-Chavin found the dogs of the area to have remarkable
scenting powers. They braved the most tangled thickets in their search
for woodcock. They were utterly fearless in crossing rivers and canals.
And they could chase a hare for at least three quarters of an hour
over rough country.

Señor Juan Pugibet of Villa Obregon, near Vera Cruz, Mexico, was
the first to bring Brittany Spaniels to North America. Señor Pugibet

French Dual Ch. and 1966 national field Ch. Laskar de Saint Tugen, owned By Madame Marchand. *Dim photo.*

began a book on the history of the Brittany Spaniel. Unfortunately, he died before it could be completed. His daughter, Monique, has made available to the author that part which he had written.

Señor Pugibet, of whom more later, translated and quoted from an article by Ronan de Kermadec. The latter was a pioneer Brittany fancier. He was a judge of all breeds in France, and he was at one time vice president of the Brittany Spaniel Club of France. The article appeared in *La Vie à la Campagne* in September, 1923. At the time, at least, de Kermadec was convinced that the Brittany Spaniel was closely related to the Welsh Springer Spaniel. Here is Señor Pugibet's translation.

"It was very tempting to suppose that the Brittany Spaniel was only a variety of the French Spaniel. But it would be very difficult for those who thought so, to explain how a long-headed and long-lined dog could have been able to produce a short-headed and short-lined dog. The character is more different yet: The French Spaniel is a very quiet dog, the Brittany full of life, activity, and as a good Welsh must be, single minded.

"The study of this dog with its swarming animation and the examination of his skull and anatomy, suggested to M. Paul Pegnin and to myself, that the Brittany Spaniel and the Welsh Spaniel were only two branches of the same origin.

"Knowing the ethnical affinities of those two countries: Wales and French Brittany, and that both have the same kind of rough coated hounds, the hypothesis built on the study of the skeleton becomes a certainty. And that resemblance is evident because an English gentleman residing in French Brittany, used to tell me: 'One day I will bring from my country a short tail Brittany Spaniel;' and (he) was always establishing a parallel between both breeds.

"It is a fact that most of the typical subjects are found among the white and orange families and the white and mahogany, sure evidence they are from French Spaniel blood, and the best among those have signs of that cross: cephalic profile and the shape of the ears. Is that the reason buyers prefer light colored dogs? Maybe it is also because mahogany and roan colored dogs are not easily distinguished in the woods for quick shooters.

"It is not only what we have said above, which connects the Brittany Spaniel with the Welsh Springer. When the woodcock hunters were so pleased with him, his setting aptitudes were weak and always (he) was ready to flush the bird when ordered, and sometimes before. He did that, barking like a spaniel.

"He flushed so much that, before sportsmen began to breed the pure Brittany Spaniels, some hunters, to make him more staunch, conceived the idea to cross him with well chosen setters. A long time ago that

Juan Pugibet, a pioneer fancier, is believed to have been the first sportsman to bring the Brittany Spaniel to America. His home was Villa Obregon, Vera Cruz, Mexico. He died there in 1945.

A group of breed immortals performing the breed's work: (l. to r.) Dual Ch. Angelique De Bretagne, Fld. Ch. Broad Archer of Richmont, Fld. Ch. Allamuchy Valley Addie and Dual Ch. Avono Happy.

cross was useful and beneficial, improving the staunchness and the power of scent and contributing to make him a more useful dog in the field. But that cross should not be continued without danger of seriously modifying the character, aptitudes, and originality of the breed, which has the special qualities of both spaniels and setters.

"To prevent the effect of new crosses, the breeders are keeping away from mating even typical dogs not born short-tailed and the Judges did not reward in shows dogs not born short tailed, this character being the base in selecting the breeding dogs from the beginning."

Some comments on this early article need to be made. Modern readers will consider the Welsh Springer Spaniel as it is today. Breeding to such a dog would be disastrous for Brittany Spaniels. The modern Welsh Springer is not very fast afield. And it is purely a flushing dog. R. de Kermadec was more knowledgeable about bench dogs than field performance. Certainly long before his time, the dogs which were to become Brittany Spaniels were staunch pointing dogs. A decade later, French breeders were to eliminate the requirement that dogs born with tails were not to be used for breeding.

On the other hand, the Welsh Springer Spaniel of today is much different than was the Welsh Springer of 1900. In those days, in England, a litter of spaniels would be born. Some might be small, and would be called Cocker Spaniels. Some would compete first as Cockers, then would exceed 25 to 28 pounds in weight and would then compete as Springers. Those Springers born liver and white or black and white, would compete as English Springers. Those born orange or red and white would compete as Welsh Springers. Yet both might have come from the same litter.

Pictures extant of the Brittany Spaniels of the 1900 period show them to look very much like the modern English Springer Spaniel field type. There is, in this breed, a wide divergence in type between bench Springers and field Springers. One could say that, at least in type, the Brittany Spaniel has vastly improved since 1900, while the field Springers have equally deteriorated. Each reader must decide for himself how de Kermadec's theory fits into the story of the Brittany.

There are several versions of the following story. It is taken from the *annuaire* (Year Book) of the Brittany Spaniel Club of France for 1933. The author was M. Mège, the well known breeder. While the story, in any form, is supposed to be only a legend, it is interesting to compare it, in both time and substance with the quotations given earlier from the Kemp book. Again, the translation is by Señor Pugibet.

"About a century ago, there were two Englishmen who came to Brittany to shoot woodcock. They settled down at Pontou, a little town situated in the valley of Bouron, bordering on the National Road, Paris to Brest, fifteen kilometers from Morlaix.

"These Englishmen brought with them several small dogs, white and lemon, long tails, in height about 17½ to 19 inches, cobby built, with small ears. They were perfect in the woods.

"An old hunter of this region, who accompanied these Englishmen, had a bitch, white and mahogany, looking very much like the English dogs. This bitch, coming in season, the old hunter bred her to one of the English dogs. The resulting litter consisted of a mixture of black and white, white and orange with long tails, and also two curiosities. One had no tail and 'pattes de grenouille' (a free translation might mean 'frog footed'). A second one was considered a curiosity as he also had no tail. This dog proved himself to be wonderful in the field and was therefore largely used for stud purposes. In all his get there were many without tails, frequently little stubs. The original were much lighter in build and in appearance, very nervous, small boned and very cobby. For a long time they were small and runty. This was undoubtedly due to the feeding which consisted largely of milk, potatoes, and pan cakes.

"From all time, this breed has been known as a dog good on all game. He hunted on a gallop with high head marking his point, very fond of brush. When hunting a hare or a rabbit he gave tongue. He was noted as being extra good in the swamps and woods, and a natural retriever. The Brittany of today is not the same in bone, head and line of back, due to careful breeding."

In his book, *Le Chien,* the renowned French veterinarian and dog authority, Dr. Fernand Mèry, has a short account of the origin of the Brittany Spaniel. As will be seen, it differs somewhat from other accounts. Dr. Mèry has very kindly given me permission to quote from it.

"It was in 1906 that the veterinarian, Major P. Grand Chavin, gave an official description of them. He described them as 'little spaniels almost all with a short tail, a nearly homogeneous breed, and with a white-mahogany, white-orange, or white-black coat. These little animals are appealing because of the wide-awake appearance, a wide-awake bearing, a good expression in the eye, and (they) appear intelligent.'

"Since 1896, one has seen French spaniels of the Breton breed in shows. But the true Breton Spaniel will not make an appearance in the great Paris Exposition until 1904. This first (one) 'Max de Callac' was the son of a little bird dog from Monts d'Arrhee, named 'Cora:'

she herself an issue of a black and flame setter, and of a French Spaniel of the light breed, and of a white-mahogany color. Descendants of 'Max' were in their turn crossed with these little spaniels, a more or less cross-breed of Braque (author: a French Pointer) which were quite numerous in the north of Finisterre, and on the coasts of the North. Forewarned, breeders managed to save and to better these families of white-liver which were for a long time the predominant strain.

"The white-orange would have as origin, Scottish setters brought to Brittany by M. de Moll. The offspring were then crossed with Welsh Springers. One knows from a sure source that there was introduced Irish Setter blood and English spaniel to favor the trips of more and more numerous English hunters, who came to Brittany with their dogs to hunt woodcock; which explains the persistance in the interior countryside of the old type white-liver, while the new white-orange breed progressed on the northern shores."

We suppose that when Dr. Mèry refers to "black and flame" setters, and to "Scottish setters," he means the Gordon Setter.

The passion of the Brittany Spaniel for woodcock, and of those sportsmen who considered woodcock hunting the supreme sport, is illustrated in a story told by Ronan de Kermadec. He had the pleasure of hunting with His Royal Highness, Prince Albert of Monaco, one of the great ornithologists of his day.

Their hunting companion was a Brittany Spaniel named Sam, and they hunted in the Forest of Rambouillet. So specialized was Sam that when he came on point, he was almost certainly pinning a woodcock.

De Kermadec tells the story of the crossing of the English Setter with the French Spaniel belonging to the Breton hunter, Lulzac. But he has Lulzac being the game keeper for M. de Pontavice, a pioneer Brittany breeder close to the end of the 19th century.

Perhaps in summary, a reasonable statement of the origin of the Brittany Spaniel is this:

The Brittany Spaniel is the result of the crossing of English Setters with small French land spaniels. This process began as early as 1850, and possibly earlier. The English Setter was itself developed from some of the swifter land spaniels of England, and possibly Wales. In the interior of Brittany, liver and white dogs predominated. In the coastal areas, orange and white colors were prominent. By 1904, the Brittany Spaniel had evolved into a distinct breed.

# 4

# The Tail-less Brittany

ALL accounts agree that at some point in French Spaniel history, a dog was born without a tail. Most accounts believe that this occurred during a French Spaniel-English Setter cross. At first, this was seized upon as a distinctive feature of the new breed.

After many arguments, it was decided that dogs born with tails could be registered. But the tails were to be docked close to the body. Later, a further relaxation was made. A short, stubby tail was to be allowed.

One is forced to wonder why sportsmen docked the tails of their hunting dogs. Some of the answers are supplied in an entry in *The Sportsman's Dictionary* by Henry James Pye, Esquire. We quote here from the fifth edition, published in 1807.

The entry is entitled: "The Benefit Of Cutting The Tip Of The Spaniel's Tail Or Stern."

> "It is necessary that this be done when he is a whelp, for several reasons: First, by doing so, worms are prevented from breeding there; and in the next place, if it be not cut he will be less forward in pressing hastily into the coverts after his game, and besides it will make the dog appear more beautiful."

One can analyze this in the following way. The tails of sheep are always docked. If they are not, flies lay their eggs in the hair about the rectum and set-on of the tail. The eggs hatch into maggots, and these invade the rectum. Infection and death are likely to follow.

Spaniels, cross-bred with Setters seem to inherit the long tail of the Setters. That is, on the English Setter, the tail tip will reach the hock joint. The same tail, upon a spaniel, will reach the ground.

Such a tail will pick up burrs. And these spaniels were being used in the copses and brushwood. They had to press into briars. Among the English Setters of today, there are those known as "tail beaters." They hunt merrily, waving or beating their tails back and forth.

Such dogs invariably slash their tails into bloody ribbons when in briar country. The scar tissue, which forms, will not permit hair to grow, and it bleeds easily. The author of the above quotation is implying that such dogs may not willingly enter heavy cover, whether it contains briars or not.

And then he adds: "and besides it will make the dog appear more beautiful." Perhaps Pye meant by this that the dog would not have a bloody, hairless, scar tissue tail. And he may have meant that an abnormally long tail would drag behind the dog and make it appear both clumsy and slow.

In the early days of the Brittany Spaniel in America, the fanciers included converts from the Pointer and Setter ranks. They felt that there was nothing so beautiful as the sky-pointing, stiffly held tail of a bird dog on point. So some sportsmen did not dock the tails of their Brittany Spaniels. Great discussions followed. But eventually, all agreed that the Brittany should have no tail, or one docked very short.

There have been other reasons why men have docked the tails of their dogs. They must be mentioned at our point in time because we cannot know what influence they had upon the custom. For a time, men believed that docking the tail prevented rabies. And the tails of fighting dogs were taken off at the body. They were a serious impediment, and they offered an easy hold for the adversary. And they bled easily. Docking neatly eliminated the problems as it did the tail.

# 5

# Why the Brittany Spaniel Became Popular

---

Two of the most common questions asked of dog fanciers are these: "How did you happen to get into the dog game?" "How did you happen to pick this breed?" As far as the first question is concerned, the answer is quite simple. Sportsmen need dogs to help them to locate game. Declining game populations have made the use of a dog mandatory, not only to locate game, but to find and to retrieve the cripples which are brought down.

The second question is less simply answered. First, sportsmen who want hunting dogs fall into many categories. The passion of one may be the trailing dog. He may be a rabbit hunter, and the voice of a Beagle stirs him as does that of no other dog. So he gets a Beagle. Another may be stirred by the sight of a pointing dog frozen on a solid point. Still another may get his greatest thrills from seeing a flushing dog outwit a running and dodging pheasant.

Cynical observers have have sometimes explained the choice of breed in this way. The sportsman cannot control the dog he has. Or it is a quitter, or it has a poor nose. He then equates all the other dogs of this breed with his own. A new breed comes along. Perhaps the propaganda for it is intense. He is ready to switch, and he does.

Yves du Cosquerou on point backed by Fenntus, his mother and Fanche, his father.

Breeders of bench dogs may find the competition too great for them. But they are hobbyists and animal lovers. They cannot defeat the established breeders, or more likely, believe that they can't. So they switch to a new breed.

Our interest is the Brittany Spaniel. To some extent all the reasons given above have been responsible for the steady rise in popularity of the breed. People have come to the Brittany Spaniel from other breeds. Some have tried Brittanies and then have moved to other breeds.

The Brittany Spaniel was never either the beneficiary or the victim of a heavy barrage of publicity. As noted in other chapters, Louis A. Thebaud was the American pioneer. Stewart J. Walpole was then the publisher of *The American Field*. It was—and is—a magazine devoted primarily to pointing dogs. Pointers and English Setters got the bulk of attention. But Walpole was one of the first to own a Brittany in the United States. His articles in *The American Field* brought the Brittany to the attention of thousands of bird dog lovers. Some of these articles appear elsewhere in this book.

An American pioneer in English Springer Spaniels was Dr. A. C. Gifford of Oshkosh, Wisconsin. His Winnebago Kennels were already well established when the Brittany Spaniel first came to America. Dr. Gifford decided to try the breed. He liked the dogs. But he was first of all a lover of flushing dogs, and secondly, his interests lay with Springer bench dogs. So he did not persevere with the Brittany.

Dr. Samuel Milbank, a prominent breeder of Wire Fox Terriers, and for years head of the Westminster Kennel Club in New York City, decided to get into field trials. He, too, tried Brittany Spaniels. But, as with Dr. Gifford, Dr. Milbank found his interests to be with the flushing dogs and retrievers. So he moved into ranks of the Labrador Retriever and English Springer Spaniel field trialers.

The reverse was also true. Edward Borger was an early competitor in English Springer Spaniel field trials in northwestern Pennsylvania and northern Ohio. But Borger's true interest was in the pointing dog. He switched to Brittany Spaniels and has remained with the breed.

Charles Frank, whose sporting dog act was for years an attraction at winter sportsmen's shows, was another who began with Springer Spaniels. His dogs first distinguished themselves in the conformation ring and in obedience. When he developed his act, Frank added Golden Retrievers. Then he became interested in Brittany Spaniels. His "Duckerbird" dogs then became prominent in the ranks of the Brittanies.

The author has asked some of the pioneers who are still with us why they decided to go with Brittany Spaniels. Speaking for her deceased husband, Mrs. Walter B. Kleeman said simply: "Walt wanted a pointing dog with which he could hunt on foot." He was one who learned of the breed through Walpole's articles in *The American Field*.

Louis A. Thebaud introduced the Brittany Spaniel to the United States. What is less well known is that he also introduced to America the breed then known as the Korthals Griffon. We now know it as the Wirehaired Pointing Griffon. Thebaud tested both breeds. The Griffon failed to meet the test of American hunting conditions and game birds. The Brittany succeeded.

Henry Briggs, M.D., lived at West Orange, N.J. He met Louis Thebaud and became interested in the breed. His brother-in-law, Edgar W. Averill, Ph.D., came to visit. Dr. Briggs had a lovely Brittany Spaniel bitch in the house. She jumped into Dr. Averill's lap, and cuddled up there. Dr. Averill was entranced. The bitch was Yvonne de Sharvogue. On Sept. 13, 1936, Yvonne whelped a litter by Gwennec de L'Argoat. That Christmas, Dr. Averill received a male puppy for Christmas. The puppy was to become Ch. Patrice of Sharvogue. Dr. Averill—"Bill" to everyone still—had been "hooked" by Yvonne. Patrice made him forever a Brittany fancier.

"All those dogs could hunt," Bill said later. "Those of us in Michigan set out to improve their looks, while keeping their hunting abilities." This the Brittany Spaniel breeders have done with remarkable success—a record of success achieved by no other breed in world history. But that story belongs in the chapter of dual—bench and field—champions. Dr. Averill hunted Ch. Patrice of Sharvogue until the dog was past 14 years old.

René Joubert, another early pioneer, lived at this time in the Detroit area. He is often listed as having been the nephew of Louis A. Thebaud. But in fact, Louis Thebaud was a first cousin of René Joubert's mother. Before her marriage to Emmanuel Joubert, she was Isabelle Thebaud. The families were of French descent, but they lived in the New York-New Jersey area.

Isabelle Thebaud's father, Dr. Jules Thebaud, was killed by an explosion of cartridges as he prepared for a hunting trip. His widow took her numerous children back to France. She never returned. Isabelle married Emmanuel Joubert in Paris. They had two sons, Jacques and René.

René inherited the passion for the outdoors and the game fields

from the Thebauds. He always referred affectionately to Louis Thebaud as "Uncle Louis." René served in the French Army in World
War I and won the *Croix de Guerre* and the *Medaille Militaire.*
He came to New York to work for the *Compagnie Générale Trans-
atlantique,* and then was transferred to Houston, where he married
his wife, Margaret.

In 1932, he was transferred to Detroit, where he remained until
the French Line office was closed in 1940. With his background,
his relationship to Louis Thebaud, his knowledge of France, and with
the rapidly burgeoning interest in Michigan and Ohio in the Brittany
Spaniel, it was natural that he should take up the breed. René Joubert
returned to Texas in 1940, but not until the Brittany Spaniel had
won its acceptance as a great American sporting dog.

In France, the Brittany Spaniel and its ancestors had demonstrated
a remarkable passion for woodcock hunting for roughly one hundred
years. In America, the dog had to prove itself upon ruffed grouse,
prairie chicken, quail and pheasant as well as woodcock. In addition,
Michigan and northwestern Ohio had the chukar, or Indian rock
partridge. Juan Pugibet had brought the Brittany Spaniel to Mexico.
There game birds were often scarce, the hunting was difficult, and
the valley quail was an entirely different sporting proposition than
in the bob white quail. The Brittany Spaniel was tested on all these
game birds, and it passed the tests brilliantly.

But not even all this will explain how and why the Brittany Spaniel
caught on and became so popular. Remember that it had to survive
the great depression, World War II, and the Korean War. Yet during
the next 25 years it moved into the first 20 of all American breeds
registered by the American Kennel Club. In 1970, it was in 18th
place with 13,400 registrations. In one recent year, 2,380 Brittanies
competed in field trials under American Field procedures. All this
the breed had to accomplish without the fantastic, and often unfair,
publicity which has been dreamed up for the promotion of other
breeds.

To understand what happened, we have to go back to Mrs. Kleeman's simple statement: "Walt wanted a hunting dog he could use
on foot." American game areas have become steadily more restricted.
In only a few areas can men follow wide ranging Pointers and Setters,
as they once did, on horseback, or in wagons or trucks. Usually the
remaining such areas are privately owned and are denied to most
sportsmen.

The passing of these great game areas somewhat lessened the need for big, fast, wide ranging dogs. More and more highways cut through the game areas. Traffic became an increasing hazard for the dogs. Sportsmen began to think in terms of smaller, less wide ranging dogs. The German Shorthaired Pointer and the English Springer Spaniel were already well established. The latter is a flushing dog; the former a pointing dog which adapts well to all the above requirements. As does the Brittany, the German Shorthair lacks sufficient tail to get torn by briars.

Both the German Shorthair and the Brittany Spaniel make excellent house dogs, and this has become an increasingly important requirement for a sporting dog. But the latter has an additional advantage. It is small enough to be easily transported in the family car.

To sum it up:

The Brittany Spaniel has passed the test upon every type of game for which pointing dogs are used. It has the disposition of the best house pets and companions, and yet a remarkable passion for hunting. It can face any kind of weather. It can be kept within the range of modern hunting conditions. It is small, yet can do a big job. And it makes an ideal dual purpose—bench and field—dog.

Ch. Tuway's Kaymore Flash, C.D. (Dual Ch. Kaymore's Dapper Dan ex Ch. Nedbalek's Ginger), holds the record as the youngest Brittany to finish a bench championship. He was eight months and eleven days old when he completed his title.

# 6

# Early Brittany Spaniel History in France

---

IN earlier chapters we have tried to indicate how and why bird dogs developed. Moreover, we have pointed out that the great period in the development of specific dog breeds came during the last half of the 19th Century, and during the first decade or two of ours. The true history of the Brittany Spaniel, as a breed, falls into two decades—from 1890 to 1910.

F. Rothschild published his book, *Notre Ami Le Chien,* in 1897. He does not mention the Brittany Spaniel specifically. But he does list the known French hunting breeds, and he devotes some space to the French spaniels. His descriptions of some of them fit the Brittany.

They were white and chestnut, white and orange, often speckled. They were 19½ to 20½ inches tall at the withers. Their hair lay flat, and some of them had short tails or no tails.

The year before, a dog of this type was shown at the Paris Exposition. He was whelped in 1892, by Printemps out of Fauville, and his name was Pincon Royal. The owner was the Viscount de Cambourg. Pincon Royal was listed as a Brittany Spaniel. In 1902, another Brittany was shown. This was Das de Magenta, whelped Jan. 20, 1898 by Kim out of Eda. He was owned by M. Laveissiere.

These two dogs had to be shown in a miscellaneous class for French spaniels. Neither impressed the judges of the time. And it seems likely that neither impressed the sophisticated sportsmen of Paris who came to see the show.

But during that same year, a Brittany Spaniel competed in a field trial for continental dogs. This means that it was a trial for pointing dogs which were required to be steady to point and flush, to be steady to shot, to mark the fall, and then to make the retrieve. Myrrha d'Amorique was the dog. She was owned and had been trained by M. Treuttel. The trial was at Cany, and Myrrha won. Today, we would call Myrrha a very poor type. She was white and liver, and she looked very much like a present day English Springer Spaniel field type. But Myrrha won, and her victory turned attention to the hitherto ignored spaniels of Brittany.

Two years later, in 1904, M. Patin showed Max de Callac at the Paris Exposition. In the preceding chapter, we have quoted from John Kemp's *Shooting And Fishing In Lower Brittany*. He mentions the dogs and the shooting at Callac. So the appearance of Max de Callac—a dog from a great woodcock territory—did bring both attention and credit to the new breed. Max became the breed's first champion in 1909.

Then in 1907, dogs owned by M. de Pontavice, M. de Fougeres, and Dr. Gastel, were shown at the Paris Exposition. They won the acclaim of sportsmen, and particularly that of men who had hunted in lower Brittany. Stories about the breed appeared in the sporting journals for that year. Brittany Spaniels were given separate classification at Toulouse that year.

John Kemp had mentioned that a railroad was to be built from Brest to Nantes, that is, along the coast. Kemp wrote in 1859. By 1907, the railroad was a reality. And major highways had also been built across and around the Brittany Peninsula. The once isolated hunting areas were now opened up to an increasing number of sportsmen. Parisian and Northern French sportsmen were now learning about a hunting area and its dogs already long familiar to the English.

For example, a highway had been built from Quiberon, on the Bay of Biscay, through Pontivy, and on to St. Brieuc on the English Channel. North of Pontivy, this road split, and one section went east through Fougeres. And there was also an excellent highway from Nantes to Rennes. One could also travel from Nantes to Carhaix. These are all important names in the history of the breed.

In 1907, Arthur Enaud, Dr. Gastel, and M. de Fougeres met with others at Loudeac. This town is some 85 miles west of Rennes, 22 miles north of Pontivy, and 68 miles east of Carhaix. It is therefore in the heart land of the Brittany Spaniel. The purpose of the meeting was to found a breed club, and to draw up a standard. This was done. The Brittany Spaniel Club was formed. The standard called for a dog about 19 and ⅝ths inches tall at the shoulder. The head was to be broad, with a rounded skull. The ears were to be rather short—a departure from the traditional long spaniel ear—and only slightly fringed with hair. Body hair was to be flat, and in no sense curly. The body was to be short—"cob"—and the tail was to be "naturally short."

A second general meeting of Breton sportsmen was held at Pontivy on June 7, 1908. A more definitive standard was drawn up. And this was again modified at another meeting at Pontivy on June 16, 1912. Field trials for continental dogs, and for French spaniels, were already being held. Dogs belonging to M. Patin, and others, were winning, and were demonstrating remarkable scenting powers, as well as both searching ability and stamina. These dogs, by proving themselves in the field, brought true recognition to the breed.

The greatest dog of the pre-World War I period was Bac du Kerlossac. Ronan de Kermadec says he was "of the blood of Fougeres." He was bred by M. de Fougeres, and he was predominantly of the strains bred in the Fougeres section of Brittany. Bac du Kerlossac did not become a champion. World War I probably prevented him from becoming one. De Kermadec wrote that although he conformed to the standard of 1908, he was of a "strengthened model" with a good Breton head on a cob body.

The great war seriously impeded French breeding. Yet the best dogs were somehow kept. Gistr, bred by M. Le Denmat, and owned by M. Patin, was born Nov. 25, 1916. He won third prize at Paris in 1919. Gistr was by Klask IV de Callac, who had been a first prize winner at Nantes in 1913. His dam was Miss, by Dick. Klask IV was by Klask de Callac. Gistr became one of the great dogs of the postwar period, and serves as an example of the conservation of their best breeding stock by the Bretons.

Names fabled throughout Brittany history now began to appear. Duck de Callac, bred by M. Patin, was whelped April 12, 1920. He was by Rac II de Callac out of Noz de Callac. The Cosquerou Kennels also appeared. M. Mège registered Miss du Cosquerou, whelped July 15, 1920, by Frileux de Cosquerou, out of Souris II de Cosquerou. Shimmy du Cosquerou was whelped Mar. 29, 1921, by Franchic out of Kiss de Cosquerou, by Pen Bas de Kerbrug.

Perhaps it should be pointed out here that, because of the war, registration activities ceased for some years. But breeders did not stop breeding, though they continued on a small scale. They kept careful records, and these were placed in the stud book years later.

Another kennel which has played a major role in Brittany Spaniel history since its founding was the Pradalan Kennel of M. Quemener. One of his first great dogs was Perlic de Pradalan, a winner at the Rennes shows of 1922 and 1923. During this period, M. Chech bred Mousse, born in April, 1919, and heavily inbred to Gistr.

The greatest dog of the 1920s, and one who has been a major stud factor in both French and American dogs, was the immortal Aotrou de Cornouaille. He was bred by Emile Bourdon, and was whelped Nov. 15, 1926. Perlic de Pradalan later came to Mexico. Aotrou remained in France where he won one hundred first and honor prizes in shows, won at several field trials, and took first in the International Brittany Spaniel Club trials in 1929. Aotrou's pedigree is given here, but it may be mentioned here that Gistr, mentioned earlier, appears in Aotrou's pedigree.

Earlier in this chapter, we pointed out that F. Rothschild did not mention the Brittany Spaniel in his list of French hunting dogs when he wrote his book, *Notre Ami Le Chien* (Our Friend The Dog). Less than 30 years later, Aotrou was to come on the scene, and the Brittany Spaniel was to become world famous. The other breeds of French spaniels either died out, or have remained relatively unknown outside their local areas of France. It is time now to place the Brittany Spaniel in North America.

French Ch. Aotrou de Cornouaille was one of the great foundation sires of American Brittany Spaniels. (Photo, courtesy of L. Bourdon, Cornouaille Kennels).

```
                                     Potic du Cosquerou
                        Potic
                                     Flute
         Ch. Potic II de Cornouaille

                                     Caür
                        Peda II
                                     Poda I
CH. AOTROU DE CORNOUAILLE

                                     Tac
                        Yan Fred
                                     Tantine Fred
         Zile de Cornouaille

                                     Flip
                        Diane de Cornouaille
                                     Potress de Pradalan
```

# 7

# The Brittany Spaniel
# Comes to North America

---

TWO men are responsible for introducing the Brittany Spaniel to North America. Both had French antecedents. They were Juan Pugibet of Villa Obregon, near Vera Cruz, Mexico, and Louis Andre Thebaud of Morristown, N.J. Of these two, Juan Pugibet comes first.

Juan Pugibet was an engineer. His father was French and his mother, Mexican. He was a lover of field sports, especially of hunting upland game birds. He was a close friend of J. A. Sanchez Antuñano, the great Mexican authority on bird dogs. Sanchez Antuñano's *Practical Education of the Bird Dog* was for years the standard American guide to bird dog training.

Sanchez Antuñano was at home with bird dogs under all the varying conditions to be found in North and Central America. Juan Pugibet was nearly as well versed. Neither appears to have known anything about the Brittany Spaniel. But Juan Pugibet went to France in the winter of 1924 where he learned about the breed. He was sufficiently impressed to want to test the breed in southern Mexico.

That September he bought the Brittany Spaniel bitch, Perlic de Pradalan. She arrived at Vera Cruz in December. Perlic was very well bred, and she adapted well to hunting conditions in Mexico.

She stood intense heat, tropical humidity, and upland dryness equally well. Yet it was four years before Pugibet decided to breed Brittany Spaniels.

In 1928, he imported Djinn des Veaux. Djinn was a grandson of one of the great dogs of his time, Rac II de Callac. Rac II de Callac appears in many of the pedigrees of dogs imported to North America. He has therefore been a stud force in Mexico, the United States, and Canada. Djinn des Veaux arrived at Vera Cruz in time to be bred to Perlic de Pradalan during her early fall heat period. Her litter—the first ever recorded in North America—arrived in December, 1928.

Pugibet imported many more Brittany Spaniels. His Casa Blanca Kennels became famous in Mexico, the United States, and Canada. Dogs bred at Casa Blanca became the foundation stock in all three countries.

One of Pugibet's imports was the famous bitch, Histr de Cornouaille, whose record and complete pedigree are included in this book. Pugibet and his daughter, Monica, took Histr to a field trial at the King Ranch in Texas. There she performed brilliantly, though competing against both Pointers and Setters.

Most of the early Brittany Spaniels to come to America were registered with the *Field Dog Stud Book* of the American Field. In addition, it was at that time possible to register Mexican dogs with the American Kennel Club. Thus, until about the time of his death in 1946, Pugibet registered all of his dogs with the American Kennel Club. In many cases, he also registered them with the *Field Dog Stud Book*.

To explain this further, Pugibet would import dogs from France. These would be registered by the American Kennel Club. Litters born in Mexico of parents registered with the American Kennel Club would then be registered by that organization. But about 1946, the American Kennel Club began to refuse such registrations. In some cases, it would register imported dogs for new owners living within the United States. But this was so only if the stud books of the country of origin were recognized by the American Kennel Club.

For example, a dog owned in France could not be registered by the American Kennel Club. Neither could a dog owned in Mexico. At this time, the American Kennel Club recognizes the stud books of England, France, Germany, Canada, Australia, South Africa, etc. If an American imports a registered dog from one of these countries, the AKC will in most cases, transfer ownership to an American owner.

But it will not do so if the dog is owned in Mexico. Moreover, the American Kennel Club does not currently recognize the stud books of the Latin American countries, including Mexico.

This accounts for the odd fact that dogs from Pugibet's Casa Blanca Kennels were not registered by the Mexican Kennel Club until after his death. Had the American Kennel Club policy of from 1946 to the present existed when Pugibet began importing and breeding, the Brittany Spaniel could not have got the start it did in the U.S. and Canada. The Casa Blanca influence in Canada is shown in the chapter dealing with the Brittany Spaniel in Canada.

Louis André Thebaud is a legend in America, and legends are sometimes hard to pin down. Legend tends to obscure facts, but many people have aided the writer in working out the history which follows. Among these is Vice Admiral Leo H. Thebaud, U.S. Navy retired. He collaborated with Robert L. de Larosiere, a retired French Naval Captain, in writing a history of the Thebaud family in both France and the United States. Admiral Thebaud has very kindly supplied me with this history, plus other information.

Louis André Thebaud and his twin brother, Edward Paul, were born Oct. 24, 1859 at Orange, N.J. They were the sons of Paul Louis Thebaud, a member of the Thebaud Brothers firm in the import-export business. This firm closed its doors in 1907. Paul Louis Thebaud was a director and officer in many New York firms, including the Atlantic Mutual Insurance Co.

It has been said that Paul Louis Thebaud was for some years a banker in Yucatan, a state in southern Mexico. It is further said that his son, Louis, spent his younger years in Yucatan, where he became a passionate devotee of both hunting and fishing. We have not been able to verify any part of this story.

In a personal letter to the author, Admiral Thebaud writes: "Neither Louis A. Thebaud, nor his father, ever lived in Yucatan. Louis Thebaud was a highly successful insurance man with Mutual Life in New York. His father was a member of the firm of Thebaud Brothers.

"All Thebauds have roots in Morristown, N.J., where the family has been well known for over a century. I was born next door at Madison, N.J. No Thebaud ever known to me ever met or heard of Juan Pugibet." Yet as stated elsewhere in this book, Juan Pugibet had planned to dedicate the book he was writing to Louis Thebaud.

Louis A. Thebaud went almost annually to France where he divided his time between an apartment in the Rue Spontini, Paris, and a

Louis A. Thebaud is considered a legend among American Brittany fanciers. He was one of the first to bring the breed to North America and played a major role in the breed's rise to prominence in the field and on the show bench.

One of the great names among the first Brittanies in the United States was that of Franche du Cosquerou (above)—Louis Thebaud's favorite hunting dog. The famous dog portrait photographer Rudolph Tauskey took this picture of Franche at the request of the American Kennel Club to represent the breed in the 1936 Edition of *The Complete Dog Book*. Franche subsequently became the property of Réne Joubert.

Réne Joubert, celebrated sportsman and breed pioneer, with two early greats; Fanche due Cosquerou (left) and Gwennec de L'Argoat.

sea coast home at St. Briac in Brittany. He is described as being "handsome, charming, and courtly" and "also a great sportsman; hunting, shooting, fishing, and sailing." He financed the building of the famous Gloucester schooner, Gertrude L. Thebaud, which was named after his wife. This schooner, under the command of Capt. Ben Pine, enhanced the prestige of New England fishermen at sea, in the international fishermen's races against the Nova Scotia schooner, Bluenose.

It is generally supposed that Louis Thebaud annually attended French field trials, and particularly those for Brittany Spaniels. But this seems not to have been true. He appears to have spent most of his time at St. Briac in sailing and fishing.

Earlier, we have pointed out the close personal relationship between the Joubert family and the Thebauds. The Jouberts had an apartment very close to the Thebaud apartment in the Rue Spontini. The two families went together to St. Briac, and the Joubert brothers always called Louis Thebaud "Uncle Louis." In a personal letter to the author, J. R. Joubert writes:

"My uncle, Louis A. Thebaud, except during the First World War years, came over to France every year from 1900 to 1939, the year of his death. He and his wife, Gertrude, usually arrived in March. Then in July and August we all went to St. Briac. My uncle was fond of fishing, but he often went on shooting parties. During the time between 1905 and 1920, he bought two or three dogs in France and brought them back to the United States, but none of them was a Brittany Spaniel." (Author's note: They were Korthals Griffons, later to be known as Wirehaired Pointing Griffons.)

"It is only between 1930 and 1939 that my uncle talked to me for the first time about Brittany Spaniels. The main reason, I think, is that my uncle thought that the breed would be very efficient for quail hunting, which he did on horseback in Florida . . . He asked me to find five . . . Brittany Spaniels for him, which I did with the greatest pleasure. My uncle never attended field trials in France, but I did it for him, with the aim of finding the finest dogs possible.

"The result was that I bought four or five dogs for him, among which were Edir (very nervous, turned mad a few times) and Clap de Callac. (Callac is the name of the Brittany village where the first Brittany Spaniel was born.) As far as I remember, this latter dog was famous.

"I went to the U.S.A. with two of the dogs, and accompanied my uncle to New York to have the breed recognized and the dogs registered on the American Kennel Club's Stud Book. Sometime later, the second World War broke out, and I was separated from my brother, to whom my uncle had given some of the dogs before his death."

One of the dogs which J. R. Joubert sent to his uncle in 1933 was the bitch, Genette du Mesnil. She was carrying a litter sired by Gredin du Mesnil. After her arrival in the United States, Thebaud shipped her to Winnipeg, to Eudore Chevrier's Avandale Kennels. There she whelped. Thus, to Canada belongs the honor of producing her litter. It is a strange story: bred in France, imported with her puppies "in utero," and then sent to Canada.

# 8

# Early History of the Brittany Spaniel in America

$A$MONG the dogs selected in France by Jacques Joubert for Louis A. Thebaud were Edir du Mesnil, Genette du Mesnil, Franche du Cosquerou, Hai du Cosquerou, and Fenntus. As stated earlier, Genette was in whelp to Gredin du Mesnil. She was sent to Winnipeg, Manitoba, to Eudore Chevrier's Avandale Kennels. After producing her litter, she was returned to Thebaud.

Franche du Cosquerou arrived in this country with the reputation of being France's finest field Brittany Spaniel. He appears not to have been brought over by René Joubert, as stated by some authors. René Joubert did not return to France during that period, according to the recollections of his brother. Franche was mated to Genette du Mesnil, and was then sent to Winnipeg to be used on Genette's daughters. Then he was returned to Thebaud.

Meanwhile, Jacques Joubert and Louis Thebaud went to the American Kennel Club to try to get the breed recognized and admitted to the stud book. They took with them two dogs—Edir du Mesnil and Genette du Mesnil. As a result, the board of directors of the AKC formally recognized the Brittany Spaniel in August, 1934.

The French Kennel Club had sent the "Standard of Perfection"

46

for the breed at Thebaud's request in July, 1934. But oddly enough, the AKC did not approve the standard until Miss Clara G. Perry had made an acceptable translation of it. Approval came on Mar. 12, 1935. Franche, described as "Mr. Thebaud's favorite hunting dog," was photographed by famed dog photographer, Ruldoph Tauskey. His picture was used to illustrate the history and breed standard in the official AKC book, *Pure-bred Dogs*. Arthur Frederick Jones, of the AKC staff, wrote the breed history. That particular edition of the book was published late in 1935, or early in 1936.

It should be pointed out here that it was much easier to gain breed recognition in the mid-1930s than it is today. Then, Jacques Joubert and Louis Thebaud could take two dogs of the breed to the American Kennel Club, present their certified French pedigrees, and import certificates, and get the breed recognized immediately.

Today that would be impossible. First, the AKC would require proof that a certain number of dogs—perhaps 600—were in the country, and well spread from coast to coast. Then they would admit the breed to the "miscellaneous class" status. A strong national breed club would have to be set up. And that club would have to establish an accurate stud book under AKC supervision. If then, some 600 dogs were registered in this stud book, and if AKC considered their pedigrees to be accurate, the breed might be elevated to full breed status. In the years since, it has taken some breeds a decade or more to achieve what Joubert and Thebaud accomplished in one day with two dogs.

Miss Clara G. Perry was also a true pioneer of the breed. She had maintained a home in France, and there she had owned Brittany Spaniels. Finding that there was an interest in the breed in the United States, she now joined Thebaud in importing dogs.

So did Louis de la Fleche, a Breton Frenchman, who was then living in the New York-New Jersey area. David Barbieri, and Dr. Henry Briggs also began importations. Later, Louis de la Fleche returned to France and remained there.

Miss Perry brought over Gilda des Causes and Douglas de l'Odet. The year was 1935. The following winter the dogs were shown at Westminster, in Madison Square Garden, and at Boston. They were the first to appear at a U.S. show. That same year, Thebaud imported Hai du Cosquerou. Juan Pugibet brought over Histr de Cornouaille, bred to Gwennec de l'Argoat. La Fleche imported Keryvon de Basgard, and Keryvette du Roselier. At about the same time, Laurence Richardson imported Meg, Barbieri and Tango.

French Ch. Potic II, an influential sire during the early history of the Brittany in North America. His name appears three times in the pedigree of Histr de Cornouaille (below).

```
                                                   Potic
                               Ch. Potic II de Cornouaille
                                                   Peda II

                     Celtic de Cornouaille

                                           Dof
                               Gliz Noz
                                           Tuss

          Int. Ch. Flist III de Cornouaille

                                           Ch. Potic II de Cornouaille
                               Ch. Aotru de Cornouaille
                                           Zile de Cornouaille

                     Dia de Cornouaille

                                           Bleiz de Cornouaille
                               Brise de Cornouaille
                                           Galope du Cosquerou

HISTR DE CORNOUAILLE

                                           Potic du Cosquerou
                               Potic
                                           Flute

                     Ch. Potic II de Cornouaille

                                           Caër
                               Peda II
                                           Peda

          Diwal de Cornouaille

                                           Tom Fred
                               Pesq-Ebrel
                                           Valse

                     Ayout

                                           Yan Fred
                               Gaït
                                           Peda II
```

Fenntus was sired by the immortal French dog, Aotrou de Cornouaille, out of Plahic by Potic II. She was closely inbred to the latter dog, since Aotrou was himself sired by Potic II. An orange and white, she was bred by M. Le Coz and whelped Mar. 6, 1931.

Hai du Cosquerou was bred by M. F. Mège, and was whelped Mar. 1, 1933. He was orange and white. He was by Esop du Cosquerou out of a bitch by Aotrou de Cornouaille.

Histr de Cornouaille was bred by Emile Bourdon, and she was born May 18, 1933. She was white and orange and was by Flist III de Cornouaille, out of Diwal de Cornouaille, by Potic II. Flist III de Cornouaille was inbred to Aotrou de Cornouaille.

Keryvon de Basgard was bred by M. Poilbout. He was born Aug. 1, 1932 by Cren de Callac out of Eyra de Basgard, by Aotrou de Cornouaille.

These dogs show the powerful influence of Aotrou de Cornouaille upon Brittany history in the United States. But there were other powerful lines to cross with that of Aotrou.

Douglas de l'Odet was by Cyrano de Ler Leo out of Coant, by Yan du Cosquerou. He was whelped Sept. 25, 1929, and was thus six years old when brought to the United States. Gilda des Causes was sired by Ali de la Marphee out of Biscotte de Callac, by Yoko de la Marphee, out of Cora V de Callac. Rac II of Callac appears twice in her pedigree.

Meg was bred in France by Miss Clara Perry. She was whelped April 8, 1934 by Sam out of Gilda de Causses. Djinn des Veaux was whelped Feb. 22, 1926, a white and orange dog bred by B. Benoist. He was by Ramus des Veaux out of Monne I des Veaux by Lac II d'Armorique. Rac II de Callac appears twice in his pedigree.

The first litter born in the United States was from the mating of Douglas de l'Odet to Gilda des Causses. That litter was born June 28, 1935. From this litter, Laurence Richardson bought Bragoubras; D. G. Mann bought Pembas; Louis de la Fleche bought Daoulas; and Mrs. Ruth B. Perry bought Bigotin. Lassie went to George E. Benson.

Louis A. Thebaud imported the great Gwennec de l'Argoat at this time. Gwennec was whelped April 6, 1932. He was a white and orange dog by Aotrou de Cornouaille out of Coantic de Cornouaille, by Potic II. Gwennec became a major stud force in the U.S., and through puppies taken to Mexico "in utero" by Histr de Cornouaille.

Brittany Spaniels now began to appear in the United States in surprisingly large numbers. For example, 11 were registered in Nov.

Pioneer fancier Walter B. Kleeman enjoying a personal moment with the celebrated Gwennec de L'Argoat.

1936. Ten of these were bred by Juan Pugibet's Casa Blanca Kennels in Mexico. But American-bred dogs were also beginning to appear.

It was in 1936 that the Brittany Spaniel Club of North America was founded. It received official membership in the American Kennel Club on Sept. 15, 1936. Louis A. Thebaud was the first president. Aldo Balsam of Bridgehampton, N.Y., was vice president. Louis de la Fleche of Farmingdale, N.Y., was elected secretary-treasurer and delegate to the American Kennel Club.

Among the members in the club's first years were Walter B. Kleeman of Springfield, O.; Laurence E. Richardson of Concord, Mass.; Dr. Chester Keogh of Chicago, Ill.; Howard P. Clements of Chicago; H. B. Conover of Chicago; René Joubert, then of Detroit, Mich.; Juan Pugibet of Villa Obregon, Mexico; George B. Perry of Boston, Mass.; Miss Clara Perry of Boston; and Western Higbie of Lynmour, British Columbia.

On Aug. 12, 1940, Alan Rutherford Stuyvesant of Allamuchy, N.J. became president. He succeeded Louis A. Thebaud who had died at the venerable age of 80. Frederick S. Wildman of Bellows & Co. became secretary. By then World War II was in progress and it was virtually to destroy the club.

Alan R. Stuyvesant, who had become a great importer of Brittany Spaniels, had joined his brother in organizing an ambulance corps. This was sent to North Africa. The Stuyvesant brothers were captured. Alan returned at the end of the war; his brother was never heard from again.

René Joubert had been the head of the French Line office in Detroit. Louis Thebaud had sent him some of his great dogs. Outdoor sports were a passion with René Joubert. And he did much to promote the breed in the Midwest. But the war brought the closing of the French Line office. Joubert moved to Houston, Tex. Louis de la Fleche would return to France at the end of the war. War duties forced other members to become inactive.

But Brittany Spaniel interest was seething. And this was particularly so in the Midwest, which was clamoring for licensed championship Brittany Spaniel field trials. Thus, the stage was set for the formation of the American Brittany Club.

# 9

# First Official American History of the Breed

<br>

W HEN the Brittany Spaniel was first recognized by the American Kennel Club, Arthur Frederick Jones was assigned to write the official history of the breed. Jones was on the staff of *Pure-bred Dogs, American Kennel Gazette,* and he would later become its editor. His history of the breed differs in some respects from others. And so we feel that it should not be entirely ignored.

Jones obtained his material from several sources. These included Louis Thebaud, and Jacques and René Joubert. Louis de la Fleche, a native of Brittany, was then living in the New York-New Jersey area. He, also, may have contributed to this history.

As respects the first Brittany Spaniels to reach America, there is a notable difference from Jones' account and those of others. It is generally accepted as a fact that the first Britts to appear at bench shows were Gilda des Causes and Douglas de L'Odet. They were shown at Boston and Westminster by their importer, Clara G. Perry, in 1935.

Westminster is a mid-February show, and Boston was, at that time, an early March show. The American Kennel Club's *THE COMPLETE DOG BOOK,* published early in 1935, contains the first offi-

Dual Ch. Amos of Edough, a famous early winner and the first Dual Ch. Brittany to win a Sporting group. *Worwick photo.*

Rumba de L'Argoat, the last dog imported by Alan Stuyvesant. *Jones photo.*

cial history of the breed. And in it, Jones says: "The first specimens of the Brittany Spaniel were imported to America in 1931, and they have been exhibited at many of our shows since that time."

Jones neither names the dogs nor the shows at which they may have been exhibited. Yet he has always been an accurate reporter. So the possibility does exist that Brittany Spaniels did appear in the Miscellaneous Class at U.S. dog shows before 1935. The following is the complete text of the Jones' history as it appeared in 1935.

### SPANIELS (BRITTANY)

"During the past few years American sportsmen have begun to realize the qualities of a French breed that has been known on the Continent for many centuries. This dog is officially known in the United States as the Brittany Spaniel, but from his size and the manner of his working he might, properly, be called a setter. He stands 18 to 20 inches at the shoulder, is liver and white or, preferably, orange and white, and is either without a tail or has one of only a few inches.

"The basic stock for all the spaniels, pointers, and setters came originally from Spain, but the migration of these dogs took place so long ago that it is impossible for anyone to say with certainty just when it occurred. The greatest development of these breeds took place in England, Ireland, and Scotland, but many of them spread through various parts of the Continent, and today there are many varieties— particularly in France—that trace back to the old Spanish strains.

"The Brittany Spaniel is one of the oldest of them all, and he was bred up from the original spaniel size in much the same manner as the British, using similar stock, produced the setters. In fact, there is reason to believe that he had attained his present size long before his cousins across the channel had attained to recognizable type.

"It is believed by some that the Brittany Spaniel was related to the red and white setter which preceded the golden red setter in Ireland. There is a strong possibility that some of the Irish chieftains, who invaded Gaul—or what is now France—during the first third of the Fifth Century A.D., carried their hunting dogs with them. These dogs, left in France may have contributed something to the development of the Brittany Spaniel. The Irish influence also is seen in the orange and white *Epagneul Ecossais,* or Scotch spaniel—especially if it is remembered that at the time of these invasions the Irish were known as Scoti.

"The first tailless ancestor of the modern Brittany Spaniel was bred, about a century ago, at Pontou, a little town situated in the Valley

This picture, taken in 1945, shows Jilo (background) and Kaer de Cornouaille on point. Both dogs were imported and owned by Alan Stuyvesant. *Jones photo.*

of Douron. It was the result of a cross between a white and mahogany bitch, owned by an old hunter of the region, and a lemon and white dog brought to Brittany by an English sportsman for woodcock shooting. Of the two tailless specimens produced in this litter, only one was considered worth keeping. He grew into a splendid dog. His work in the field has been described as wonderful, and because of this he became a popular stud. All his litters contained puppies either without tails or with short stubs.

"The modern history of the Brittany Spaniel dates back only to the beginning of the present century. At that time, the breed had degenerated badly, principally because it had been closely inbred, but also because it had not been regarded as a show specimen. Eventually it caught the attention of Arthur Enaud, a French sportsman with a biological turn of mind. He admired the all-around working qualities of the breed so highly that he undertook to improve its appearance.

"M. Enaud went about his work very thoroughly, and he did not try to accomplish too much in too short a time. He was forced to use certain crosses, but after each cross he returned immediately to the old breed. Unfortunately, like many breeders who have done the same thing with other breeds, he left no clear record of the different dogs that entered into this restoration. In fact, it is only through a study of the other breeds available that it is possible to follow this period in the history of the Brittany Spaniel.

"The intensification of the desired orange and white color was one of the chief aims of M. Enaud, and for this he found two breeds that had not only the colors but keen scenting ability. One was the *Italian Bracco,* or pointer, and the other was the *Braque de Bourbonnais,* also a pointer. This second breed was the more suitable for his purposes, for besides its other points it was possessed of a very short tail.

"The only drawback to the use of pointers was that the coat of the Brittany Spaniel might be affected, but as sparing use was made of crosses and the rest was a matter of selective breeding after improving the blood lines, the modern dog was still the counterpart of his ancient Breton ancestors. By 1907 the breed had been restored to all its former glory.

"The first specimens of the Brittany Spaniel were imported to America in 1931, and they have been exhibited at many of our shows since that time. The breed has proved a capable gun dog, and like most of the Continental-bred setters and pointers it can be trained very easily as a retriever. The original use of the breed in France was for woodcock hunting, but it is far from a specialist. And it has proved already that it can hold its own in field trials, for, the first time in competition in America, a Brittany Spaniel carried off a prize against a field of more experienced dogs from other breeds."

Thus ends the first official American history of the Brittany Spaniel. As is so often the case in breed histories, it leaves a lot of questions unanswered. We know that Franche du Cosquerou placed third in the Jockey Hollow shooting dog stake on April 20, 1935. This is the first officially recorded placing of a Brittany in an American field trial. Yet the last sentence in the official history would indicate that a Brittany Spaniel had placed in, or won, some trial earlier. For the Jockey Hollow trial came too late for Franche's placing to be mentioned in that history. But the dog and the trial elude us.

Ch. Allamuchy Valley Joe on point with Fld. Ch. Allamuchy Valley Addie backing. *Niper photo.*

Officers of the American Brittany Club posed for this photo in November of 1950. They are (l. to r.) Alan Stuyvesant, Coy Conwell, Walter B. Kleeman, William Averill and Howard Clements. *Shafer photo.*

This photo shows (l. to r.) Walter B. Kleeman with Ch. Buckeye De Klemanor, Hilmer Peterson with Duffy of Chippewa and Tommy Cox with Fld. Ch. Allamuchy Valley Addie.

# 10

# Organization of the American Brittany Club

---

$F$OR many years, the American Kennel Club has had a recognition policy for parent breed clubs. The first club to be organized would be considered as the parent club for that breed. This was occasionally harmful to the breed, since the club might be entirely local in scope, and might be dedicated to only one facet of the sport of dog breeding. For instance, the club might be interested only in conformation and shows, or in field trials.

In recent years, the AKC policy has been more rigid. Before recognition, the breed would require 600 or more dogs, spread over the country, and registered in a breed stud book. But such was not the case when the Brittany Spaniel Club of North America was founded. World War II had hurt the club. Some officers and members could not be located, or were in no position to work for the club or for the breed.

Meanwhile, some of the best of the Thebaud dogs had gone to Rene Joubert in Michigan. Walter B. Kleeman had bought Parisienne from her breeder, Andre Vaudoyer of Winnipeg, Manitoba. She was, you will remember, by Franche du Cosquerou out of Genette de Mesnil.

Dr. Chester H. Keogh of Chicago had established his famed MacEochaidh Kennels, and had bought a son of Gwennec de l'Argoat, named Mirabile Dictu. He had also imported Leltic de Pradalan, and the great Idoc de Cornouaille. He also bought dogs from Juan Pugibet.

Kleeman had produced a litter from Parisienne, sired by Gwennec de l'Argoat. The famed all-breed judge, George S. Thomas, had bought Louis Quatorze of Tintagel from Juan Pugibet. Dr. Samuel Milbank, later to be a power in English Springer Spaniels and Labrador Retrievers, and for some years an officer of the Westminster Kennel Club, bought Marie Therese of Tintagel from Pugibet. Alan Stuyvesant's great imports had included Kaer de Cornouaille, a son of Idoc of Cornouaille out of Hem'za de Cornouaille, by Flist III de Cornouaille.

Eugene D. Britton of Fort Worth, Texas had established a kennel under his own name. Dr. Edgar W. Averill, a brother-in-law of Dr. Henry Briggs, had received Patrice of Sharvogue from Dr. Briggs. Patrice, whelped Sept. 13, 1936, was by Gwennec de l'Argoat out of Yvonne de Sharvogue. J. G. White of Walla Walla, Washington, had bought Kelov of Casa Blanca, by Jalov of Casa Blanca out of Jenoff of Casa Blanca.

Thus, Brittany Spaniels had spread across America. But the great importer-breeder, Alan Stuyvesant, was a prisoner of War. Louis A. Thebaud was gone. And the Midwest was seething with Brittany Spaniel activity. The time had come to found a new parent club, one which would be national in scope.

What follows is taken from the first issue of *The Brittany Field and Bench,* dated October, 1942. Dr. D. B. Ruskin of Karomish Kennels, Caro State Hospital, Caro, Mich., was editor. Jack L. Whitworth of Avon, O., was business manager. Until his retirement in August, 1971, Whitworth operated the print shop at Hotel Cleveland, later the Sheraton-Cleveland. Dr. Ruskin wrote the following text.

"The American Brittany Club was founded on May 16, 1942, in the Lafayette room of the Hotel Fort Shelby in Detroit. With the Honorable Judge Homer Ferguson, presiding, the meeting was called to order. Those present were Dr. and Mrs. Chester Keogh of Chicago, Mr. and Mrs. H. P. Cline of Rocky River, Ohio, Mr. and Mrs. A. H. Ady of Detroit, Mich., Mrs. Kathryn Adams of Detroit, Mich., Mr. Edgar W. Averill of Birmingham, Mich., Mr. Jack L. Whitworth of Cleveland, Ohio, Mr. Thomas C. Fitzpatrick of Pontiac, Mich., Mr. William K. Martin of Detroit, Mich., Dr. Charles C. Lynch of Detroit,

Dr. Chester H. Keogh and four of his early Brittanies. Dr. Keogh was extremely active with Brittanies and played a large part in their early progress. The dogs with him are (l. to r.) Mirabile Dictu, Leltic de Pradalan, Idoc de Cornouaille and Banba MacEochaidh.

Mich., Mr. Don Waller of Farwell, Mich., Mr. Ralph E. Hughes of Lansing, Mich., Mr. R. B. McCurdy of Detroit, Mich., and Dr. D. B. Ruskin of Caro, Mich.

"The meeting opened with a discussion on the advisability and purpose of organizing a club of Brittany Spaniel owners on a national scale, such a club to further the interests of Brittany Spaniels, obtain recognition of the FDSB and the AKC, and to further develop the breed for field and bench.

"Formal action was then taken to form a club, national in scope, of Brittany Spaniel owners, to be called the American Brittany Club. It was then necessary to elect officers and it was decided that there should be a three man Board of Directors who, in turn, would be the officers of the Club. The members elected to the Board are: Mr. A. H. Ady, Mr. E. W. Averill, and Dr. D. B. Ruskin, and by action of the Board, Dr. Ruskin was elected as secretary of the Board and the Club.

"All owners of registered Brittany Spaniels are eligible to membership and any member of their immediate family is eligible to associate membership. More information on membership can be found elsewhere in this publication.

"The members present at the meeting of May 16th also showed their appreciation for the work done and the services rendered the Brittany Spaniel Club by voting honorary memberships to Dr. Chester H. Keogh and to Mr. René Joubert. This is a life sentence, folks.

"At a later date, the Board of Directors met and drew up a constitution and by-laws which was subjected to the criticism of the members, and when all the smoke cleared a final draft was drawn up. We include it in this issue for your pleasure and ask you to keep it for future reference.

"A membership campaign was then started, and we already are getting results. This is truly becoming a national club. Memberships from all parts of the country. To those who live too far away to be active in the parent organization, we say that in the near future we will be able to assign regions for local chapters. You will then be a member of both the local chapter and the parent organization, and will profit from the activities of both."

This was the beginning. But the road was to be difficult. The American Kennel Club had recognized the older club. The new one could not hold licensed field trials or specialty shows without permission from the Brittany Spaniel Club of North America. Partly because of the inability to communicate with many of the officers and members of the latter club, such permission could not be obtained.

The services of two people were enlisted. One was the author. The other was Frank L. Grant. The author was a dog columnist for the *Cleveland Press,* and was the president of a Springer Spaniel field trial club. Grant was then the show chairman of the Western Reserve Kennel Club. He was a Doberman Pinscher breeder, and an original obedience trainer before the American Kennel Club established obedience trials. He was also delegate to the American Kennel Club and as such had represented several show giving clubs.

Both the author and Grant made several trips to New York to plead the cause of the American Brittany Club. Henry D. Bixby was then vice president. It was his policy to defend member and parent clubs even when they had not entirely lived by the American Kennel Club's rules. He also thought it would be unfair to kick out the Brittany Spaniel Club of North America just because it had been so badly crippled by the war. Bixby also had reservations about the new club's name. He felt that "Brittany" should not stand alone, and that the name should be American Brittany Spaniel Club. But many in the new club objected. A spaniel, they felt, was a flushing dog, the Brittany a pointing dog, and therefore not a true spaniel.

A compromise was finally worked out. This was mainly brought about by Grant, and with the advice of Judge Homer Ferguson. The compromise consisted of merging the two clubs. The name would be the American Brittany Club. Members of the Brittany Spaniel Club of North America would, if they wished, automatically become members of the new club. All the members of both clubs would be permitted to vote on the merger. In the meantime, with a sort of tacit approval by the older, and still parent club, the American Brittany Club was to be allowed to have licensed, or championship, field trials and shows.

All of this was not accomplished within a couple of weeks or months. It was slightly more than two years after its founding that the American Brittany Club became what its letterhead already stated "Sponsor of the Brittany Spaniel." That letterhead listed A. H. Ady, president; E. W. Averill, vice president; W. B. Kleeman, second vice president; R. B. McCurdy, vice president at large; and Jack L. Whitworth, Avon, Ohio, secretary-treasurer.

Because of its historic importance, we are reprinting in full the official merger letter which was sent to Henry D. Bixby. It is self explanatory.

June 6, 1944

Dear Mr. Bixby:

"We are happy to inform you that the American Brittany Club and the Brittany Spaniel Club of North America have merged. As you were one of the first to recommend this merger, we feel certain the American Kennel Club will approve it.

"The attached joint resolution was agreed upon by the officers of the Brittany Spaniel Club of North America, namely Mr. Louis de la Fleche, Mr. Laurence E. Richardson, and Mr. René Joubert, nephew of the late Mr. Louis Thebaud, former president and organizer of that club; and by Mr. A. H. Ady, Mr. E. W. Averill, Mr. W. B. Kleeman, Lt. Robert B. McCurdy, and J. L. Whitworth, officers of the American Brittany Club. Mr. Alan Stuyvesant, acting president of the Brittany Spaniel Club of North America, and also an active member of the American Brittany Club, is out of the country and cannot be reached, but his manager, Mr. Arthur Danks, assures us he will be in favor of any move that will help the breed.

"A copy of this resolution was mailed along with a ballot to the active and voting members of both clubs. List of members of the Brittany Spaniel Club of North America furnished by its secretary, Mr. de la Fleche. List of members of the American Brittany Club furnished by its secretary, Mr. Whitworth. Both lists were given to Mr. Frank L. Grant, Euclid, Ohio, who was selected to mail, check, and receive the returned ballots.

"Under the terms of the Merger, as outlined in the joint resolution, fourteen days were allowed for the return of the ballots. A majority was to mean a majority of the actual ballots returned.

"112 ballots were mailed to the members of the American Brittany Club, and 20 ballots were mailed to the members of the Brittany Spaniel Club of North America. Two letters addressed to members of the American Brittany Club were returned by the Post Office marked 'incorrect address,' and three addressed to members of the Brittany Spaniel Club of North America were returned. Two were marked 'addressee deceased', and one was marked 'addressee returned to France.'

"A total of sixty-one (61) ballots were returned to Mr. Grant, fifty nine of them (Author's note: an apparent discrepancy) were from members of the American Brittany Club and all of them voted 'YES' for the merger. There were eleven (11) ballots returned from members of the Brittany Spaniel Club of North America, and all of them voted 'YES' for the merger. There was not a single vote against the merger.

"Therefore, subject to A. K. C. approval, the merger will take effect immediately. The name of the club will be changed from the Brittany Spaniel Club of North America to the American Brittany Club.

"The constitution and a list of members are enclosed.

"The officers of the club until the next election in November are as follows: A. H. Ady, president. E. W. Averill, vice president. W. B. Kleeman, 2nd vice president. R. B. McCurdy, vice president at large. Jack L. Whitworth, secretary-Treasurer. Delegate to the A. K. C., Louis N. de la Fleche.

"The Board of Directors are: Alan Stuyvesant, Laurence E. Richardson, Louis N. de la Fleche, René Joubert, A. H. Ady, E. W. Averill, W. B. Kleeman, R. B. McCurdy, and J. L Whitworth.

"We sincerely hope the above meets the full approval of the American Kennel Club, and ask an early acknowledgment, so that future plans may be made for the advancement of the breed.

Very truly yours,

American Brittany Club          Brittany Spaniel Club of North America
Jack L. Whitworth, Secretary  Laurence E. Richardson Vice President

Immediate approval was given, and the parent club of the breed became the American Brittany Club. In the ensuing years it has expanded, and its officers and members have worked tirelessly for the breed. It is worth pointing out here that, in the very beginning, the club meant to give each member a voice in the club's operation by establishing regional clubs. This policy, difficult and never easy to administer, has paid in great dividends to the breed, and to clubs and individuals within it.

The Eastern New England Trial of 1970 was a memorable one for the Suzabob Brittanies. All four placings were won by dogs from this breeding. First through fourth (l. to r.) are Dual Ch. Suzabob's Hum Dinger, owned by Robert Young; Fld. Ch. Suzabob's Frisco Frannie, owned by Gerald Supplee; Dual Ch. Suzabob's Gigolo, owned by Nancy Dilliplane and Fld. Ch. Suzabob's Errol of Flynn, owned by James Dilliplane.

# 11

# The Brittany Spaniel
in Canada

THE history of the Brittany Spaniel in Canada is intimately tied into that of the United States and Mexico. The breed gained its initial impetus from Louis A. Thebaud of the United States and Juan Pugibet of Mexico. In Canada, there was a third pioneer— Eudore Chevrier, a Frenchman by extraction.

Chevrier operated a breeding and sales kennel which he registered. It seems probable that he named the kennel Avandale in order to link it to then famous Avendale Kennels of England. Avendale bred English Springer Spaniels, and Chevrier bought, bred, imported, and sold hundreds of this breed.

Chevrier had a remarkable ability to sense well in advance the rising popularity of a given breed. He was essentially interested in sporting dogs. He imported hundreds of dogs in the sporting breeds, used them for breeding, and often then resold them. His puppy sales mounted into the thousands.

The connection between Eudore Chevrier and Louis A. Thebaud is not entirely clear. But this much is known. Thebaud imported Genette Du Mesnil from France. She was born Jan. 6, 1932, a white and orange bitch bred by G. Metayer from Escault Du Mesnil out of Crevette de Hirondelle. Before shipping her, Metayer bred her to Gredin du Mesnil, a grandson of the immortal Aotrou de Cornouaille, through his son, Emir du Cosquerou.

Earlier accounts state that Genette du Mesnil arrived in the United States on Aug. 6, 1933. But this would appear to be an error. If one allows at least six days for travel, Genette could not have been mated before Aug. 1. Yet, as will be shown, the mating must have taken place much later.

Upon her arrival in the United States, Thebaud shipped her to Eudore Chevrier at Winnipeg. There she produced a litter of six living puppies on Oct. 12, 1933. This is the whelping date, as certified by the Canadian National Livestock Records and the Canadian Kennel Club Stud Book. If Genette arrived on Aug. 6, then her puppies would have to have had a gestation period of 73 days or more, or at least 10 days longer than normal, which seems improbable.

The Brittany Spaniel was not recognized by the Canadian Kennel Club until 1935, when the breed was given official stud book admission by both the Canadian and American Kennel Clubs. Thus, Chevrier did not register Genette du Mesnil until after the breed's recognition in 1935.

The first of Genette's litter to be registered was Yvette of Avandale in 1935. Although she was "whelped the property of Chevrier," and was given his Avandale kennel name, Yvette was registered by her second owner, Andre Vaudoyer of Winnipeg. In 1936, Chevrier registered one of the litter which he had kept, Agincourt of Avandale.

In the meantime, Thebaud had imported Franche du Cosquerou from France. He sent Franche to Winnipeg. Andre Vaudoyer bred Yvette of Avandale to Franche. Her litter, born Oct. 31, 1934, included the famous Parisienne. Chevrier bought Parisienne from Vaudoyer, and later sold the dog to Walter B. Kleeman of Springfield, Ohio. Parisienne was entered in the Greater Winnipeg Kennel Club show in 1936 to become the first Brittany Spaniel ever entered in a Canadian dog show.

After using Agincourt of Avandale at stud, Chevrier sold the dog to A. Miller McKay who showed him at the Picton, Ontario, show in 1937 and got best of breed.

But Brittany Spaniel activity in Canada remained weak until 1940. Chevrier seems to have lost most of his interest in Brittanies. In 1940, five Brittany Spaniels were registered in the Canadian Kennel Club Stud Book. These were Iva de Sainte-Yveline, Izel, Langoat of Casa Blanca, Loquirec of Casa Blanca, and Lossac of Casa Blanca.

The Casa Blanca dogs all came from the kennels of Juan Pugibet of Villa Obregon, Mexico. Iva de Sainte-Yveline was whelped in France on July 25, 1934. She was bred by Louis Pigassou. Alan Stuyvesant imported her to the United States, then sent her to Canada. Her sire was Frileux, a son of Cassis du Cosquerou, and her dam was Era de l'Etat by Vite 2nd de l'Etat.

Izel was bred in France by Emil Le Jannick, and was imported by Samuel B. Wells. He sold the dog to Alan Stuyvesant. The latter sold her to F. H. Hatheway of Fredericton, New Brunswick. Izel was white and orange roan in color.

Langoat and Lossac of Casa Blanca were both by Jilgrim of Casa Blanca, out of the famous Histr de Cornouaille. Pugibet sold them both to J. Harold McMurray of Fredericton, N. B. They were whelped Aug. 19, 1937. Loquiric of Casa Blanca, a white and orange dog whelped Oct. 9, 1937, was by Kobold of Casa Blanca out of Jaiet of Casa Blanca. His Canadian owner was H. G. Chestnut, also from New Brunswick.

In 1941, only four dogs were registered. Hatheway registered Gunner of Lincoln, by Loquirec of Casa Blanca out of Izel. Frank Shute of Fredericton registered three puppies under his Sunstead name— Jacques, Jalna, and Jeanette of Sunstead. They were whelped Sept. 3, 1939 by Langoat of Casa Blanca out of Iva de Sainte-Yveline.

There were eight registrations in 1942. Two of the more important ones are mentioned here. C. Leslie Laing of Vancouver, British Columbia, bought Allamuchy Valley Pierre, later a champion, from Alan Stuyvesant. Pierre was by Allamuchy Valley Mike out of Iane de Cornouaille. A. J. Pocock of Beebe, Quebec, bought Allen's Tex from R. C. Ward of Missoula, Montana. Tex was by Ace of Brittany, a son of Gwennec de l'Argoat, out of Pride of Brittany. Tex was whelped Sept. 19, 1940, and was described as being brown and white.

Brittanies now began to appear at dog shows. Bob Along of Langoat, owned by R. E. Healy of Moncton, N.B., was best of breed at the Moncton show in 1942. Mae De Cornean, owned by W. R. Willgrass of Burnaby, B.C., was best of breed at the International Kennel Club of Vancouver show in the same year.

In 1943, Lucien Ufford of Bellows Falls, Vermont, took Loufel Daisy to Moncton where she won best of breed. Mae De Cornean was best of breed at the International Kennel Club of Vancouver show of 1943, and at the Taunton House School Kennel Club. Pierre De Basgard was best of breed at London, Ontario, and Voyageur

Canadian Dual Ch. Vic's Winsome Whirlwind, owned by Francis Benson.

Canadian Dual Ch. Kipewa's Breton Belle, owned by William McClure, is a Brittany with accomplishments in field, bench and as a producer. She won the ABC 1966 Grouse Classic and has 32 field wins. She is also the dam of two show champions and two field winners. *McNeill photo.*

A gathering of the contestants at the New Brunswick woodcock trials in 1949. In the back row (l. to r.) are John Pettit, Ott Hicks, Jack T. Mayer, Dave Griffith, Al Gray and Stewart Jones. Those in the front row are (l. to r.) Grover Torrens, Lucien Ufford and Alan Stuyvesant.

This picture, taken at the New Brunswick cover trials on woodcock, shows some of the well-known fanciers that participated in the event. In the back row (l. to r.) are Leigh DeVoe, Dick Hoyer, Walter Kleeman and Herbert Farnsworth. The gentlemen in the front row are (l. to r.) J. W. Mayer, Frank McGinley, A. Gray and Alan R. Stuyvesant.

Judges of the New Brunswick trial Dr. John Likely (left) and Charles Bennett (center) with Bill McClure, columnist for *Dogs in Canada* and noted field trialer on both sides of the border.

MacEochaidh was best of breed at the second Vancouver Island K. C. show.

There were only seven dogs shown in 1944, but the sudden surge of interest in the breed in the Pacific Northwest resulted in the crowning of the first three Brittany Spaniel champions in Canadian history. All three were owned in the area of Vancouver and Western British Columbia. In all, 33 dogs competed at shows that year.

The three champions were: Nan of Chippewa, bred by Hilmer Peterson of Brandon, Minnesota, and owned by Western Higbie of Lynmour, B.C.; Pierre de Cornean and Voyageur Mac Eochaidh, both owned by W. R. Willigress of New Westminster, B.C.

Pierre de Cornean, or Pierre of Cornean, as he was also known, was unregistered at the time he became a champion. There was a technical defect in his registration application, so registration was refused. He was whelped on Feb. 4, 1944, by Jotek Jr. out of Mae de Cornean. In Oct. of 1947, the Canadian National Livestock Records granted him registration under Article 33, Section 7, of the rules. This rule permits the registration of a champion when there is only a technical error in the pedigree. Pierre won his championship while still a puppy.

Interest in the breed now grew rapidly. There were 120 registrations in 1946, and four dogs completed championships. These were Allamuchy Valley Pierre, Mae de Cornean, Cecile of Westhaven, and Pride of Westhaven.

Perhaps the greatest name in the Canadian field trial history of the Brittany Spaniel is that of Jack T. Mayer. Even before 1940 Mayer was training field dogs, and he is still doing so. His headquarters are in the great woodcock and grouse area around Moncton, N.B., near Gunningsville and Coles Island. Mayer began training Pointers and English Setters. But these breeds are—ideally—wide ranging dogs. In the thick, wooded cover of New Brunswick they were apt to get out of sight and hearing, and therefore out of control. Thus, unless trained to work rather closely, they were not ideal for New Brunswick hunting. Mayer later developed a method of "range training" the wide going dogs, but in the early days this was extremely difficult.

Mayer was a close reader of the *American Field*. And in early Brittany Spaniel history, both the American and Canadian Brittanies were registered with the American Field's *Field Dog Stud Book*. It was in the *American Field* that Mayer first read about the close

This is Jack
Mayer, a pioneer
trainer of Brittany
Spaniels in
Canada.

Coverdale Mitzie, owned by Jack Mayer, was a famous
Canadian field trial performer in the earlier days of the
breed. She is shown here on point.

working French pointing spaniels. They appeared to be perfect for New Brunswick woodcock and grouse hunting.

One day he showed an *American Field* article to a Massachusetts client. Then he asked: "What is the use of getting our arms pulled off trying to bring the big dogs back into range? Why don't we try one of these Brittany Spaniels?"

Along with the article there was an advertisement for Brittany Spaniel puppies owned in Kansas. The Massachusetts man immediately sent off a telegram to purchase one. Later, he sent the pup to Mayer for training. She was only six months old, and when Mayer first took her into the field he was amazed to see her point and retrieve without training. She was named Coverdale Mitzie. Coverdale is Mayer's kennel name. She was by Duke of Windsor out of Wallic Warfield.

Mayer believes that Iva de Sainte-Yveline was the first Brittany to arrive in New Brunswick. And he recounts that Alan Stuyvesant had a policy of placing Britts where they would bring the most attention. Thus, Iva went to his New Brunswick hunting companion, Frank Shute, of Fredericton. Later, he placed Izel with Hatheway.

In the fall of 1940, Lucien Ufford of Bellows Falls, Vermont, was experimenting with Gordon Setters. These were slower and closer ranging dogs than Pointers and English Setters. Ufford took his dogs to the Moncton area for the woodcock shooting season.

On the first morning, Jack Mayer hunted with Ufford and the Gordons. Not a single grouse or woodcock was brought down. That afternoon, the Gordons were kenneled, and Mayer brought out his bitch, Coverdale Mitzie. The men got their game limits. Ufford said later that Mitzie's work had been nothing short of fantastic. He was instantly converted to the breed. Within weeks, he had bought the famous Mollie de Ver Der Mont. She was by Puchyan Britt out of Leostic of Casa Blanca.

The success of the New Brunswick Brittany Spaniels brought about the organization of the Maritime Brittany Club. On Oct. 26–27, 1946 Ufford and Alan Stuyvesant judged the first trial given by this club. A. D. Gray and Grover Torrens, both of Moncton, were in charge.

Of this trial we know only that Gray's Brittanies were major winners. The following year, there was a trial at Charlottetown, Prince Edward Island. In it, the Brittany Spaniels had to compete against Pointers and English Setters. Alan Stuyvesant's Allamuchy Valley Addie, though still young enough to compete as a puppy, won the open all-age-stake.

Mexican Authority, Yves Besnier, with Alan Stuyvesant's import, Thais du Roc' Hellou.

Ray Goland, Brittany fancier and field trial judge, hunting woodcock with Ch. Pepper of Loufel in New Brunswick, Canada in 1946. *New Brunswick Gov't Information Bureau photo.*

The following year, the Maritime Brittany Club gave its second trial. It stands out as one of the greatest of all the early trials. The dates were Oct. 27–28, 1947, and the courses were over the famous Rampasture Covers near Elgin. There were 44 dogs entered, of which 36 were American, and eight were from New Brunswick and Prince Edward Island.

The judges were Raymond Hoyer and Robert Farnsworth, both from Andover, Mass. A report of the trial said: "The judges placed the winners solely on merit and ability to find birds." Tommy Cox and Bill Kull had strings of dogs with them. Cox had four puppies entered and placed all four in the puppy stake. Yves Besnier, a Mexican fancier and a representative of the Mexican Kennel Club, attended. The trial was held under the rules of the American Brittany Club.

Broad Archer of Richmont, owned by Dr. R. C. Busteed, then of Savannah, Ga., won the open all age stake, with Cox handling. Avono Jill of Karomish, owned by Jack L. Whitworth of Avon, O., and handled by Kull, was second. Iza Mac Eochaidh, owned by Dr. H. E. Longsdorf of Mt. Holly, N.J., and handled by Jack Mayer, was third. Aotrou's Jacques, owned and handled by J. T. Sprague of Honeoye Falls, N.Y., was fourth.

Bill Kull handled the first and second dogs in the Derby. They were Georges of Leeway, owned by John W. Lee of Indianapolis, Ind., first, and Calatin Mac Eochaidh Sam, owned by Dr. T. J. Talbott of Lima, O., second. Third went to Rouge Kaer de Klemanor, owned and handled by Walter Kleeman, then president of the American Brittany Club. A. J. Hicks of Gunningsville, handled his Meil du Shepodie to fourth.

The open shooting dog stake was won by Buckeye de Klemanor, owned and handled by Kleeman, who also handled his Brittany House Abner into second. Parky's Joan, owned by Eral Larsen of Minneapolis, Minnesota, was third. And Brittany House Ann, owned by Dr. Talbott, was fourth.

Ray Goland handled his Pepper of Loufel to first in the shooting dog stake. An odd feature of the trials was that Allamuchy Valley Addie, winner of the open all age stake the week before on Prince Edward Island, got only a second in the puppy stake, and was otherwise unplaced.

The Maritime Brittany Club had actually originated field trials in New Brunswick. In 1948 its affiliate, the Moncton Brittany, Pointer & Setter Club, held trials at Turtle Creek. Jack T. Mayer served as field marshall. His son, Jack T. Mayer Jr., made his debut as a trainer-handler. The Coverdale affix was now making a name for itself all over Canada. Three of the four first place winners were bred by Mayer and carried the Coverdale name.

Jack Mayer Jr. handled Coverdale Eva, owned by Alan Stuyvesant, to victory in the puppy stake, and to second in the Derby. First place went to a Pointer. Coverdale Slug, owned and handled by G. B. Wetmore of Hillsboro, N. B. won the open all age. Mayer had also bred Luke's Allamuchy Chesta, owned and handled by Alan Stuyvesant, which won the shooting dog stake. He had also bred the Pointer, Shawinigan Brown-Eyed Susan, winner of the derby.

Allamuchy Kaergirl of Loufel, handled by Cox for Mrs. Rene Espourteil of Angle Point, Ore., was second in the all age. The Pointer was third. Alan Stuyvesant handled Rumba de L'Argoat to fourth. All told, Americans captured 10 of 16 placements. But the work of the outnumbered Canadian dogs proved that they were the equal to any in North America.

Ever since the early days, Brittany Spaniels have competed against each other on both sides of the border. Perhaps three American dogs should be mentioned here. The First was Dr. Edgar W. Averill's American Ch. Diane de Beauch, U.D. Diane won her bench championship in Canada, and also completed a C.D.X. title there.

American Dual Ch. Way-Kan Jeff also won a Canadian dual championship. He is the first dog of any breed ever to do this. Way-Kan Jeff died in the summer of 1971 at the age of 12. During that same month Bernie's Butch, owned by Bernus Turner of Kent, Washington, joined Way-Kan Jeff by winning his Canadian and American dual championships. Other Brittany Spaniels have starred on both sides of the border. Their records appear in the Canadian statistics given below.

Up to this writing, Canada had produced five dual champions— show and field. It had crowned 73 show champions and 10 field champions. Nineteen Brittany Spaniels have won Companion Dog (C.D.) titles only. Five have won Companion Dog Excellent (C.D.X.) titles. And two have won Utility Dog (U.D.) degrees. In addition, one Brittany Spaniel has won a Tracking Dog (T.D.) title.

Besides American Ch. Diane De Beauch, U.D., American Ch. Sun Tan's Happy Hi Tone, C.D., also won both a Canadian show title and a Canadian C.D. Canadian Ch. Jocko's Tic Toc Spice also won a C.D.X. title. Canadian Field Ch. Corky De Leigh and Can. Ch. Poplar Hill Riptide also won C.D. degrees.

The first dual champion of the breed was Britt of
Bellows Falls owned by Lucien Ufford.

Brittany Spaniels won first and third places in the Open Shooting Dog Stakes
at the 12th annual New Brunswick Field Trial Club's trial in 1971. First was
Peggy's Friend (left), owned by Harold Hatfield, and third was Corky De
Leigh, owned and handled by Basil Hawkins.

The following lists show the dogs that have won dual championships, utility degrees and tracking degrees in Canada:

## CANADIAN DUAL CHAMPIONS

Bernie's Butch (U.S. Dual Champion)
Kipewa's Breton Belle
Salisbury's Pal of Span-Haven
Vic's Winsome Whirlwind
Way-Kan Jeff (Also U.S. Dual Ch.)

## CANADIAN UTILITY DOG TITLE HOLDERS

Renee Cottrell
Westburn Spreckle

## CANADIAN TRACKING DOG TITLE HOLDER

Speckles Dark Loon

Canadian Ch. Kipewa's Paradise Rex, owned by William McClure, has placed in the Sporting group and is the sire of two field winners.

Coquette of Bonnechere, owned by William McClure, is the dam of two field winners.

# 12

# The First Field Trial Tests

T HE first Brittany Spaniels to come to North America came to hunt. Their reputation had been made in France, principally as superb woodcock and grouse dogs. But Louis Thebaud thought they might be ideal for quail hunting. Others thought they might be suitable for use in rather restricted hunting areas where men wanted a pointing dog which could be used by a man on foot. Others were eager to try the new breed on pheasants.

So it was that the first Brittany Spaniels were eagerly tried under American shooting conditions. They quickly proved their merit. Yet for most sportsmen a big question remained. How would these dogs compare to Pointers and English Setters? So sportsmen tended to reserve judgment until the dogs had proven themselves on American game birds in field trials. There were plenty of these in most sections of the U.S. and Canada, and there were also trials in Mexico. Almost all of them were run under the procedures set up by the American Field and the Amateur Field Trial Clubs of America. These trials had become virtually "breed specific." That is, Pointers and English Setters dominated them to so great an extent that few dogs of other pointing breeds competed against them. For most of the sportsmen who competed, the Brittany, a spaniel, seemed a ridiculous possibility for their trials.

79

Ch. Avono Jake (left) and Ch. Kaerson of Loufel at the breakaway of the American Brittany Club Trials of 1948.

Allamuchy Valley Luke, owned by Walter Clements, was a trailblazer that brought fame to himself and his breed. A French-bred, he competed successfully against pointers and setters at American field trials.

Trial procedures in some countries, and in some areas of these countries, differed. In England, and in some areas of continental Europe, a dog was required to point. Then, upon command, it went in to flush. Some trials required that the flushed bird be shot. The dog might be sent in to flush, or the handler might flush it. The handler, or a professional gunner might do the shooting. The dog would have to be steady to flush, mark the fall, and then make the retrieve.

A somewhat similar situation exists today in the United States at trials for Gordon Setters. Eastern clubs normally require the owner or handler to flush the bird. The handler fires a blank pistol. At Pacific Coast trials, the handler flushes the birds. Professional gunners then bring them down. The dogs must mark the birds and retrieve to hand.

But at pointing dog trials under the procedures of the American Field, the handler flushes the bird, then fires a blank cartridge. For the new Brittany Spaniel owners, this was a change from European procedures. So some slight retraining of the dogs was necessary. Still, these sportsmen were anxious to test their dogs against the well established, and highly competent Pointers and English Setters.

We do not know when the first Brittany Spaniel appeared in an American field trial. There are hundreds of informal events which go unreported. But the Jockey Hollow Field Trial Club in New Jersey was already an old, well established club, and one hallowed by long tradition. At its event on April 20, 1935, Franche du Cosquerou, owned by Louis A. Thebaud, placed third.

Shortly thereafter, Brittany Spaniels began to appear in trials in Mexico, in many areas of the United States, and in British Columbia. Histr de Cornouaille ran creditably in Mexico and Texas. Meanwhile, Alan Stuyvesant, a member of Jockey Hollow, had seen the Thebaud dogs. He imported Iane de Cornouaille in 1936. Iane had been whelped in France before Histr went to Mexico. Iane placed in American events, as did Ebob's Jannick Kay, a son of Hart de la Casa Blanca, and a fully bred Mexican dog.

It must be remembered that Louis Thebaud began importing Brittany Spaniels at an age when most men have retired to the fireside. He was 76 years old when Franche du Cosquerou placed third in the Jockey Hollow trials. Now Thebaud sent his three finest dogs to his near nephew, René Joubert, at Detroit. The three were Franche du Cosquerou, Fenntus, and Hai du Cosquerou. René Joubert has said that hunting and field sports were a way of life for him.

In this photo of Parisienne de Klemanor one can observe correct shoulder angulation in the long extension of the left front leg.

Int. Ch. Wanda de L'Argoat pointing pheasant.

Consequently, he spent as much time as he could with the three dogs. Under his handling, Fenntus placed second in the members' shooting dog stake at the Royal Oak Club trials. The next spring, in April 1937, she won the stake.

In the years that followed, Michigan, Ohio, and the Chicago area became a great triangle in which Brittany Spaniel activity increased greatly. In the fall of 1939, the first all-Brittany trial was held in the Detroit area. The winner was Fanche's French Line (usually called Napoleon). Since René Joubert represented the French Line shipping company, the relationship to René Joubert's dogs is obvious. Fanche's French Line was owned and handled by Judge Homer Ferguson. The dog defeated Franche du Cosquerou and Gwennec de l'Argoat. The following year, Kaer de Cornouaille won with Fanche's French Line second. It is of note that Judge Ferguson did most of the legal work in the founding of the American Brittany Club. But his work with Brittany Spaniels ended shortly after the club's organization when he became the United States Senator from Michigan.

At these early Michigan trials, the birds were shot. Consequently, most of the dogs had to run under entirely different conditions at different trials. Above, we have mentioned the victory of Kaer de Cornouaille. He is one of the great dogs in American Brittany Spaniel history. He competed in trials against Pointers and English Setters in this country and Mexico, and the brilliance of his performances did much to give the Brittany Spaniel its place in the American bird dog field.

Kaer was whelped on Aug. 1, 1936. He was bred by the great Frenchman, Emile Bourdon, at his Cornouaille Kennels. A short pedigree of him reads like this: By Idoc de Cornouaille out of Hem'za de Cornouaille, by Flist III de Cornouaille out of Diwal de Cornouaille, by Potic II out of Ayout. Idoc was a son of Huch de Bleun Brug, out of Gaud de Guilben by Dag de Basgard, out of Dora de Carigne, by Bath de Callac out of Yotte de Basgard. Idoc de Cornouaille was brought to America by Dr. Chester H. Keogh of Chicago.

Alan Stuyvesant imported Kaer de Cornouaille in Sept. 1938. Some two months later, Kaer ran in the trials of the Jockey Hollow Field Trial Club. He placed third in the shooting dog stake. *The American Field* report says that "Kaer ran the course with good judgment and with considerably better pace and range than most of the pointers and setters running against him. A nice find, followed by a good retrieve, climaxed his race."

Kaer took a second the following month in the members' shooting dog stake at Jockey Hollow. He then placed second at trials near Vera Cruz, Mexico. Kaer won first place in finals of the Jockey Hollow gundog competition for 1941. Jockey Hollow had a series of trials, with the winners of each to compete in a final event. Having won a preliminary, Kaer now won the finals. The victory made him the best shooting dog to be owned by a member.

Howard Clements had bought Allamuchy Valley Luke from Alan Stuyvesant. In 1940, Luke took a second in the all age stake at the Chicagoland trials. And he was voted the second best all around shooting dog in the trials. Walter Kleeman's Parisienne also was placing in trials, in competition with Pointers and English Setters.

Then a critical time had come for the Brittany Spaniel in America. Louis Thebaud had died in 1939. Alan Stuyvesant, who had seen Thebaud's dogs at Jockey Hollow, had begun an astonishing import program. But Europe was involved in World War II. Alan Stuyvesant and his brother had entered the war on the side of France. They had organized and equipped an ambulance corps. Alan was now a prisoner of war; his brother was to be forever "missing in action." The Brittany Spaniel Club of North America had virtually ceased to exist. The American Brittany Club was organized, in part, because Brittany Spaniel owners could not make contact with the parent club. In part, also, the center of Brittany activity had moved into the Michigan, Ohio, Illinois triangle. At its October, 1942 meeting, the club could report that 59 per cent of its members came from these three states. But the club had members in 17 states, and Juan Pugibet in Mexico.

At that meeting Dr. D. B. Ruskin reported that, for more than a year, mail sent to the Brittany Spaniel Club of North America had been returned unclaimed. Meanwhile, there had been seven trials for Brittany Spaniels alone in the Michigan area. Dr. Ruskin had been named correspondent, and official columnist on the breed for the official AKC magazine, *Pure-bred Dogs, The American Kennel Gazette.*

Cries were being heard all over America for an official trial. But ideas as to procedure differed. Some wanted to follow the procedure at American Field trials, in which the pointed game was flushed but not shot. Others wanted the birds flushed, marked, and retrieved— the procedure which had been used in the trials for Brittany Spaniels alone. And Allamuchy Valley Luke had won the last.

The American Brittany Club now sponsored a formal national amateur shooting dog stake. It was held at the Outland Riding Club,

14 miles from downtown Detroit, on Oct. 11, 1942. R. B. McCurdy
was field trial chairman. The judges were Hunter Gaines of Lansing,
Mich., and Robert Herndon of Detroit. In addition to the shooting
dog stake, there was a derby and a puppy stake. In the national
amateur shooting dog stake, two pheasants were planted in the bird
field for each brace. In some cases, the birds had flushed before the
dogs entered the bird field.

In its second issue, December, 1942, *The Brittany Field & Bench*
gives an official report of the trial:

"FIRST PLACE went to Suzette of Chippewa, owned and handled
by Hilmer Peterson of Brandon, Minn. Suzette broke fast and ran a
beautiful field. She made her find in the bird field, but the bird flew
low and towards the gallery, and there was no kill. She was later called
back to work in the bird cover. She made her find. Peterson killed
the bird and the dog made a perfect retrieve.

"SECOND AWARD was won by Reliew Rene, owned and handled
by C. L. Williams of Birmingham, Mich. Reliew Rene was in the
fifth brace and by that time the day was getting quite warm. Reliew
Rene made her find and Williams got the bird. The dog retrieved
nicely.

"THIRD was taken by Marron Glace, owned by Dr. Keogh of Chicago, and handled by Mr. Thomas W. Cox of South Dakota. She
broke fast, made her find and point. Mr. Cox dropped the bird with
a wing shot. Marron Glace was unable to make the find or retrieve.
Marron Glace was called back to work in bird cover, being braced
with Suzette of Chippewa, and made a sight back while Suzette made
her find.

"Other entries in the all age stake were:

"Sorcha Mac Eochaidh, owned and handled by Mr. Peterson. Sorcha
made her find, the bird flushed wild, but Sorcha was steady to wing.

"Potainne de Sharvogue, owned and handled by E. W. Averill of
Birmingham, Mich.

"Patrice de Sharvogue, owned and handled by E. W. Averill. The
bird flushed wild, but was brought down by Mr. Averill. But Patrice
refused to retrieve.

"Betsy de Bonaventure, owned and handled by R. B. McCurdy of
Detroit, made the retrieve of the bird brought down by Mr. Averill.

"Tutti Frutti Mac Eochaidh, owned by Dr. Keogh and handled by
Mr. Cox, was paired with Suzette of Chippewa, and backed her nicely.

"Kiki Mac Eochaidh, owned and handled by C. L. Williams

"Beau de Bonaventure, owned and handled by R. B. McCurdy, made
his find. The bird flushed wild and out of shooting range, Beau was
called back to cover the bird field, but no find resulted.

"Gwennec's Pascey, owned and handled by Mrs. Mildred Ady and handled by Al H. Ady, Detroit, Mich., was paired with Reliew Rene. One bird flushed when planted and Reliew Rene made the find on the other bird.

"Gwennec D'Etoile, owned and handled by Mrs. Kathryn Adams. Etoile broke fast and ran a nice field. Her bird ran, following a hedge row across the field and flushed wild. Etoile was steady to flush.

"Aotrou Mac Eochaidh was a by-dog, owned and handled by Mr. Ady. The bird ran and the dog bumped him and then chased him out of sight.

## SUMMARY

"First—Suzette of Chippewa, bitch, by Morris de l'Argoat Basgard ex Sorcha Mac Eochaidh. Hilmer Peterson, owner and handler.

"Second—Reliew Rene, dog, by Gwennec de l'Argoat ex Franche's Smarty. C. L. Williams, owner-handler.

"Third—Marron Glace Mac Eochaidh, bitch, by Idoc de Cornouaille ex Leltic de Pradalan.

## DERBY

"The derby was run over the same field and one bird was staked out in the field for the dogs to work on. There were 13 entries.

"First place went to Brit of Bellows Falls, owned by Mr. Lucien H. Ufford of Bellows Falls, Vermont, and handled by Mr. Cox.

"Second place went to Chipps Brit of Chippewa, owned and handled by Mr. Peterson.

"Third place went to Chartreux Mac Eochaidh, owned by Dr. Keogh, and handled by Mr. Cox.

"Other entries in the Derby were:

"Ogma Mac Eochaidh, owned by Dr. Yant of Cleveland and handled by Mr. Cox.

"Andre Phillipe de Bonaventure, owned and handled by E. B. Galloway, Grosse Pointe, Mich.

"Andre de Carnac, owned and handled by Mr. J. Whitworth of Avon, Ohio.

"Brit Les Chien, owned and handled by Dr. Batson of Mt. Pleasant, Mich.

"Brehon Mac Eochaidh, owned by E. Wood of Wisconsin, and handled by Mr. Cox.

"Suzette of Chipewa, owned and handled by Mr. Peterson.

"Zuk de Beauchamps, owned and handled by Mr. Gayek of St. Clair Shores, Mich.

"Bonne de Beauchamps, owned by Mr. Whitworth and handled by Mr. Averill.

The famous Ch. Patrice of Sharvogue, owned by Dr. Edgar W. Averill, was best of breed at the first national Specialty. This early great narrowly missed becoming a dual champion.

"Benedictine Mac Eochaidh, owned by Mr. Cline of Cleveland, Ohio, and handled by Mr. Cox.

"Macaron Mac Eochaidh, owned by Dr. Keogh and handled by Mr. Cox.

## SUMMARY

"First—Brit of Bellows Falls, dog, by Kaer de Cornouaille ex Oged de la Casa Blanca, owned by Mr. Ufford and handled by Mr. Cox.

"Second—Chipps Brit of Chippewa, dog, by Morris de l'Argoat Basgard ex Sorcha Mac Eochaidh, owned and handled by Mr. Peterson.

"Third—Chartreux Mac Eochaidh, dog, by Idoc de Cornouaille ex Leltic de Pradalan. Dr. Keogh owner, Mr. Cox handler.

## PUPPY STAKE

"The puppies were run on a shorter course. There were five entries.

"First place went to Chiquo of Chippewa, dog, by Morris de l'Argoat Basgard ex Sorcha Mac Eochaidh, owned by Mr. H. Wassau of Minnesota and handled by Mr. Peterson.

"Second place went to Brit Les Chien, dog, by Calatin Mac Eochaidh ex Bakers Flirt, owned and handled by Dr. Batson.

"Third place went to Jacques de Bonaventure, dog, by Beau de Bonaventure ex Betsy de Bonaventure, owned by Mr. Fitzpatrick of Pontiac and handled by Mr. Scully of Pontiac.

"Others entered were Jojo of Chippewa, owned by Mr. Dell of Minnesota, and handled by Mr. Peterson, and Biddy of Briarcliff, owned by Mr. MacMichaels (handler not known)."

Notably this trial brought out two dogs which were to be among the first dual champions of their breed—Brit of Bellows Falls, and Aotrou Mac Eochaidh. A system of trial points was worked out, with five for a win, three for a second, and one for a third. Walter B. Kleeman, who had to miss the trial, gave a special silver trophy for the person who won the most points. The trophy, given to stimulate multiple entries, was won by Hilmer Peterson.

# 13

# The First Licensed
# Trial and Show

Both members and non-members of the American Brittany Club were now clamoring for a championship field trial and a licensed bench show, or specialty show as it is usually called. Under American Kennel Club rules, the Brittany Spaniel Club of North America was the parent club of the breed and would have to give permission. But its president, Alan Stuyvesant, was a prisoner of war in Italy, and its secretary could not be reached. The American Kennel Club at last agreed to license both a field trial and a bench show without parent club permission. But it did suggest that an experienced, but non-Brittany club, act as host for both events.

The Ravenna Field Trial Club at Ravenna, Ohio, had been conducting licensed trials for English Springer and Cocker Spaniels. It had also held Pointer and English Setter trials until told by the American Kennel Club that it could no longer do so. That is, it had been told that it would have to be a spaniel or a pointing dog club. And it had settled for the former, but it did have experienced personnel for both types of trials.

The American Kennel Club then agreed to allow the Ravenna club to act as host club for the Brittany field trial and bench show.

The author was selected as field trial and bench show chairman. The trial and show were to be held in conjunction with a trial for English Springers and Cocker Spaniels. Today, it must appear to have been an odd arrangement, especially since the writer was also field trial chairman for the flushing dog trials. Yet it worked out very well.

The situation in Ohio in 1943 was this. An attorney general had ruled that domestically raised and banded game birds became the property of the State of Ohio at the instant of release. They could not be shot, except during the hunting season, and hunting was not allowed on Sunday. So the Springer and Cocker trials had to be held during the hunting season, and in this case, on Saturday. But the American Brittany Club had decided not to permit the shooting of flushed birds. So their club's trial could be held on Sunday.

The Springer and Cocker trials were thus held on Saturday, Nov. 27, 1943. The two clubs held a joint field trial dinner at the Masonic Temple at Ravenna. Afterward Jerome N. Halle judged the bench show. Mr. Halle helped later to revise the standard, and became an honorary lifetime member.

There were 28 dogs at the specialty show. Winners dog and best of breed was Patrice of Sharvogue, owned and shown by Edgar W. Averill. Winners bitch and best of opposite sex to best of breed was Madame Patricia, owned by Robert M. Spangler of Massillon, Ohio. Reserve winners dog was Avono Jack of Karomish, owned by Dr. David Ruskin, Caro., Mich. And reserve winners bitch was Benedictine Mac Eochaidh, owned by Hal P. Cline of Rocky River, O.

The following day, Sunday, Nov. 28, 1943, the first licensed Brittany Spaniel field trial was held. The judges were William T. Windsor and James Talmadge. Windsor was a bird dog field trial man of long experience, and he was an officer in the Ohio Department of Conservation and Natural Resources. Talmadge also was an experienced bird dog field trial man. With his father he operated what was then one of the largest pheasant farms in the world.

Here is the official report of the trial, as written by Dr. Ruskin. It appeared in the Jan. 1944 issue of *Pure-bred Dogs, The American Kennel Gazette.*

"Although it had snowed on Saturday, during the American Brittany Club Specialty Show, Sunday, Nov. 28, turned out to be clear, brisk, and with a slight breeze. The trial was held on the Hohing Farm, two miles south of Ravenna, O., which was thickly covered with briars, and which provided excellent cover for both the planted

Some of the officials at the National Trials in 1944. They are the author (mounted at left), Edward Dana Knight (mounted at right). The bird planter is Jack Murphy and field marshall, Lee French, stands before Mr. Knight. The horseman in the center is unidentified.

Ch. Buccaneer de Klemanor (Ch. Buck of Chippewa ex Ch. Jule of Loufel), owned by Walter B. Kleeman.

pheasants and for those which had made the farm their natural home. The short, flat, wavy coat of the Brittany, and the absence of tail, or at the most, a stub of tail, proved of considerable advantage to the dog, and enabled him to work in cover which would ordinarily turn back any other pointing breed.

"Under the judging of James Talmadge and Bill Windsor, the open all-age stake was run in the morning with six braces before a rest period was called, during which time the officials and others took the opportunity to warm up in a tent provided on the grounds, where sandwiches and hot coffee were enjoyed by all. It was already evident by this time that the caliber of the competition was high, and that there would be considerable difficulty in selecting the winners.

"This was borne out later by the fact that several dogs were called back after the first series, among them being Allamuchy Valley Luke, Brit of Bellow Falls, Parisienne de Klemanor, and Aotrou Mac Eochaidh. Unfortunately, Mr. Kleeman had left for home before the first series was completed, and was therefore unable to give Parisienne a chance at a second series.

"After considerable weighing of the pros and cons, the judges placed the dogs as follows: First, Aotrou Mac Eochaidh, owned and handled by A. H. Ady; second, Brit of Bellows Falls, owned and handled by L. H. Ufford; third, Allamuchy Valley Luke, owned and handled by H. B. Clements; and fourth, Betsy de Bonaventure, owned and handled by R. B. McCurdy; special commendation, Parisienne de Klemanor, owned and handled by W. B. Kleeman, and Benedictine Mac Eochaidh, owned and handled by H. P. Cline.

"A. H. Ady received a glass cocktail shaker, chrome tray, and six glasses for the open all-age winner. For the first time in the history of this country, a dual award was given. This too was won by Aotrou Mac Eochaidh by virtue of being the all-age winner and also qualifying by placing first in one of the classes of the bench show held the night before. This dual award was symbolized by a Handscraft Baked Bean Service Set.

"The puppy stake began about 2 p.m. and included entries born after Jan. 1, 1942, thereby combining in competition puppies and derby dogs. This stake was run over the same course and three of the four ribbons went to older dogs. They finished as follows: First, Bientot Mac Eochaidh, owned and handled by E. W. Averill; second, Babette of Brookcliff, owned and handled by L. H. Ufford; third, Avono Jack of Karomish, owned and handled by Dr. D. B. Ruskin; and fourth, Geoffre de Beauchamps, owned and handled by J. F. Powers.

"Special thanks are due to so many for the success of the events

Dual Ch. Tigre de Klemanor (Ch. Buccaneer de Klemanor ex Int. Ch. Wanda de L'Argoat), owned by Walter B. Kleeman.

Ch. Andre De Carnac (left) and Ch. Avono Jake.

These five men were among the founders of the American Brittany Club.
They are (l. to r.) A. H. Ady, Jack L. Whitworth, Walter B. Kleeman, W. E.
"Bill" Averill and Dr. D. B. Ruskin.

This picture was taken in 1948 and shows four famous early field trainers.
They are (l. to r.) Buck Bissell, Bill Kull, Lee Holman and Tommy Cox.

that a listing of the deserving people would run counter of national emergency and paper shortage. However, we would like to thank those who came from a distance to swell the entries, and those officials mentioned above, and all to give our thanks to Jack L. Whitworth, without whose industry and enthusiasm all this would have been impossible, and to Mr. Lee French who so ably helped him.—D. B. Ruskin, M.D."

It should be added here that Lee French, mentioned in Dr. Ruskin's report, had a small bird dog training kennel not too far from the Whitworth residence. He laid out the course, and members of the Ravenna Springer Spaniel group planted the birds.

So successful were this trial and show that the American Brittany Club never again had to seek permission from another breed club to hold a licensed trial or show. And never again did it have to have a "foreign" club act as host. It was successful in another way as well. The club, when finally it became the recognized parent club of the breed, decided that, wherever possible, it would hold joint trials and shows. In this way, it would keep the concept of the dual purpose dog before its members. As a result, and excepting German Shorthaired Pointers, the Brittany Spaniel has produced more dual champions—bench and field—than have all the other sporting breeds and hounds combined.

The caliber of the men who competed in the first field trial also is worth noting. Not a single one of the dogs which placed in either stake was handled by a professional. All were owner-handled. This means that they were thoroughly experienced bird dog men. They had been schooled under fire, as it were, and they knew exactly what they wanted in the Brittany Spaniel. Their knowledge and judgment made the great history of the breed possible.

Ch. Tudor du Roc' Hellou, owned by Alan Stuyvesant, finished his bench championship at the International Kennel Club of Chicago.

# 14

# The Brittany Spaniel
# as a Show Dog

W HEN, in 1943 and 1944, the American Brittany Club decided
to revise the breed standard, a number of people were asked to help.
This is discussed at greater length in the chapter on the History
of the Standard. Yet it is important to repeat part of it here. Edward
Dana Knight argued that, if the Brittany Spaniel was to make any
impression at dog shows, it would have to conform to the standards
of beauty of show dogs. These would include close clipping of the
neck and shoulders, some barbering of body coat, and heavy feathering
on the legs, belly and on the rear of the thighs.

Jerome Halle was a bench show judge. But while still in college
at Cornell University, he had run Pointers in field trials. At the time
of the discussions, Knight was a justly famous show judge. But he
was running both English Setters and English Springer Spaniels in
field trials, and he was judging Pointer, Setter, Springer and Cocker
Spaniel field trials. A division between English Setter bench and field
dogs had already taken place.

Halle and the author argued that, to prevent such a split, the
standard should be such that a Brittany Spaniel could leave a field
trial and complete successfully at a show. Even then the author was

97

noting that Springer Spaniels were being split into separate breeds, bench and field. So Halle and the writer argued that it was up to the American Brittany Club to teach the bench show judges exactly what a good Brittany Spaniel should be, and to understand the aims of the American Brittany Club. On their part, Brittany Spaniel owners should cooperate by competing in both branches of the sport.

This policy has, in large part, proven itself. The Brittany Spaniel has more dual champions—bench and field—than any other breed. In fact, excluding the German Shorthaired Pointer, it has more than all the other breeds combined. In another way, it has been less successful. Fewer Brittany Spaniels have won groups and best in show than should be the case. Here let us quote from that excellent book *The Brittany in America* by Fred Z. White, M.D., second edition:

> "I wish to repeat, formally and sincerely, that I mean no disrespect to the bench show judges who have done their best, with usually very little thanks for the trouble they have taken to judge our Brittanies as they saw them. The fault, if any, lies with us, the Brittany owners, breeders, and club members who may be confused about what we are trying to achieve, and for not having been able to properly instruct our judges about what we consider the most important characteristics of our breed."

This indicates his own dissatisfaction and that of many Brittany Spaniel owners with the majority of bench show judges. Yet there are several factors which must be mentioned. The American Brittany Club still needs to educate sporting dog judges. For the roster of such judges is constantly changing. Names disappear from it, and new ones appear.

A second factor needs to be discussed. E. W. "Bill" Averill once said that the Midwest Brittany Spaniel owners and breeders set out to improve the looks of their dogs. Alan Stuyvesant used to say that the Brittany is not a good looking dog, but is only a superb hunting machine. Can a dog be both? The answer is: "Yes, of course." But you have to apply the old proverb: "Handsome is as handsome does."

Can you say that an English Bulldog is beautiful? Probably most people would roar "no." But, if you are a breeder of English Bulldogs, and if the dog conforms closely to the standard, then you can say that the dog is beautiful. It follows that if breeders can teach judges to see beauty in a Bulldog, Brittany Spaniel breeders should be able

Dual Ch. Gringo De Britt owned by Drs. T. L. and T. E. Poling, shows the style and intensity on point that made him a field trial champion. This dog is a many faceted winner with titles in bench, field and obedience, and was the winner of the U.S. Open Championship in 1969.

Dual Ch. Gringo De Britt, C.D., is shown here making a win under judge Alvin Maurer, handler Catherine Murphy. *Shafer photo.*

to teach them to recognize a good Brittany. But then, in respect to the latter, other factors must be considered.

Many of the early Brittany Spaniels, and some of those today, were flat footed and straight in stifle, that is, with insufficient angulation at the stifle joint. Theoretically, flat feet should contribute to lameness in field work, and to some loss of stamina. Theoretically, too, straight stifles should contribute to loss of stamina. The straight stifled dog does not drive as far forward with each step as does a better angulated dog. Thus, the same amount of energy produces more forward motion in the well angulated dog. Or, the straight stifled dog must use more energy to move forward the same distance and at the same speed as does the dog with better angulation. Loose elbows are universally condemned. It is supposed that they may contribute to loss of stamina and to lameness in a field dog.

Note we have used such terms as "theoretically" and "supposed." This is for several reasons, one of which we will discuss. The other is that, even in hunting, dogs are seldom driven to the point where points of unsoundness will become a serious factor in performance. One hour to three hour heats at field trials and all day hunting would be cases where unsoundness would begin to affect performance.

Factors which might operate to mitigate the effects of unsoundness are: intensity of hunting desire, refusal to quit, stamina from other sources, wisdom, field experience, and trainability. No bench show judge can assay these qualities. He cannot know that the straight stifled dog has the stamina, intensity, and experience to be a great field dog. He cannot know whether the dog can face any kind of weather, the roughest terrain, briars and heavy cover, or whether, under these circumstances it will quit. The judge cannot, in short, estimate what we call "heart" or "guts."

The judge then has to base his decisions on soundness, on his conception of the standard of perfection of the breed, and upon temperament. Temperament is one attribute by which he can come close to guessing field performance. He cannot know whether a given dog will range out from the owner to search birdy cover. But he does know that most shy dogs will not. He can guess, and be close to right, that the noise-shy dog in the ring, will show some degree of shyness in the field. He recognizes and usually penalizes shyness because he knows that shy dogs should never be used for breeding; that no excuses should ever be made for them. He also knows that neither viciousness or sharpness are Brittany qualities. So if he recognizes them in any dog, he penalizes the dog for them.

Ch. Elcia's Lil'Hoss of Greenfield, owned and handled by Theda F. Stell, finished his championship at the same show where his sire, Ch. Beelflower Dirty Dan was best in show. *Ludwig photo.*

```
                        Ch. Royal Prince of Duckerbird
            Dual Ch. Rusty of Beelflower
                        Sandy of Beelflower

    Dual Ch. Sir Robert of Beelflower

                        Casa Blanca Mike
            Rusty of Fontana
                        Terry's Jane of Paradise

Ch. Beelflower Dirty Dan

                        Dual Ch. Albear Valley Dingo
            Dual Ch. Pacolet Sam
                        Dual Ch. Pacolet Cheyenne

    Pacolet Sam's Pierrette

                        Dual Ch. Tex of Richmont
            Fld. Ch. Riviere Valley Suzette
                        Ch. Ruby of Edough

CH. ELICIA'S LIL' HOSS OF GREENFIELD

                        Ch. Ultra-Mend Valgo Cracker
            Ch. Vitchy Valley Zipp
                        Le Gras' Midget

    Ch. Zipp's Feather Merchant

                        Ch. Yacko du Roc Hellou
            Larsen's Mitsie
                        Ch. Messer's Honey

Greenfield Gai Comique

                        Ch. Zip's Feather Merchant
            Honey's Tigar
                        Ch. Messer's Honey

    Gepsey's Mey-Len

                        Petar of Edough Duval
            Petite Femme DeLa Bois
                        Petite Femme d'Allamuchy
```

Recently, a professional handler who has spent his life, since he was 16, showing sporting dogs, said to the author:

"I can't understand why this Brittany Spaniel hasn't won groups. He is certainly good enough to win his share of them, and even an occasional best in show."

Now this comment comes from a professional who must have won several hundred best in show awards and countless sporting groups during his life. So if he asks such a question, or at least complains, every Brittany Spaniel owner is entitled also to ask: Why?

One reason is that, to most judges, the Brittany Spaniel is not a pretty dog. It doesn't catch the eyes of either the judges or of the galleries. A second reason is that too few judges understand what a Brittany should be. And a third is that some judges are just plain afraid to give a group to a Brittany Spaniel even when they feel that it deserves to win.

A famous judge, now dead, once said to the author: "You crazy damn fools can put up those garbage breeds. I'll stick to the standard breeds." Well, it isn't the way to judge dog shows. But there are usually so many good dogs in the sporting group that no one can prove they are simply sticking with the "standard" breeds. Another factor is that too few of the judges come from a Brittany background. So they have less sympathy for the breed than do those who are more familiar with it. Again, it is a job of education. In that respect, not enough Brittany Spaniels are being shown to educate these judges properly.

Now within its breed, the Brittany Spaniel has produced its share of bench champions. Following are the records of some of the Brittany Spaniels which have won in show competition with other sporting breeds.

The first Brittany Spaniel to win first in the sporting group was Ch. Queen of Paradise. She was owned by Walter S. Oberlin of DeKalb, Ill. Queen was one of the earliest champions. Her sire was Crepe La Brilliante, a son of Kaer de l'Argoat. Her dam was Suzette de Mirabeau, a son of Tango. The circumstances of her victory are interesting.

Oddly enough, the place of her victory was Ravenna, Ohio, the place where the first Brittany licensed show and field trials were held. The event was the Ravenna Kennel Club's all breed show. It was not a large one, since there were only 400 dogs in competition. The date was Sept. 14, 1946. Mabel Pyle, one of the earliest professional

Ch. Ti War Chip de Triumph, owned and handled by R. B. Edwards, shown winning fourth in the Sporting group at the Blennerhassett Kennel Club under judge Henry Stoecker. The dog was ten years old at the time of the win. *Norton of Kent photo.*

handlers of her sex, showed Ch. Queen of Paradise. William L. Kendrick judged the breed and the group.

Mabel Pyle was a noted handler of pointing breeds. On this day, she won best of breed with the Brittany, with the Irish Setter, Ch. Janet of Aragon, with the English Setter, Ch. Bohemia of Aragon, and with a Pointer. Of course, she could not show all these dogs in the group. And Brittany Spaniels never placed anyway. So she put Queen of Paradise into a crate, and loaded her into her van along with beaten dogs. She elected to show the Irish Setter, and turned the English Setter and the Pointer over to other handlers.

When the sporting group started, Mr. Kendrick asked about the Brittany. The writer, as show chairman and chief steward, had to report that it was absent. But Mr. Kendrick refused to judge until it had been brought into the ring. The committee unloaded Miss Pyle's crates and found Ch. Queen of Paradise in the last crate to be unloaded. An exhibitor was asked to take the dog into the ring, and Mr. Kendrick sent it into first place. A Parti-color Cocker Spaniel placed second, the English Setter third, and the Irish Setter was unplaced.

The second Brittany Spaniel to win a sporting group was Dual Champion Amos of Edough. Lee Holman showed him at the Lima, Ohio, show in 1950. The author was the judge. Amos was an exciting dog, both at shows and in the field. He remains the only dual champion Brittany Spaniel ever to win a group.

The third dog to win a group was a California bitch, Cherie D'Oiseau. She was owned by S. Roose, and was shown by him. The show was the 29th annual Del Monte K. C. show at Pebble Beach, Cal., May 30, 1954. The author was also the judge at that event. Cherie had come up from the classes to go best of breed, and then went on to her group first. She completed her championship later. She was sired by Count Chanteur and her dam was Countess d'Oiseau Belle.

The years from 1956 to 1960 were truly great ones for the breed. In 1956, Havre Des Bois Henri completed his championship. He was bred and shown by Paul R. Vollmar of Clinton, Mich. He was by Sonny's Mate of Cyrus out of Ch. Wild Haven Dottie. The following year, he made breed history by becoming the first Brittany Spaniel to win best in show at an all-breed event.

Ch. Havre Des Bois Henri was best in show at the Livonia Kennel Club show, Sept. 15, 1957. There were 555 dogs competing in the

This picture shows an historic occasion. Ch. Amos of Edough is being presented with the award of best Sporting dog at the Lima Kennel Club, 1946. This is the first time a dual champion Brittany won the Sporting group in the United States. The judge was the author of this book and the handler was Lee Holman.

Ch. Havre Des Bois Henri, owned by Paul Vollmar, was the first Brittany Spaniel to win best in show at an all-breed show. He was handled by the late Horace Hollands and is shown winning a Sporting group first under judge Gordon Parham. *Norton of Kent photo.*

show. Judge Selwyn Harris gave him first in the sporting group, and then best in show. He had defeated 22 other Britts under Mrs. Marie B. Meyer. Later that year, Ch. Havre Des Bois Henri won the national specialty show under Judge Gordon Parham. The following year Havre Des Bois Henri won the sporting group at Canton, O., and at Columbus, O. He also had eight other group placements. Until 1971, he remained the only Brittany Spaniel ever to win best in show at any American all-breed event.

Ch. Bonnie Kay's Ricki's Image now came onto the scene. He was bred by Ken Holemo, who put him in the name of his daughter Bonnie, for whom he had also named the dog. He was by Happy Hunter's Buster Brown out of Joy De Lune. Ricki's Image was best of breed 71 times, twice won the sporting group, and had 18 other group placements. He was best of breed at the national specialty show three times, in 1959, 1960, and 1961. Edgar W. Averill's Ch. Patrice De Sharvogue had won this show three times, in 1943, 1944, and 1945.

Two dogs now came along with truly great show records. The first was Ch. Bonnie Kay's Duke of Sequani. He is a son of Ch. Bonnie Kay's Ricki's Image, out of Alf's Queen, by Jay Jay's Rusty. He had 84 best of breed victories as of Sept. 1, 1971, two group firsts, eight seconds, eight thirds, and 14 fourths. Thus, he broke his sire's record. He was best puppy at the national specialty in 1964, and was best of breed in the 1968 event.

Duke was now followed by his son, American and Bermuda Champion Sequani's Dana MacDuff. His dam is Dana's Jody of Kaymore, C.D., by Dual Ch. Doctor Joe of Kaymore. As of Sept. 1, 1971, Dana MacDuff had won 70 bests of breed, 10 group firsts, nine group seconds, five group thirds, and five group fourths. He also had two group thirds in Bermuda. He retired in June 1973 with 14 group firsts.

Dana MacDuff had the unusual distinction of winning his championship by placing four times in the sporting group. He was twice best of breed at the American Brittany Club's summer specialty shows, and he was best of breed at eight regional shows. Both dogs were bred at the Sequani Kennels of Mr. and Mrs. Frederick Murphy, Far Hills, N.J.

We now come to Ch. Beelflower Dirty Dan. He won the coveted best in show award at Salinas, Cal., in mid-August, 1971, in an entry of over 2000 dogs. He is owned by Paul and Linda Mooney, and was shown by Mrs. Mooney. Here let us quote from the *American Brittany Magazine* which adequately gives the dog's background.

Ch. Sequani's Dana MacDuff (Ch. Bonnie Kay's Duke of Sequani ex Dana's Jody of Kaymore, C.D.), owned by Mrs. F. H. Murphy and N. Rigoulot and bred by D. and N. Rigoulot. This dog is the most successful show ring campaigner in the history of the breed and retired with 14 firsts in the Sporting group. *Tauskey photo.*

|  |  |  |  |  |
|---|---|---|---|---|
|  |  | Happy Hunter's Buster Brown |  | Ch. Bonnie Kay's Ricki |
|  | Ch. Bonnie Kay's Ricki's Image |  |  | Lady of Woodworth |
|  |  | Joy de Lune |  | Pride of Mansfield |
| Ch. Bonnie Kay's Duke of Sequani |  |  |  | Midge de Kremanor |
|  |  | Jay Jay's Rusty |  | Lubilt of Huntsmore |
|  | Alf's Queen |  |  | Frosty Zipper |
|  |  | Ray Kay's Gal |  | Ch. Lucky de Rosevere |
| CH. SEQUANI'S DANA MACDUFF |  |  |  | My Gal Trixie |
|  |  | Jud of Pasatrou |  | Pasatrou's Rex |
|  | Dual Ch. Doctor Joe of Kaymore |  |  | Pasatrou's Judy |
|  |  | Lady Godiva de Basgard |  | Jack O'Maine de Basgard |
| Dana's Jody of Kaymore, C.D. |  |  |  | Lexington Penobscot Jilo |
|  |  | Dual Ch. Tex of Richmont |  | Allamuchy Valley Warrior |
|  | Kaymore's Sumthin Special |  |  | Soize MacEochaidh |
|  |  | Woody's Buttons |  | Pontac's Hero |
|  |  |  |  | Fld. Ch. Buttons and Bows, C.D. |

"Dirty Dan is a winner that fulfills all the breed's specifications. He is sired by a Dual Champion, Sir Robert of Beelflower and his grandsire is a dual as well, Rusty of Beelflower. Rusty's sire was a champion and his grandsire was Ch. Duckerbird's Sir Guy de Beauch, a field winner, which took best of breed from the classes at the second largest assemblage of Brittanies ever held (a Michigan specialty show).

"Dan's dam (Pacolet Sam's Pierette), has produced three field winners and is a daughter of Dual Champion Pacolet Sam and Field Ch. Riviere Valley Suzette. Sam is, as students know, a son of the duals Albedo Valley Dingo and Pacolet Cheyenne. Suzette is sired by Dual Ch. Tex of Richmont and from the bench champion Ruby of Edough.

"To add a little frosting to the cake, not only does Dan have a dual studded pedigree, he has placed himself in trials, twice in puppy stakes. He is OFA certified (Editor's note: which signifies he is free of hip dysplasia). We wonder if any other breed can boast a comparable BEST IN SHOW winner."

The author can only add that, to the best of his knowledge, the answer is "no." He was bred by Virgil I. Davidson, and was whelped April 23, 1968.

One of the great show dogs of the 1960s was Ch. Miss Sue's Gad-A-Bout. He was owned by Richard and Anne Smith of Roswell, Ga. In some 15 months, he won 40 bests of breed; 12 group placings, of which three were firsts; and a Companion Dog degree in obedience.

We single out one other dog for special mention here. Ch. Ti-War Chip de Triumph, owned by R. H. Edwards, won first in the sporting group at Lorain, Ohio, when he was nearing 10 years old. He was shown by Daniel Sweeney, who was 17.

Our search of the records indicates that at least the following dogs, not mentioned above, have won group firsts. They are:

Ch. Glenn-Pat's Rusty Shadow, Ch. Ultra-Mend Ace High, Ch. Ultra-Mend Jacques, Ch. Ffynant's Trouble, Ch. Fun Galore Chummie, Ch. Holley Haven Suzette, Ch. Lakeside Secret Joy, Ch. Havre Des Bois Seigneur, Ch. Lincoln's Skipper of Kaymore, Ch. Star Raiser, and Ch. Laddie Star.

Ch. Beelflower Dirty Dan, owned and handled by
Linda Mooney, was best in show at the Salinas Kennel
Club under the author. This is only the second Brittany
to win best in show at an all-breed dog show.
*Stillman photo.*

```
                    Ch. Duckerbird Sir Guy de Beauch
        Ch. Royal Prince of Duckerbird
                    Duckerbird Su of Holley Haven

    Dual Ch. Rusty of Beelflower

                    Ch. Freckles of San Diego
        Sandy of Beelflower
                    Gil's Bella Gal of Bu-Can

    Dual Ch. Sir Robert of Beelflower

                    Teddy of Sharvogue
        Casa Blanca Mike
                    Britt Brees Three Star

        Rusty of Fontana

                    Don's Terry of Paradise
        Terry's Jane of Paradise
                    Howdy's Beauty of Paradise

CH. BEELFLOWER DIRTY DAN

                    Dual Ch. Pontac's Dingo
        Dual Ch. Albedo Valley Dingo
                    Rousse de Raou

    Dual Ch. Pacolet Sam

                    Dual Ch. Tex of Richmont
        Dual Ch. Pacolet Cheyenne
                    Ch. Ruby of Edough

    Pacolet Sam's Pierrette

                    Allamuchy Valley Warrior
        Dual Ch. Tex of Richmont
                    Soize MacEochaidh

        Fld. Ch. Riviere Valley Suzette

                    Hello Mike
        Ch. Ruby of Edough
                    Iolet of Edough
```

# 15

# The First American Brittany Spaniel Standard

THE first American standard for the Brittany Spaniel was a translation of the French standard of 1933. Miss Clara Perry, who had raised Brittany Spaniels in France, and who had been an early importer, made the translation. But the standard of 1933 had, with some alterations, existed since the first standard was drawn up in September, 1907.

In 1907, three colors were allowed. These were white with liver; white with orange; and white with black. The white and liver dogs were preferred and white and orange dogs were almost barred. The reason was that the white and liver dogs had shown up well in field work, while some of the white and orange dogs had performed poorly.

French breeders were interested first in performance and second in type. Some of the white and orange dogs were oversized, and probably represented a late cross with English Setters. In the end, it was the white and black dog which was to disappear.

It will be remembered that a tailless Brittany Spaniel had been born. Many of his offspring were either tailless or had a very short tail. They were born pre-docked, so to speak. Early French breeders considered that the true Britt should be born either tailless or with

Ch. Windy Hill's Sweet Bippy (Dual Ch. Lund's Trooper ex Ch. Edgewater's American Beauty), owned by Rich and Mary Sabit. She is shown with her handler Robert Eldridge. *Ritter photo.*

Ch. Windy Hill's Troopers Tuffy (Dual Ch. Lund's Trooper ex Ch. Edgewater's American Beauty), owned by Robert Edwards and bred by Al Langan. *Olson photo.*

a naturally docked tail. So the standard of 1907 said: "Always short at birth, not over six inches at the very most, sometimes a little twisted and terminating with a tuft of hair." One wonders if a screw-tailed Bulldog got somehow mixed into the breed to produce that twisted tail. A second reason for specifying a tailless or naturally docked dog was that early breeders felt this requirement would prevent crossing the Breton dogs with English Setters.

By 1933, this danger had apparently disappeared. But also, breeders were beginning to understand that great field dogs could be born with long tails. It was therefore absurd, and even tragic, to bar dogs born with natural tails.

There is another point which should be mentioned here. Some of the early French fanciers feared that the Breton Spaniel might become too small. So the 1907 standard called for a dog 50 to 56 centimeters tall, when measured at the highest point of the withers. In inches, this is 19½ to 22 inches. Our own early breeders feared that the dog might grow too large. The modern standard calls for a shorter dog. But some Britts do grow too tall. Thus, the problem of size has been with us since 1907. And although standards change, the problem will in all likelihood, remain.

Herewith, we give the "Description and standard of points" as adopted by the American Kennel Club on March 12, 1935. It is of particular interest because of the earlier standard and later changes.

## General Appearance

**Height**—17 inches minimum; 19¾ maximum with toleration of ¾ inch more for males, back short; head rounded; muzzle rather pointed; with lips close fitting; ears short rather than long and placed high, relatively but little fringed; hair close on body; fringes wavy; never curly, a compact cob type; tail always naturally short, about 4 inches. (See note at end).

**Nose**—Nostrils well open; color brown or rose according to whether the dog is white and liver; or white and orange.
   **Faults**—Black and shiny; tight or snipy.

**Muzzle**—Medium length narrowing toward nose; straight or very slightly curved.
   **Faults**—Too short or too long.

**Lips**—Fine, close fitting, the upper lip overlapping the under lip by very little.

**Faults**—Thick or too overlapping.

**Crown of Head**—Medium length, rounded; each side of the depression well marked and rounded; well defined stop though sloping gently and not too abrupt.

**Faults**—Square; narrow; apple-headed; stop too abrupt.

**Eyes**—Deep amber, bright and expressive.

**Faults**—Too light, mean look.

**Ears**—Placed high, short rather than long, slightly rounded, but little fringe, though the ear should be well covered with wavy hair.

**Faults**—Placed low; falling; large; curly.

**Neck**—Medium length, well placed on shoulders; without dewlap.

**Faults**—Too long; too thin; too short, or too heavy.

**Shoulders**—Slightly oblique and muscular.

**Faults**—Straight or too oblique

**Arm**—Muscular and bony.

**Faults**—Fatty or too fine.

**Chest**—Deep, reaching quite to level of elbow; sides rounded enough and quite large.

**Faults**—Chest narrow; not deep, sides flat.

**Back**—Short, withers well marked; never hollow or saddle backed.

**Faults**—Long or hollow.

**Loin**—Short and strong.

**Faults**—Long; narrow or weak.

**Flanks**—Well tucked up but not to excess.

**Faults**—Fat; falling.

**Hind Quarters**—Broad—strong and muscular.

**Croup**—Slightly sloping.

**Faults**—Too narrow; too straight; too sloping.

**Tail**—(See note at end)—Straight and carried low; always naturally short; about 4 inches long, often screw tail ending in a mesh of hair, or *anoure*.

**Front Legs**—Very straight; forearm slightly oblique, fine and muscular; fringes not heavy but wavy.
**Faults**—Forearm too straight or too oblique; without fringes or too heavily fringed.

**Hindlegs**—Thighs large, well muscled, well fringed and wavy half down thigh, canon well set with hock and not too angular.
**Faults**—straight thighs, without fringes or too oblique.

**Feet**—Toes close with a little hair between them.
**Faults**—Large; long, fat, too round or open.

**Skin**—Fine and fairly loose.
**Faults**—Thick or too loose.

**Coat**—Hair flat on body, fine but not to excess and quite smooth or slightly wavy.
**Faults**—Long, curly or too silky.

**Color**—Liver and white preferably with roan ticking, or orange and white preferably with roan ticking.

**As a Whole**—A small dog, closely knit and strong though elegant, very vigorous; energetic of movement; intelligent expression; presenting the aspect of a thoroughbred cob.

(**Note**—The question of Brittany Spaniels born with tails being admitted to the Show Ring was voted on in the General Assembly of 1933 and it was decided that a cut tail was not disqualification either in the Show Ring or the Field Trials.)

# 16

# Modern Standard
# for the Brittany Spaniel

A breed standard is often called the "standard of perfection" for that breed. Sometimes, it is claimed that the standard was based upon a certain dog. This is almost never true. Often, standard writers do discuss the points of one or more dogs. But a standard is an idealization—the perfect dog. Such a dog is seldom, or never, achieved.

Standard writers may use the head of one dog, the neck of another, the body of a third, and the legs and feet of still another. Thus, they achieve an ideal, but in their minds only.

One often hears an owner say: "I wish this dog had the head of that one." Or: "I wish that dog had the drive of this one." Again, these are only wishes, and wishes are only idealizations and not realizations. There are two reasons why this is so. First, a dog is a going unit. It has been said that the great Greek nudes were idealizations; that human beings couldn't be built that way. This is to some extent true of dogs.

A more important reason is that, as a working unit, a dog is the sum of its parts. You cannot say, for example, that this dog's hind legs would fit on that dog's body. Nor can it be said that this dog's head would be perfect on that dog's neck. If you could take two or three dogs apart and rearrange their parts, you would almost certainly come up with a horrible monstrosity. It would not be the sum of the good parts of all the dogs, but much more likely, a badly balanced dog which could not function with half the efficiency of any of the dogs from which some of its parts came.

One must, therefore, regard the breed standard as a useful guide. But one must inevitably regard the dogs it describes as working units. Each is a whole. Successful breeders and judges study the standard. They note the good points and faults, as listed in the standard. Then they examine the dogs as more or less successful working units.

In the previous chapter, we gave the Brittany Spaniel standard as it was first approved by the American Kennel Club. Miss Clara Perry had translated it. Those who read it will recognize that it was virtually unintelligible. Yet at the time, students who wished to understand it had an advantage which is denied to most of us today. Most of the dog shows were benched, and dozens of them were two-day events.

This meant that one could take the standard and go down the stalls, studying each dog. Arguments, or friendly discussions, would take place. Owners would take their dogs off the benches and pose them for study. Perhaps more important, Brittany Spaniels could be compared to other sporting breeds. Such comparisons could often make points in the Brittany Spaniel standard clearer. A good feature in another breed might be a fault in a Britt, and the student would realize why this was so.

If one reads that first American standard, one can understand why the American Brittany Club was thoroughly dissatisfied with it. So a standards committee was set up. The year was 1946.

Dr. David Ruskin obtained the latest standard from France, and translated it. Much of the information Dr. Ruskin obtained from France was far too technical, and therefore hardly understandable.

As the author remembers it, the main committee consisted of Dr. Ruskin, Jack Whitworth, Jerome N. Halle, Edward Dana Knight, and the author. Knight was a fine sporting dog judge. He was a great student. He exhibited English Springer Spaniels at shows and trained them for field. He also ran English Setters in American Field trials, and he usually had an American Foxhound or two.

Jerome Halle had run Pointers in American Field field trials while an undergraduate at Cornell University. He, too, was a fine sporting dog judge. His early, and long association with Brittany Spaniels is well known.

These two, and the author, were thoroughly familiar with the tragic split of the English Setter into two breeds—bench and field. Knight, and the author, were watching the split of English Springer Spaniels into two breeds. Both fought against this split and lost.

However, Knight felt that, if the Brittany Spaniel was to get anywhere as a bench dog, it would have to develop the heavy coat and feathers of modern sporting bench dogs, and the rounded fatness of so many of them. American Brittany Club officers and members did not want this to happen because the inevitable result would be a split of the breed into two varieties, bench and field.

Halle, and the author, argued that the Brittany standard should be so written that no such split would be possible. One result was that the American Brittany Club began a policy of holding bench shows along with field trials. That meant that field dogs could come out of the field and compete, as they were, for bench championships. It is this factor which caused the standard writers to prescribe a dog without excessive coat and feathering.

Halle and the author also argued that the Brittany Spaniel could compete on equal terms with other breeds in the sporting group at dog shows if sporting dog judges could be properly trained. Judges had to be told that a hard, lean, field conditioned Brittany without heavy leg feathering, or a fine, silky and long coat, was to be desired.

This policy has, to some extent, failed. One reason is that a new generation of sporting dog show judges has developed. And we have done nothing to educate them as we did an earlier generation. Yet in another sense, the policy has worked well. It is proven in the number of dual champions—bench and field—which the breed has produced. And it remains as an argument for conducting bench and field events at the same meeting.

The first American standard tried to explain the meaning, and the reason for each point. It has survived with but a few changes since. In 1946, it was feared that the breed would grow too large. Dogs from other lands did tend to grow larger. In most cases, this was temporary, and dogs tended to return to their basic size. But in 1946, several champions were larger than the agreed upon height. It is to the credit of the owners of those dogs that they agreed upon a height which would disqualify their dogs.

It is imperative for Brittany Spaniel owners to study the present standard in the light of the past. And they should understand the reasons behind each point in the standard so that a great and un-spoiled breed may continue to improve, as it has in the past. Here then is the present standard, as it was approved by the American Kennel Club, Sept. 13, 1966. It represents the thoughts and experi-ences of Brittany Spaniel people since 1907. But it also is the result of the breeding, training, field trialing, and exhibiting by Brittany owners in America since 1946.

## *Official Standard of the Brittany Spaniel*

### GENERAL DESCRIPTION

A compact, closely knit dog of medium size, a leggy spaniel having the appearance as well as the agility of a great ground coverer. Strong, vigorous, energetic and quick of movement. Not too light in bone, yet never heavy-boned and cumbersome. Ruggedness, without clumsi-ness, is a characteristic of the breed. So leggy is he that his height at the withers is the same as the length of his body. He has no tail, or at most, not more than 4 inches.

**Weight**—Should weigh between 30 and 40 pounds.

**Height**—$17\frac{1}{2}$ to $20\frac{1}{2}$ inches—measured from the ground at the highest point of the shoulders.

**Disqualifications**—Any Brittany Spaniel measuring under $17\frac{1}{2}$ inches or over $20\frac{1}{2}$ inches shall be disqualified from bench-show competition. Any black in the coat or a nose so dark in color as to appear black shall disqualify. A tail substantially more than 4 inches in length shall disqualify.

### COAT

Dense, flat or wavy, never curly. Texture neither wiry nor silky. The ears should carry little fringe. The front and hind legs should have some feathering but too little is definitely preferable to too much. Dogs with long or profuse feathering or furnishings shall be so se-verely penalized as to effectively eliminate them from competition.

### COLOR

Orange and white or liver and white in either clear or roan pat-terns. Some ticking is desirable. The orange or liver is found in standard parti-color or piebald patterns. Washed out colors are not desirable. Black is a disqualification.

# HEAD

**Skull**—Medium length (approximately 4¾ inches). Rounded, very slightly wedge-shaped, but evenly made. Width, not quite as wide as the length (about 4⅜ inches) and never so broad as to appear coarse, or so narrow as to appear racy. Well defined, but gently sloping stop effect. Median line rather indistinct. The occipital crest only apparent to the touch. Lateral walls well rounded. The Brittany should never be "apple-headed" and he should never have an indented stop. (All measurements of skull are for a 19½ inch dog).

**Muzzle**—Medium length, about two thirds the length of the skull, measuring the muzzle from the tip to the stop, and the skull from the occipital crest to the stop between the eyes. Muzzle should taper gradually in both horizontal and vertical dimensions as it approaches the nostrils. Neither a Roman nose nor a concave curve (dish face) is desirable. Never broad, heavy, or snipy.

**Nose**—Nostrils well open to permit deep breathing of air and adequate scenting while at top speed. Tight nostrils should be penalized. Never shiny. Color, fawn, tan, light shades of brown or deep pink. A black nose is a disqualification. A two-tone or butterfly nose should be penalized.

**Eyes**—Well set in head. Well protected from briars by a heavy, expressive eyebrow. A prominent, full or pop eye should be heavily penalized. It is a serious fault in a hunting dog that must face briars. Skull well chiseled under the eyes, so that the lower lid is not pulled back to form a pocket or haw for catching seeds, dirt, and weed dust. Judges should check by forcing head down to see if lid falls away from the eye. Preference should be for darker-colored eyes, though lighter shades of amber should not be penalized. Light and mean-looking eyes to be heavily penalized.

**Ears**—Set high, above the level of the eyes. Short and leafy, rather than pendulous, reaching about half the length of the muzzle. Should lie flat and close to the head, with the tip rounded very slightly. Ears well covered with dense, but relatively short hair, and with little fringe.

**APPEARANCE:** Compact; closely-knit, strong; rugged without clumsiness; energetic, vigorous, agile; leggy

**EARS** short, leafy; set high above eye level; reach half-length muzzle; flat, close to head; very slightly rounded tips; relatively short hair, little fringe

**NECK** medium length; strong; well-set into shoulders; not throaty

**SHOULDERS** sloping; muscular; blade forming nearly 90-degree angle with upper arm; perhaps 2-thumb-widths between blades

**BACK** short, straight; slight slope from withers to tail-set; short (3-4 finger widths) from last rib to upper thigh; slight drop from hips to tail root

**TAIL** high-set; tailless, natural or docked, not over 4"

**HINDQUARTERS** broad, strong, muscular; powerful thighs; rounded, fairly full flanks; hips well-set into short, strong loins; well-bent stifles; hocks firm, turning neither in nor out; hock to heel fairly short

**COAT** dense, flat, wavy; not too fine; never curly or silky; feathering moderate (excessive severely penalized). Skin fine; fairly loose

**RIBS** well-sprung

**ELBOWS** turning neither in nor out; height to elbows approx. equal distance elbows to withers

**SIZE:** Height, 17½"-20½", measured from ground at highest point of shoulders; weigh, 30-40 lbs. Body length (point of forechest to rear of haunches): approx. same as height

**DISQUALIFICATIONS:** Measuring under 17½" or over 20½"; black in coat; nose so dark as to appear black; tail substantially more than 4"

**SKULL** medium length (approx. 4¾"), width less (approx. 4⅜"); rounded, evenly-made; very slightly wedge-shaped, lateral walls well-rounded; never coarse, "apple-headed" or racy; occiput crest only apparent to touch; indistinct median line

**EYES** well-set; dark colors preferred; expressive; eyebrows heavy

**STOP** well-defined; gentle sloping; never indented

**NOSE** fawn, tan, light brown shades, deep pink; nostrils well-open; neither Roman nor concave curve (dish-face) desirable; (butterfly two-tone) severely penalized)

**LIPS** tight; dry. Upper lip overlapping lower jaw only to cover under lip. Flews penalized

**TEETH** well-joined; scissors bite; neither under- nor overshot

**MUZZLE** medium—2/3 length of skull (measuring muzzle from tip to stop, skull from occipital crest to stop); tapering gradually toward nostrils; never broad, heavy, snipy; well-chiseled under eyes

**CHEST** deep; reaching elbow level; neither too wide nor too rounded

**FORELEGS** perpendicular; not too wide apart; bones clean, graceful, not too fine; supple. Pasterns slightly bent

**FEET** strong; proportionately smaller than other spaniels; close-fitting, well-arched toes; thick pads

**COLORS:** Dark orange and white; liver and white; some ticking desirable (not enough for belton pattern). Roan patterns or factors of orange or liver (found in std. parti-color or pied) permissible; washed out or faded colors not desirable; tri-colors (liver, white with some orange markings) severely faulted

Lips—Tight to the muzzle, with the upper lip overlapping the lower jaw only sufficiently to cover under lip. Lips dry, so that feathers do not stick. Drooling to receive a heavy penalty. Flews to be penalized.

Teeth—Well joined incisors. Posterior edge of the upper incisors in contact with anterior edge of lower incisors, thus giving a true scissors bite. Overshot or undershot jaw to be penalized heavily.

## BODY

Neck—Medium length. Not quite permitting the dog to place his nose on the ground without bending his legs. Free from throatiness, though not a serious fault unless accompanied by dewlaps. Strong, without giving the impression of being overmuscled. Well set into sloping shoulders. Never concave or ewe-necked.

Body Length—Approximately the same as the height when measured at the withers. Body length is measured from the point of the forechest to the rear of the haunches. A long body should be heavily penalized.

Withers—Shoulder blades should not protrude much. Not too widely set apart with perhaps two thumbs' width or less between the blades. At the withers, the Brittany is slightly higher than at the rump.

Shoulders—Sloping and muscular. Blade and upper arm should form nearly a 90 degree angle when measured from the posterior point of the blade at the withers to the junction of the blade and the upper arm, and thence to the point of the elbow nearest the ribs. Straight shoulders do not permit sufficient reach.

Back—Short and straight. Slight slope from highest point of withers to the root of the tail. Never hollow, saddle, sway, or roach-backed. Slight drop from hips to root of tail. Distance from last rib to upper thigh short, about three to four finger widths.

Chest—Deep, reaching the level of the elbow. Neither so wide nor so rounded as to disturb the placement of the shoulder bones and elbows, which causes a paddling movement, and often causes soreness from elbow striking ribs. Ribs well sprung, but adequate heart room provided by depth as well as width. Narrow or slab-sided chests are a fault.

Flanks—Rounded. Fairly full. Not extremely tucked up, nor yet flabby and falling. Loins short and strong. Narrow and weak loins are a fault. In motion the loin should not sway sideways, giving a zigzag motion to the back, wasting energy.

Fiddle Front          Out at Elbow          Straight Front

Down in Pastern          Knuckled Over          Straight Front

Cat Foot          Hare Foot          Paper Foot          Correct
                                                          Foot

Level Back

                                    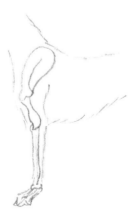

Sloping Shoulder                          Straight Shoulder

Poor Rear
Movement

Good Rear
Movement

Cow-Hocked

**Hindquarters**—Broad, strong and muscular, with powerful thighs and well-bent strifles, giving a hip set well into the loin and the marked angulation necessary for a powerful drive when in motion. Fat and falling hindquarters are a fault.

**Tail**—Naturally tailless, or not over four inches long. Natural or docked. Set on high, actually an extension of the spine at about the same level.

**Front Legs**—Viewed from the front, perpendicular, but not set too wide as in the case of a dog loaded in shoulder. Elbows and

Correct Front
Movement

Paddling

Weaving

feet turning neither in nor out. Viewed from the side, practically perpendicular to the pastern. Pastern slightly bent to give cushion to stride. Not so straight as in terriers. Falling pasterns, however, are a serious fault. Leg bones clean, graceful, but not too fine. An extremely heavy bone is as much a fault as spindly legs. One must look for substance and suppleness. Height to the elbows should be approximately equal distance from elbow to withers.

**Hind Legs**—stifles well bent. The stifle generally is the term used for knee joint. If the angle made by the upper and lower leg bones is too straight, the dog quite generally lacks drive, since his hind legs cannot drive as far forward at each stride as is desirable. However, the stifle should not be bent as to throw the hock joint far out behind the dog. Since factors not easily seen by the eye may give the dog his proper drive, a Brittany should not be condemned for straight stifle until the judge has checked the dog in motion from the side. When at a trot, the Brittany's hind foot should step into or beyond the print left by the front foot. The stifle joint should not turn out making a cowhock. (The cowhock moves the foot out to the side, thus driving out of line and losing reach at each stride). Thighs well feathered, but not profusely, halfway to the hock. Hocks, that is, the back pasterns, should be moderately short, pointing neither in nor out; perpendicular when viewed from the side. They should be firm when shaken by the judge.

**Feet**—Should be strong, proportionately smaller than other spaniels, with close-fitting, well arched toes and thick pads. The Brittany is not "up on his toes." Toes not heavily feathered. Flat feet, splayed feet, paper feet, etc. are to be heavily penalized. An ideal foot is halfway between the hare and cat-foot.

**A Guide to the Judge**—The points below indicate only relative values. To be also taken into consideration are type, gait, soundness, spirit, optimum height, body length and general proportions.

### Scale of Points

| | | | |
|---|---|---|---|
| Head | 25 | Running gear | 40 |
| Body | 35 | Total | 100 |

## DISQUALIFICATIONS

Any Brittany Spaniel measuring under 17½ inches or over 20½ inches. Any black in the coat or a nose so dark in color as to appear black. A tail substantially more than 4 inches in length.

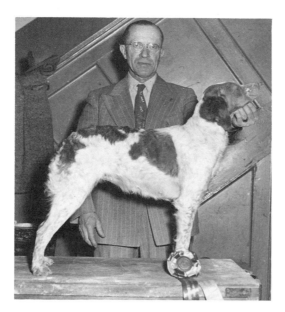

Ch. Retta of Avono was an early specialty winner. She was handled by Lee S. Wade.

National field and National Specialty show winner, Dual Ch. Pacolet Cheyenne Sam, owned by Ken and Erin Jacobson. *Roberts photo.*

# 17

# The National
# Specialty Show

In Chapter 13, we have told of the first Brittany Spaniel licensed specialty show and field trial. These were held at the same time for a very good reason. The organizers of the American Brittany Club clearly intended that the breed should not be split into two-bench dogs and field dogs. They had seen this happen in other breeds, and they were determined that it should not happen with the Brittany Spaniel.

It was felt that this could best be prevented by holding bench shows and field trials together. In so doing, dogs could compete in both. Thus, ever since Nov. 27–28, 1943, the national bench show has been held with the national field championship.

This policy has been slightly altered in the last couple of years to permit the holding of a separate summer bench show, held in conjunction with an all-breed show. The system has been to designate the classes at a given show as the American Brittany Club's summer specialty.

In the following table, we give the winners of the national specialty alone. As will be seen, both the national specialty and the national championship trials have gone steadily westward.

Ch. Bonnie Kay's Duke of Sequani, owned by Mr. and Mrs. Frederick H. Murphy, was sired by Ch. Bonnie Kay's Ricki's Image and is himself the sire of the breed's top winner Ch. Sequaini's Dana MacDuff. Here he is winning a strong Sporting group at the Somerset Hills Kennel Club under the author. *Gilbert photo.*

## Best of Breed at National Specialty

(In the following tabulation, the numbers indicate dogs in competition. Then follow the winners and owners.)

1943. Ravenna, Ohio. 29. Patrice of Sharvogue, Edgar W. Averill. Victory made Patrice a champion.

1944. Cleveland, Ohio. 42. Ch. Patrice of Sharvogue.

1945. Detroit, Mich. 52. Ch. Patrice of Sharvogue

1946. Smithfield, Ohio. 50. Ch. Avono Happy, Jack L. Whitworth.

1947. Pontiac, Mich. 65. Avono Retta, Jack L. Whitworth.

1948. Rensselaer, Ind. 57. Dual Ch. Avono Happy, Jack L. Whitworth.

1949. A special show was held on May 16, 1949, in honor of the famed French breeder-judge, Maurice Allaire. 58. Dual Ch. Avono Happy, Jack L. Whitworth. Regular show was held at Allamuchy, N.J. Dogs 64. Tudor Du Roc-Hellou, Alan R. Stuyvesant.

1950. Carbondale, Ill. 41. Ch. Buccaneer de Klemanor, Walter B. Kleeman.

1951. Carbondale, Ill. 40. Ch. Buccaneer de Klemanor, Walter B. Kleeman.

1952. Marion, Ill. 44. Ch. Amos of Edough (later a dual champion), Edward Staunton.

1953. Carbondale, Ill. 46. Ch. Avono Corky, Charles W. Morse.

1954. Carbondale, Ill. 32. Ch. Do-Car's Flashy Showman, Earl Gray.
1955. Carbondale, Ill. 64. Best of Breed: Tigre Par le Tigre de L'Argoat. Owner: John Doak.
1956. Carbondale, Ill. 50. Ch. Avono Corky, Charles W. Morse.
1957. Carbondale, Ill. 53. Ch. Harvre de Bois Henri, Paul Vollmar.
1958. Carbondale, Ill. 67. Dual Ch. Dingo's Little Mike, George Wilson.
1959. Carbondale, Ill. 70. Ch. Bonnie Kay's Ricki's Image, Bonnie Kay Holemo.
1960. Carbondale, Ill. 61. Ch. Bonnie Kay's Ricki's Image, Bonnie Kay Holemo.
1961. Carbondale, Ill. 53. Ch. Bonnie Kay's Ricki's Image, Bonnie Kay Holemo.
1962. Carbondale, Ill. 40 Ch. Juchoir's Tuffy, James and Helen Rookard.
1963. Carterville, Ill. 55. Ch. Juchoir's Tuffy, James and Helen Rookard.

Dual Ch. Suzabob's Hedgerow Happy (Dual Ch. Shenango Valley Dingo ex Ch. Suzabob's Seminole Sadie).

1964.   Carterville, Ill. 78. Ch. Chief of Appanoose, Len E. Stolz.

1965.   Carterville, Ill. 58. Ch. Sams Son Buckshot, C.D., L. F. Oltman

1966.   Carterville, Ill. 55. Ch. Sams Son Buckshot, C.D., L. F. Oltman

1967.   Carterville, Ill. 39. Elcon's Shotgun Smoke, L. L. Conable Jr.

1968.   Ardmore, Okla. 74. Ch. Bonnie Kay's Duke of Sequani, Mrs. F. H. Murphy and Mrs. R. E. Smith.

1969.   Paducah, Ky. 74. Ch. Suzabob's Hedgerow Happy, D. W. Buster.

1970.   Paducah, Ky. 50. Dual Ch. Pacolet Cheyenne Sam, K. & E. Jacobson

1971.   Ardmore, Okla. 65. Ch. Sequani Dana MacDuff, Mrs. G. H. Murphy and Nancy Rigoulet.

1972.   Paducah, Ky. 99 dogs competing (largest Brittany entry ever held in America) Ch. Merchant of Breton's Lightning. Henry Riske.

## American Brittany Club Summer Specialty Shows

After long consideration, the American Brittany Club decided to back a national summer specialty show. This show would not be separate from an all-breed event. Instead, the American Brittany Club would consider the classes at an all-breed show as its national summer specialty show. The show would be supported by the regional club in that area.

The first such show was held in 1968. The Northern California club was the host, and the Redwood Empire show served as the locale. There were 84 entries. Best of breed was Ch. Frenchman's Yankee Nickel, owned by Dorothy MacDonald. Nickel then placed fourth in the sporting group.

The North Jersey club acted as host in 1969 at the Twin Brooks all-breed show. Best of breed went to Ch. Sequani's Dana MacDuff, owned by Mrs. G. H. Murphy and Nancy Rigoulot.

The following year, Ch. Sequani's Dana MacDuff repeated his 1969 victory. Host club was the Ohio Brittany Club, and the show was the Ravenna, Ohio, all-breed event.

In 1971, the Greater Milwaukee Brittany Club served as the host group at the Waukesha, Wisconsin, show. The best of breed winner was Ch. Barry The Fierce, owned by Jacob E. Perica.

Ch. Barry the Fierce (Heatherlane's Peppy Fella ex Ginny's Girl Snapper), owned by Jacob Perica, is shown winning best of breed at the 1971 summer specialty of the ABC under the author, handler Dick Cooper. Note this dog's typical expression in the inset headstudy at the upper right. *Ritter photo.*

The 1972 show was held in conjunction with Del Monte, at Monterey, California. Best of breed was Ch. Kip Tam's Little Guy, owned and handled by Don Luiz. There were 88 dogs competing.

All of these events have had between 60 and 80 dogs in actual competition. And they have been supported by field and dual champions, as well as by conformation title holders.

Fld. Ch. Suzabob's Frisco Frannie, owned by Gerald Supplee.

# 18

# The National Championship Stake

NATIONAL championship stakes have been held for Pointers and English Setters for many years under the rules of the American Field and its *Field Dog Stud Book*. But the concept of such a championship did not reach the American Kennel Club until much later. Under AKC rules, a national championship stake was first set up for retrievers.

Parent bodies of other breeds then began to petition the American Kennel Club for permission to hold such stakes. Brittany Spaniels, English Springer Spaniels, and others then were granted permission to hold national championship events.

It was not until 1957 that the American Kennel Club permitted the American Brittany Club to hold an actual national championship stake. The winner has ever since been officially designated as the national champion.

Yet to give a more complete history of Brittany Spaniel field trials in America, it seems correct to list all the winners of the American Brittany Club's annual national trials.

However, a major difference should be noted. At all the American Brittany Club national trials, the open all age stake was, as its name indicates, open to all. And as usual, four places were given. A change was made when the first true national championship stake was held. To be eligible, dogs had to win or place at earlier regional club trials. And instead of making four placings, only the national champion was named.

As field trial interest spread across North America, the necessity for a central trial location became evident. Since the trials would be held in late November or early December, some consideration of weather conditions had to be made.

The State of Illinois had set up an immense wildlife area, called Crab Orchard. This is located in the Carbondale-Marion-Carterville area of Southwestern Illinois, southeast of St. Louis, Mo., and not far from Paducah, Kentucky. Included in the area were large, well managed lands suitable for field trials. Both retriever and English Springer Spaniel national championships were moved to Crab Orchard. In 1950, the American Brittany Club also began to hold its trials there.

The year was 1950. Until, and including that year, trials were half hour heats. But in 1951 this was changed. It was felt that a national champion should be able to carry his work over an hour period.

Trials have been held elsewhere, for instance, at Paducah, Kentucky, and Ardmore, Oklahoma. Always they have been held on well-managed areas suitable for reasonably wide ranging pointing dogs.

Famed French sculptor, Jacques Fath, modelled a statuette of the great French Brittany, Kaer de Cornouaille. Alan Stuyvesant had owned Kaer. He purchased the statuette and offered it to the American Brittany Club as a "travelling trophy." That is, it was to be held by the winner for one year. However, it could be won permanently if won by the same dog, or the same owner, three times.

This happened in 1959. The great Dual Champion Towsey, owned by Tom Black, and handled by Delmar Smith permanently retired the trophy. Towsey won in 1955, 1957, and 1959.

Mrs. Mary Kleeman, the widow of Walter, then replaced the trophy with an identical one. However, Mrs. Kleeman changed the conditions. The statuette cannot be permanently won. It belongs to the American Brittany Club, and it can be held for one year only. There is obvious merit to this. For each year, the names of great dogs can be inscribed on the base. And each year, tradition hallows further this memorial to a great dog, and to those which have followed.

The following are the winners and their owners from 1943 until the time of writing.

Dual and 1967 National Fld. Ch. Colorado's Yankee Timber, owned by Lucas Ruiz. This dog was sired by the former National Fld. Ch. Hellou's Yankee Timber.

Ch. Way-Kan Fritts, a liver and white owned by Ronald Stevenson, holds the National Open Field Championship for 1969.

## Winners of National Championship Stake

1943.  Aotrou MacEochaidh. A. H. Ady.
1944.  Tess of Chippewa. Hilmer Peterson.
1945.  Aotrou MacEochaidh. A. H. Ady.
1946.  Tess of Chippewa. Hilmer Peterson.
1947.  Allamuchy Valley Addie. Alan R. Stuyvesant.
1948.  Bonaire Bob. R. H. Cribbs.
1949.  Jersey Jeff. Dr. J. F. Weisert.
1950.  Butch's Lad. E. Waterman.
1951.  Pontac's Dingo. H. H. Crippen.
1952.  Pontac's Dingo. H. H. Crippen.
1953.  Tennessee Luke. H. P. Clements.
1954.  Miste de Klemanor. W. B. Kleeman.
1955.  Dual Ch. Towsey. Tom Black.
1956.  Jeffrey of Argard. LeRoy Magnuson.
1957.  Dual Ch. Towsey. Tom Black.
1958.  Fld. Ch. Hellou's Yankee Timber. Bernard Neiberger.
1959.  Dual Ch. Towsey. Tom Black.
1960.  Fld. Ch. Holliday Britt. J. T. Cahill.
1961.  Fld. Ch. Yankee Boy's Tommy. John A. Costelow.
1962.  Miller's Desert Dust. Louis Miller.
1963.  Fld. Ch. Crab Orchard Duke. Ray Trimble.
1964.  Dual Ch. Shenango Valley Dingo. Robert Seger.
1965.  Fld. Ch. Rendezvous Skipper. L. D. LaFleur.
1966.  Bazooka's Brandy. A. H. Pillow.
1967.  Dual Ch. Colorado's Yankee Timber. Lucas & G. H. Ruiz.
1968.  Fld. Ch. Goldstone's Duke. G. Pester. (Held at Ardmore, Okla.)
1969.  Way Kan Fritts. Dr. Terry Poling. (Held at Paducah, Ky.)
1970.  Fld. Ch. Augustus of Rivers. J. J. White. (Held at Paducah, Ky.)
1971.  Dual Ch. Pacolet Cheyenne Sam. K. & E. Jacobson. (Held at Ardmore, Okla.)

# 19

# The American
# Brittany Futurities—
# Bench and Field

$\mathrm{A}$ futurity is an event in which a purse has been built up over a period of time by specific payments. In most futurities, a mated bitch is nominated at some period before she whelps. There is a cash nominating fee. After the litter is born, a second payment is made. Other payments may be required at specified times. Actual competitors then pay an entrance fee. The total purse is divided in various ways, according to the terms of the specific futurity. After expenses, some futurities divide the purse between the breeder and the owner—often the same person. More often, the purse is split to permit second, third, and fourth place winners to participate.

Here is an example. Let us suppose that 100 breeders nominate their bred bitches at $8 each thirty days before whelping. There is then $800 in the purse. Thirty days after the litter is whelped all the breeders make a second payment of $8. There is now $1,600 in the pot. Then if 30 dogs actually compete in the futurity, another $240 is added, to make a total purse of $1840. While this is much simplified, it shows how the system works.

As a rule, part of the purse goes to the sponsoring group. This pays the cost of administration, and also adds money to the sponsoring organization's treasury. The American Brittany Field Futurity is run under *Field Dog Stud Book* and American Field rules. The conformation, or show futurity, is held under American Kennel Club rules. However, under AKC rules, a futurity's classes are non-regular and carry no championship points.

The first futurity began with an enrollment period of Oct. 31, 1946 through July 1, 1947. Fifty-nine bitches were nominated, and 43 were given second nominations. There were 37 actual starters. The trial was run at Inkster, Mich., Oct. 1, 1948.

One of the highest purse trials was that of 1961. There were 197 original nominations, and 142 completions. Seventy-nine dogs actually started. That made a net purse of $3300. This trial was held at Carbondale, Ill.

The first of the bench show, or conformation futurities, was held in 1963. There have been far fewer nominations for this event. Yet it has become one of the most important of the parent club's activities. Both futurities are now held in conjunction with the national trials.

The rules for the two futurities are the same. To be entered in either, a dog must be registered with the American Kennel Club. But those entered in the Field Futurity must be registered also with the *Field Dog Stud Book*. Here are the rules for the futurities.

"American Brittany Futurities shall be open to every pure-bred Brittany Spaniel bitch owned by an American Brittany Club member bred on or after October 30 of any year, and all her progeny born on or after January 1st of the year following, the dams of which have been duly nominated, and whose litters have been enrolled with the American Brittany Club.

"All dams nominated and all sires bred to must be registered or eligible for registration. Nominations and entries must be made on blanks furnished free of charge by the American Brittany Club.

"Nominations of dams must be made within thirty days after the bitches have been bred, at which time the sum of $8 for each field and bench nomination ($5 for field and $3 for bench) must be paid on each dam nominated. Before the litter shall have reached the age of thirty days, the second and final nomination payment of $8 for each field and bench nomination must be made ($5 for field and $3 for bench). This payment will entitle each puppy of this particular litter to be entered for the American Brittany Futurity purses after the dog has been properly registered in a recognized stud book, ABC membership of owner required.

"Nominations of dams may be made on or after October 30 of any year and shall close positively July 1st of the year following, for the

Tony De Fontaine Vallee.

American Brittany Futurities to be run the year subsequent to the closing date.

"If a bitch fails to whelp or gives birth to a dead litter, her nominator may substitute another, or transfer the nomination to another person in the same or next succeeding stake, subject to the approval of the American Brittany Club, provided said nominator shall give notice within thirty days after the time the bitch should have whelped. If notification is not made in accordance with this requirement, first nomination fee shall be forfeited."

Perhaps we may clarify this a bit further by giving a time-table for the 25th field and the 10th bench futurities, to be run in the fall or winter of 1972. To be eligible, bitches had to be bred on or after Oct. 30, 1970. The last day for breeding bitches was July 1, 1971. First nominations had to be made within 30 days after the mating, and the second nomination, or forfeit as it is called, within 30 days after whelping. Nominating blanks for these trials carry space for the registration numbers of both sire and dam in both the *AKC Stud Book* and the *Field Dog Stud Book*.

## ABC Field Futurity Winners

1948. Ch. Peg B. of Loufel. Breeder-owner-handler: Lucien Ufford.

1949. Allamuchy Valley Slim. Breeder: Mike Burnham. Owner: Alan Stuyvesant.

1950. Pontac's Hero. Breeder-owner: Coy Conwell.

1951. Allamuchy Valley Rusty. Breeder: Lee Holman. Owner: Alan Stuyvesant.

1952. Fld. Ch. Juchoir's Martin. Breeder: Dr. Thomas J. Talbott. Owner: James Williams.

1953. Hero's Master Spot. Breeder-owner: Dr. Harry E. Lee.

1954. Dingo's Little Mike. Breeder: Howard Crippen. Owner: George Wilson.

1955. Hels Oklahoma Topper. Breeder: M. F. Guest. Owner: Doyle Friel.

1956. Hels Oklahoma Rainbow. Breeder-owner: Melba Guest.

1957. Holliday Britt. Breeder: George Carver. Owner: S. Rowe Hill.

1958. Chien Fox. Breeder: Russell Cookingham. Owner: Richard Fox.

1959. Edandot Buzzer. Breeder: Edward Borger. Owner: Jerome N. Halle.

1960. Chip of LaRue. Breeder: C. P. Plyler. Owner: Louis E. Frank.

1961. Swanee Belle of LaRue. Breeder: C. P. Plyler. Owner: Glenn Eades.

1962. Skyline Banjo. Breeder: Harold Reed. Owner: Earl Chappell.

1963. Juchoir Termison Tiger. Breeder: Nicky Bissell. Owner: Dr. W. Heap.

1964. Diane of Leeway. Breeder-owner-handler: John W. Lee.

1965. Juchoir's Trooper Jill. Breeder-owner: Ted Hames.

1966. Jocko's Poker Chip. Owner: John Munson. Breeder: Gary and Rosalie Graney.

1967. Not held until the winter of 1968.

1968. (February) Highland Ginger Go Go. Breeder-owner-handler: Wendell Burdick. (Nov. 1968) Marmalade Sarah. Breeder-owner: Clifton Boggs.

1969. Hi Spirit Bazooka's Pistol. Owner: Darrell Gaynor. Breeder: William McNutt.

1970. Jinx's Jim Dandy. Breeder-owner: Curtiss Weyer.

1971. Flint's Dust Commander. Breeder-owner: Gene Spires.

The late Henry Holleyoak of the Holley Haven prefix. He is shown here winning the National Furturity in 1966 with Ch. Holley Haven Bret. Bret is owned by Gordon and Michele McIntyre.

1972.   Cheyenne Sam's Repeat. Owner-handler, Mrs. Marie May. Breeder: Terry Anderson.

## The Bench Futurity

1963.   Doc's Shotgun Popper. Breeder-owner: John Schuckert, D.D.S.
1964.   Ch. Edandot Iane. Breeder-owner: Edward M. Borger.
1965.   Ch. Holley Haven Tam of Twin Oaks. Owners: Donald and Mary Moloney. Breeder: Henry Holleyoak.
1966.   Holley Haven Brett. Breeder-owner-handler: Henry Holleyoak.
1967.   Not held until February, 1968.
1968.   (February) Dave O'Star Speckles. Owner: Evert Davis Jr. Breeder: Herman Bonine. (November) Trooper's Northwest Buddy. Owners: Pat and Bob Spring. Breeders: Del and Pat Foltz.
1969.   Belle's Allamuchy Terry. Owner: Patrick O'Shaughnessy. Breeder: Clarence Goering.
1970.   Scott's Super Trooper. Breeder-owner: Virginia Scott.
1971.   Freck's Boy Pete. Breeder-owner: Louis Gombert.
1972.   Ch. Sir Lancelot of Edwards. Breeder-owner-handler: R. H. Edwards.

# 20

# The National Amateur Championship Stake

---

T HOSE familiar with the first trials held for Brittany Spaniels know that there were hundreds of arguments as to what constituted an amateur handler. The argument was not, of course, limited to Brittany Spaniels. Eventually, the American Kennel Club defined the term as it applies to the pointing breeds. We quote the AKC definition in full.

> "An amateur owner or handler is a person who, during the period of two years preceding the trial, has not accepted remuneration in any form for training or handling dogs in any form of dog activity, and who at no time in the past has for any period of two years or more operated as a professional trainer or handler of field trial dogs."

This means that, while no professional trainer can handle a dog in an amateur stake, the dog may still have been professionally trained. Thus, an owner or a friend, might handle a dog in an amateur event, and then turn the dog over to its professional trainer to be handled in an open all age stake. The dog might then win an amateur all age stake when handled by an amateur and, at the same trial, win the open all age stake when handled by its professional trainer-handler.

The American Kennel Club also has spelled out the basic rules for a national amateur championship stake. Herewith, we quote these rules in full.

"The National Amateur Championship Stake for Brittany Spaniels shall be held no more than once in any calendar year, and shall be for dogs which by reason of wins previously made qualify under regulations submitted by the Parent Club and approved by the Board of Directors of The American Kennel Club. The stake shall be held by the Parent Club which shall file an application for permission to run it under procedures approved in advance by The American Kennel Club. The winner of this stake, if registered in the American Kennel Club stud book, shall be recorded an Amateur Field Champion of The American Kennel Club, and may be designated 'National Amateur Brittany Spaniel Field Champion for 19 –.' "

The first National Amateur Championship stake was held at Carbondale, Ill. in 1951. There were 14 competitors. It is an important record in the history of the breed that the winner that year was American and Canadian show champion, Diane de Beauch, U.D. For she was handled by her breeder-owner, Edgar W. "Bill" Averill. Bill, who has his doctorate in mathematics, was a founding member of the American Brittany Club.

Diane's record is one which may never be beaten. Besides her American and Canadian championships, she had an American Utility Dog title, and a Canadian C.D.X. Then, to the highest bench and obedience titles she could win, she added the National Amateur Championship. Since a dual championship with the famous Patrice of Sharvogue had so narrowly escaped him, Dr. Averill's victory with Diane must have been especially pleasing.

## Winners of the National Amateur Championship Stake

1951. Can. and Am. Ch. Diane de Beauch, U.D. Owner-handler: Dr. Edgar W. Averill.

1952. Domino de Klemanor. Owner-handler: Walter B. Kleeman.

1953. Ch. Belloaks Ginger. Owner-handler: Marcelle Bell.

1954. Dual Ch. Holley Haven Duchess. Owner: Henry Holleyoak. Handler: Reid Troutman.

1955. Holley Haven Dan. Owner-handler: William Szubielak.

1956. Fld. Ch. Ferdinand of Leeway. Owner-handler: John W. Lee.

1957. Dual Ch. Saxon of Fredan. Owner-handler: Dr. Fred Z. White, M.D.

1958.  Fld. Ch. Ferdinand of Leeway. Owner: John W. Lee. Handler: Mrs. Ruth Lee.

1959.  Dual Ch. Belloak's King. Owner: J. B. Bell Jr. Handler: Marcelle Bell.

1960.  Fld. Ch. Gladwin Smokey. Owner-handler: Amos Greer.

1961.  Fld. Ch. Jeff of Minnehaha. Owner-handler: Richard L. Culbert.

1962.  Ferd's Cannonball of Leeway. Owner: John W. Lee. Handler: Mrs. Ruth Lee.

1963.  Fld. Ch. Epper of Siouxland. Owner-handler: Dr. Adolph Utzinger.

1964.  Dual Ch. Tigar's Jocko. Owner-handler: John Munson.

1965.  Fld. Ch. Towsey's Bub. Owner-handler: M. D. Nelson.

1966.  Fld. Ch. Towsey's Bub. Owner-handler: M. D. Nelson.

1967.  Fld. Ch. Little Rapa Luke. Owner-handler: Dr. Edna Cree.

1968.  Fld. Ch. Holliday Britts Ed. Owner-handler: N. Cathey.

1969.  Fld. Ch. Gringo De Britt. Owner-handler: Dr. Tim Poling.

1970.  Fld. & National Amateur Ch. Gringo De Britt. Owner-handler: Dr. Tim Poling.

1971.  Dual Ch. Char-Lee O'Dee. Owner-handler: Francis Clasen.

1972.  Colorado Jumping Gypsy. Owner-handler: Bill Cline.

# 21

# The American Brittany Classics

As noted in the history of the breed, Brittany Spaniels spread rapidly about North America. Very shortly after their introduction, they spread from Mexico to British Columbia, and from Southern California to New Brunswick and Nova Scotia. This meant that the Brittany Spaniel was being used on all kinds of feathered game—woodcock, prairie chicken, grouse, partridge, quail, and pheasant.

When national trials came into being, it soon became evident that dogs from one section of this vast area might have to work on game birds with which they were not familiar. Moreover, a dog which could perform superbly on one type of feathered game might always be in the shadow because, at trials it had to work other species. The American Brittany Club solved this problem by setting up its "Classic Stakes."

These were to be—and are—just slightly less important than the national championship events. They are officially given by the American Brittany Club, but regional clubs act as hosts for the events.

The Classics are limited open all age events for Brittany Spaniels only. They are the Pheasant Classic, Quail Classic, Prairie Chicken Classic, and Grouse Classic. The American Brittany Club limits the entry to dogs which have qualified in other events. For example, a dog must have won a first place in a derby or open all age in order to qualify.

Here are the winners and their owners in each Classsic since its beginning.

## Pheasant Classic

1964. Ch. White Flash's Nikki. W. G. Thompson.
1965. Fld. Ch. Juchoir's Chocolate Candy. L. Prefountaine.
1966. Fld. Ch. Juchoir's Chocolate Candy. L. Prefountaine.
1967. Baroness Allamuchy Babs. Al. J. Barone Jr.
1968. Foltz's Freckles. Del and Pat Foltz.
1969. Dual Ch. Les-Lee's Red Ryder. Dave Lachance.
1970. Dual Ch. Tigar's Jocko. J. Munson.
1971. Dual Ch. Black Butte Ricochet Trooper. Ejner and Gilda Lund.
1972. Fld. Ch. Brandy's Bullet. William Norvell.
1973. Dual Ch. Pacolet Cheyenne Sam. Ken and Erin Jacobson

## Quail Classic

1962. Detective Neal of Kaymore. Herbert Farnsworth.
1963. Kaymore's Joe of Weymouth. J. B. Bell, Jr.
1964. Scuffletown Quito. D. H. Wilson.
1965. Le Bonabe. Dr. R. D. Bolton.
1966. Le Petite Blanche. Dr. R. D. Bolton.
1967. Rendezvous Skipper. L. D. LaFleur.
1968. Worrelwind's Bucky Weaver. Rufus Worrellwind.
1969. Skysan. R. Evans.
1970. Augustus of Rivers. James J. White.
1971. Fld. Ch. Sodak Sandy Sioux. Richard L. Culbert.
1972. Tondee's Sandy Duke. Stephen Tardy.

## Grouse Classic

1961. First place withheld.
1962. First place withheld.
1963. Event was cancelled.
1964. Summit Star. Thomas Howell.
1965. Not held.
1966. Kipewa's Breton Belle. W. A. McClure.
1967. Fld. Ch. Kaymore's Dappled Desire. Mrs. James Bell.
1968. Dual Ch. Joel's Copper Jacques. John G. & Ellyn Lee.

Fld. Ch. Juchoir's Chocolate Candy, (left) a Pheasant Classic winner with breeder-handler Nicky Bissell. The dog at the right is Fld. Ch. Juchoir's Bronze Bigwig with owner Grant Chadbourne.

This group of field winners all were sired by Dual Ch. Pierrot de Fontaine Vallee out of Juchoir's Shady Lady. All carry the "Juchoir" prefix. They are (l. to r.) Fld. Ch. Light Lodestar with James Rookard, Fld. Ch. Chocolate Candy with owner Larry Prefountain, Fld. Ch. Bronze Bigwig with owner Grant Chadbourne, Fld. Ch. Termison Tiger with owner Dr. Heap, Bright Bangtail with owner William Summey and Dual Ch. Shady Scamp with owner William Brown.

1969. Ch. Suzabob's Hum Dinger. Robert E. Young.
1970. Aud's Barney Boy. A. Gohlke.
1971. Not held.
1972. Not held.

### Prairie Chicken Classic

1964. Way-Kan Pete. Donald Davis.
1965. First place withheld.
1966. Not held.
1967. First place withheld.
1968. Juchoir's Choctaw. M. F. Guest.
1969. Suzabob's Rip Snorter. Harry B. Robb.
1970. Ch. Majestic Jake. O. E. Hoover.
1971. Fld. Ch. Augustus of Rivers. James J. White.
1972. Dual Ch. The Little Joker. George Wilson.

Most of these dogs were not field or bench champions at the time
of their victories. In some cases, the victory made the dog a field champion. In most other cases, the dogs later became field champions.

# 22

# How a Brittany Spaniel Becomes a Champion

T HE American Kennel Club sets up the rules governing the awarding of championships. In the case of field championships, it consults the parent clubs, or governing bodies, of all the breeds in a given classification. For example, it sets up rules for Brittany Spaniels, Pointers, German Short-haired Pointers, German Wirehaired Pointers, English Setters, Irish Setters, Gordon Setters, Vizslas, Weimaraners, and Wirehaired Pointing Griffons. These are all pointing breeds

The awarding of championships at field trials is based partly on performance, and partly on the competition. A dog has to win 10 points to become a field champion. This applies to all of the pointing breeds listed above. A dog can win points only by winning first place in a regular stake.

The regular stakes are Open Puppy, Open Derby, Gun Dog (Open or Amateur), All-Age (Open or Amateur) Limited Gun Dog (Open or Amateur), and Limited All-Age (Open or Amateur). The point schedule is as follows:

| | |
|---|---|
| 4 to 7 starters | 1 point |
| 8 to 12 starters | 2 points |
| 13 to 17 starters | 3 points |

18 to 24 starters .......................... 4 points

25 or more starters ...................... 5 points

Now the general rule for pointing dogs is that the dog must win its points in at least three licensed or member club trials. It must have won at least one three-points or better Open All-Age, Open Gun Dog, Open Limited All-Age, or Limited Gun Dog Stake. It cannot count more than two points each which have been won in Open Puppy and Open Derby stakes. And not more than four points of the 10 can be counted if won in Amateur stakes.

For Brittany Spaniels, there is an additional condition which makes the winning of a championship much more difficult. It must have won a three-points of better Open Gun Dog, Open All-Age, Open Limited Gun Dog, or Open Limited All-Age Stake in which only Brittany Spaniels were eligible to compete.

There are both national and national amateur titles open for competition to Brittany Spaniels. These can be won only at National Amateur and National Open championship stakes which are held only once in each calendar year. The rules for eligibility to compete in such trials are made by the American Brittany Club. But they are subject to American Kennel Club approval.

The winner of such a stake gains the title of "National Brittany Spaniel Field Champion of 19. . ." or "National Amateur Brittany Spaniel Field Champion of 19. . ." The winning of these titles does not automatically carry with them a field championship title. But the conditions for entry make it certain that the dog which wins is already a field champion, or will become one by winning. The point rating given above applies in the National Open Championship Stake.

## Conformation Championships

It is customary to speak of championships won in conformation as "bench championships." For at least 70 years, all dog shows were benched. Now benched shows are rare. But the term "bench" championship still remains. In France, people often speak of a "beauty" championship.

As in the field, conformation championships are won on a point system. A dog must win 15 points. At least six of these points must be won at two shows with a three points or better rating each and under two different judges. Some of the balance of the points must be won under a judge or judges other than those referred to above.

Dual Ch. Pierrot de Fontaine Vallee (left) is distinguished as one of the great performers and sires in the breed. Shown with him is Ch. Juchoir's Some Shoveller. Both dogs are owned by Mrs. Nicky Bissell.

Dual Ch. Destry, owned by Frank Vulgamore.

Dual Ch. Jacques des Rocheuses, owned by Lucas Ruiz.

Championship points are awarded in winners classes only. The so-called regular classes are puppy, novice, bred-by-exhibitor, American-bred, and open. If a dog wins first, it gets a blue ribbon, and then it enters the winners class. It competes there with the other class winners for points.

Championship points are based upon the number of actual competitors in the regular classes. The dog which is awarded winners dog, or winners bitch, then gets the championship points. The dog which gets best of winners may get extra points by doing so. Let us suppose that the winners dog won three points and the winners bitch, five. If the dog now is awarded best of winners, he would be entitled to five points, that being the number won by the bitch. He cannot add on the three points he won to make eight. That is, he cannot win double points. The most points that can be won at any show is five.

If a dog wins best of breed over champions, it cannot count these dogs in figuring championship points, since these can be won only in the classes. However, if the dog goes from the classes to first in the sporting group, and then on to best in show, it would be entitled to the highest point rating won by any dog in the group or in the show.

Let us suppose a Brittany Spaniel won only one point in breed competition. If it now wins the group, and an Irish Setter had won three points in its breed, then the Brittany would be credited with three points instead of only one. If it wins best in show, and a Maltese had won five points in its breed, then the Brittany would be given five points.

The American Kennel Club divides the country into seven divisions. It then makes up point ratings for each division by a complicated system. This is based upon the number of dogs of a breed registered in the entire country, the number registered from a given division, and the number being shown in that division. The purposes are to make it reasonably difficult for a dog to win a championship, but not so difficult that it cannot win one.

Following are the points for each division, effective May 15, 1972, as they apply to Brittany Spaniels. "D" stands for dogs; "B" for bitches.

## Division One

Maine, New Hampshire, Vermont, Massachusetts, Rhode Island, Connecticut, New York, Pennsylvania, New Jersey, Delaware, Mary-

Ch. Ches-Val's Sparky, owned by Charles Dodson, is shown winning the first of three consecutive bests of breed at the Maryland Brittany Club Specialty. The judge is Glenn Sommers and the handler is George D. Edge, Jr. *Shafer photo.*

Ch. Suzabob's Freckled Miss, owned and handled by Edwin Jeffreys, Jr. *Ashbey photo.*

land, District of Columbia, Virginia, Ohio, Michigan, Indiana, Illinois, and Wisconsin.

| One Point | | Two Points | | Three Points | | Four Points | | Five Points | |
|---|---|---|---|---|---|---|---|---|---|
| D | B | D | B | D | B | D | B | D | B |
| 2 | 2 | 4 | 4 | 7 | 7 | 9 | 9 | 14 | 12 |

## Division Two

West Virginia, Kentucky, Tennessee, North Carolina, South Carolina, Georgia, Florida, Alabama, Mississippi, Louisiana, Arkansas, Oklahoma, Texas, New Mexico, Arizona, Minnesota, Iowa, Missouri, Kansas, Nebraska, and Colorado.

| One Point | | Two Points | | Three Points | | Four Points | | Five Points | |
|---|---|---|---|---|---|---|---|---|---|
| 2 | 2 | 4 | 4 | 6 | 6 | 9 | 8 | 14 | 12 |

## Division Three

California

| 2 | 2 | 5 | 5 | 8 | 8 | 10 | 10 | 15 | 15 |
|---|---|---|---|---|---|---|---|---|---|

## Division Four

North Dakota, South Dakota, Montana, Wyoming, Utah, Nevada, Idaho, Oregon, and Washington.

| 2 | 2 | 5 | 4 | 9 | 7 | 11 | 8 | 16 | 10 |
|---|---|---|---|---|---|---|---|---|---|

Alaska, Hawaii and Puerto Rico

| 2 | 2 | 3 | 3 | 4 | 4 | 5 | 5 | 6 | 6 |
|---|---|---|---|---|---|---|---|---|---|

Before closing this section, we should add that it is often possible to increase the points at a given show by combining the sexes. This is often done in areas where there are very few dogs in a given breed. Let us suppose that the sexes are combined at an Alaskan show. There are then six Brittany Spaniels entered, three dogs and three bitches. There would be just one winners class, but that dog or bitch would then win five points instead of two.

## Canadian Bench Championships

Canadian Kennel Club rules for wining a championship are roughly the same as those of the American Kennel Club. There are these differ-

Ch. Sewall's Rex, owned by Glenn Sewall, and shown here with his handler John G. Lee. *Klein photo.*

American and Canadian Ch. Windy Hills Spike (Gus's Liberty Buck ex Pawnee Princess), owned by Al Langan and bred by the famous trainer Lee Holman. He is handled in the ring by Robert Eldridge. *Ritter.*

The main winners at the Susquehanna Brittany Club Specialty 1971. They are (l. to r.) Ch. Ffynant's Happy Time, owned by John Mattinson and Joan Coluccio, best of breed; Ch. Suzabob's Seminole Sadie, owned by Robert Young, best of opposite sex; Suzabob's Freckled Miss (now a champion), owned by Edwin Jeffreys, Jr., best of winners. The judge is Clark C. Thompson. *Shafer photo.*

ences. A dog must win 10 championship points under at least three different judges. In figuring championship points, champions are counted, provided the class dog defeats them. It must defeat dogs of its own breed at least once, or it must place in groups in which five or more breeds are competing. It is important here to point out that, in Canada, a dog must compete in all classes for which it is eligible, or any points it may have won will be cancelled. Thus, if a dog wins five points in its breed and goes best of breed, it must compete in the group or it will lose its points.

The Canadian Kennel Club also divides its country into zones. Point ratings are figured by breed only, and are not divided by sex as in the United States. At the present time, the point ratings for Brittany Spaniels are the same in all parts of the country. One dog, if it gets winners, receives one point. Three dogs get two points; four get three; six get four; and eight get five.

## Canadian Field Championships

To become a field champion in Canada, a Brittany Spaniel must win 10 points at licensed field trials under Canadian Kennel Club rules. At least three of the points must have been won in an unrestricted senior open stake, and not more than two points can be won in puppy stakes. An unrestricted stake is one in which all pointing breeds are allowed to compete. Senior stakes are all stakes other than puppy or derby stakes.

American and Canadian Ch. Torbec Filibuster, owned by Gordon and Michele McIntyre.

Ch. Torbec Little Rover, owned by Gordon and Michele McIntyre.

In puppy stakes with five or more starters, the winner gets one point. In derby stakes with eight or more starters, the winner gets two points. The rating for senior stakes is as follows.

|                          | First | Second | Third |
|--------------------------|-------|--------|-------|
| 6 to 7 dogs competing    | 1     | 0      | 0     |
| 8 to 11 dogs competing   | 2     | 1      | 0     |
| 12 to 15 dogs competing  | 3     | 1      | $\frac{1}{2}$ |
| 16 to 19 dogs competing  | 4     | 2      | 2     |
| 20 or more dogs competing| 5     | 3      | 2     |

The official stakes at Canadian trials are the Open Puppy, Open Derby, Gun Dog (Open or Amateur) and All-Age (Open or Amateur).

Ch. Stillmeadow's Rambler, C.D., owned by William McClure. *Nicholls photo.*

Dual Ch. Jacque of Connie, owned by C. Kent Lipsey.

# 23

# Official Field Trial Classes

### American Kennel Club

OPEN PUPPY. For dogs six months of age and under 15 months on the first advertised day of the trial.

OPEN DERBY. For dogs six months of age and under two years on the first advertised day of the trial.

GUN DOG STAKE (Open or amateur). For dogs six months of age and over on the first advertised day of the trial.

ALL-AGE STAKE (Open or amateur). For dogs six months of age and over on the first advertised day of the trial.

LIMITED GUN DOG STAKE (Open or Amateur). For dogs six months of age and over on the first advertised day of the trial, which have won first place in an Open Derby Stake or which have placed first, second, third, or fourth in a Gun Dog Stake. A field trial-giving club may give an Amateur Limited Gun Dog Stake in which places that qualify a dog have been acquired in Amateur Stakes only.

LIMITED ALL-AGE STAKE (Open or Amateur). For dogs six months of age and over on the first advertised day of the trial, which have won first place, second, third, or fourth in any All-Age Stake. A field trial-giving club may give an Amateur Limited All-Age Stake in which places that qualify a dog have been acquired in Amateur Stakes only.

In an Amateur Stake at a licensed or member field trial, all dogs must be owned and handled by persons who, in the judgment of the Field Trial Committee, are qualified as Amateurs.

### Canadian Kennel Club

OPEN PUPPY STAKE. From January 1st to July 1st in each year, for dogs whelped on or after January 1st of the year preceding, and from January 1st to July 1st in each year for dogs whelped on or after January 1st of two preceding years.

OPEN DERBY. From July 1st to December 31st in each year for dogs whelped on or after January 1st of the year preceding, and from January 1st to July 1st in each year for dogs whelped on or after January 1st of two years preceding.

GUN DOG STAKE (Open or Amateur). For dogs six months of age and over on the first day of the trial.

ALL-AGE STAKE (Open or Amateur). For dogs six months of age and over on the first day of the trial.

At any field trial there shall not be more than one of each of the stakes described in this section, except that both open and amateur stakes may be held in Gun Dog and All-Age stakes. And no club shall hold more than two of these stakes in one calendar year unless justified by unusual circumstances and approved by the Canadian Kennel Club. Dogs running in an amateur stake must be owned by an amateur and handled by an amateur.

Here we should add another rule of the Canadian Kennel Club. "A dog is not eligible to be entered in any stake in a licensed field trial, if the judge of that stake, or any member of his family has owned, sold, held under lease, boarded, trained or handled the dog (EXCEPT IN AN AMATEUR STAKE) within six months prior to the date of the field trial.

Ch. Jeffrey De Klemanor, owned by Walter B. Kleeman.

The judges and winners at an early field trial assemble for the camera. Judges are James Tallmadge (left) and R. L. Sutton. The dogs and their handlers (l. to r.) are Fld. Ch. Georges of Leeway, with owner John W. Lee; Ch. Avono Jake, with Buck Bissell; Burt's Buddy Fentress, with Bill Kull; and Luke's Allamuchy Valley Fury, with Lee Holman.

## Standards of Procedure

Both the American and Canadian Kennel Clubs have published carefully worked out procedures, both for operating trials, and for evaluating performances. The American Kennel Club booklet is called *Registration and Field Trial Rules and Standard Procedures for Pointing Breeds, Dachshunds, Retrievers, and Spaniels.* This booklet may be obtained by writing to the American Kennel Club, 51 Madison Ave., New York, N.Y., 10010. Single copies are free upon individual request. When ordered in quantity, the cost is 25 cents per copy.

The Canadian Kennel Club has a similar booklet *Field Trial Rules and Regulations for Pointing Breeds.* It also has a booklet, *Standards of Judicial Practice and Field Trial Procedure.* Single copies of these are free upon request by writing to the Canadian Kennel Club, 1173 Bay St., Toronto, Ontario, Canada.

French and International Ch. Noric de Saint Tugen, owned by Mme. Marchand. Noric is also a field champion. *Dim photo.*

# 24

# The Brittany Spaniel in France Today

by Genie Rundle

*The author is indebted to Madame Genie Rundle for the present information on the Brittany Spaniel in France. Mrs. Rundle visited with many of the great breeders of today to get this information. Although part of this has been covered in earlier chapters, there are slightly different conclusions. And therefore, the information is given just as Mrs. Rundle wrote it. This will enable readers to reach their own conclusions as to the origin and development of the breed.*

ACCORDING to the largest, and most recent publication in France, *Le Grand Livre Du Chien* published in that country in 1970, The Brittany Spaniel was only recognized as a distinct breed during the 19th Century, although it had existed since the time of the Celtic flight into Brittany when the Anglo-Saxons invaded Wales, at which time the Celts took with them the Springer Spaniel. This breed, when crossed with the existing French type of working spaniel, gave rise to the type so well known today. That is to say, rustic and cobby.

163

French Dual Ch. Stop de Morwandoy. *Bonnet photo.*

An international show and field titleholder is the French dog, Ch. Quetche De Kestellic, owned by M. Le Brosse.

Ch. Quodic De Kestellic, owned by M. Le Brosse, like his brother Quetche, holds international titles in both field and bench.

In fact, the 'crouching dog' of the Middle Ages is certainly the ancestor of all French types of spaniel, as well as some others with longer coats, such as the three types of setter: English, Irish, and Gordon. It dates back as far as the First Crusades, at which time it was usual for the knights of France and Arabia to exchange dogs and horses which they used for hunting. These, in turn, being crossed with several other types of dog then known, such as the Sloughi from the Orient, and various hunting dogs from Spain, gave rise to the original (crouching dog). This dog is very often depicted in early French paintings and tapestries, and which, during the 16th Century, became the French Spaniel.

In those days, these were widely spread across the Brittany regions of France, and were strongly built dogs with long, silky coats. It was after this that the Springer made its entry into the same territory. And thus was born the Brittany Spaniel, very similar to the one we know today.

There is a more recent account, which appears to be authentic, and which was related to me by Monsieur Jacques Piraux. He is the owner of the dog with the present day's highest number of awards, though not yet a champion. He tells that 70 or 80 years ago "a game-keeper named Lulzac, entered the service of the Vicomte du Pontavice. Lulzac owned a red and white Springer type of Spaniel, and the Vicomte bred English Setters. These two dogs were purposely bred and their progeny gave rise to the color, orange and white."

Monsieur Piraux goes on to say:

"I learned a few months ago from an industrialist who owned these dogs that only the liver and white Brittanies were physically able to withstand the rigorous North African climate. For that reason, sportsmen living in Morocco were the sad eye-witnesses of the general disappearance of these orange and whites, along with several other breeds, and setters, which could not survive the intense heat.

"The breed is essentially sporting, and although it can be used on big game, it is generally preferred for pointing and retrieving under all weather conditions, and in the thickest, most prickly undergrowths. The Brittany Spaniel will swim into the iciest water to retrieve its game and is tireless in all its efforts. It is one of the gentlest of breeds, willing to submit to its master's orders. It is also affectionate, sensitive, and an ideal companion."

There are at the present time over 230,000 Brittanies registered with the L.O.F. of the *Societe Centrale Canine* (the official French Kennel

French Dual Ch. Sacha de Saint Tugen, owned and bred by
Mme. Marchand, is one of 16 champions bred by this famous
kennel since 1956.

Fld. Ch. Quito de Saint Tugen, owned and bred by Mme. Marchand,
was winner of the 1971 national field trial championship of France.
Mme. Marchand trains and handles all her own dogs.

Club), and the present annual rate of registration is about 5000. However, since the Brittany is the most sought after sporting dog in the world, field trials are obviously where it is most prized. The most hotly disputed competition, other than in France, is in Switzerland, and in both North and South America.

In France, field trials are divided into three categories. Those which take place on partridge are held in the spring, and number about 30 held during April. During the summer—in August—five or six are held on partridge and quail. Then there are about 20 autumn trials, which include the wing shooting of partridge and pheasants, and the shooting of rabbits and hare. Retrieving is required. In addition, there are two special field trials on woodcock and snipe.

The most important trial of the year is the one organized by the Societe Centrale Canine, since it is here that the title Champion of France is awarded to the winner. At this trial only selected dogs can compete. Another most important trial is that held by the *Club de l'Epagneul Breton,* in which as many as 150 dogs compete in a single day.

Today the Club de l'Epagneul Breton proudly acknowledges as its head, President Gaston Pouchain. President Pouchain is also at present president of the Societe Centrale Canine, with which the Brittany Club is affiliated. There are two vice-presidents, Dr. Roguet and M. Pambrun. The secretary is M. Dages, and the assistant-secretary, M. Baudot. The treasurer is M. Valeyrie, and the assistant treasurer, M. Le Chat. Other members of the committee, of which there are 12 in number are: M. Arnaud, Dr. Bazin, L. Bourdon, Combanaire, Derouet, Freville, Guyemer, Jeangirard, Labrosse, Lamour, Lelong, and Moncet. The headquarters address is: 25, rue du Renard, Paris, 4e. The secretariat is at 24, Place de la Chapelle, Paris, 18c.

There are now three recognized colors for the breed: liver and white; orange and white; and black and white. This latter, although once banned in order to avoid the "blue" which was cropping up as the result of undesirable crossings, is now re-established.

Note: The L. Bourdon, to whom reference is made earlier, is Louis Bourdon, the son of Emile Bourdon, founder of the famed Cornouaille Kennels. Louis Bourdon continues the kennels of his father. Cornouaille is the Breton term for Cornwall.

## THE MODERN FRENCH BREED STANDARD

**General Appearance—Height:** Maximum 51 centimeters (19.89 inches); minimum, 46 centimeters (17.94 inches). Ideal height for males: 48 to 50 centimeters (18.72 inches to 19.50 inches); and for bitches, 47 to 49 centimeters (18.33 to 19.11 inches). The ideal **weights** are: 15 kilograms (33.07 pounds) for males; and 13 kilograms (28.66 pounds) for bitches. A compact dog, ears short and set high, skull rounded with tight lips, coat flat, lightly fringed, fringes wavy never curly, cobby type, tail about 10 centimeters (3.9 inches) long; natural bob tail permitted.

**Nose**—Colored according to whether the dog is white and orange, white and liver, or white and black. Nostrils open, well shaped. **Faults:** Bare nose patches (butterfly nose), too light nostrils that interfere with scenting.

**Lips**—Tight with upper lip slightly overlapping the lower. **Faults:** Thick or with heavy flews.

**Muzzle**—Medium length, about two thirds the length of the skull. **Faults:** Too long or too short.

**Skull**—Medium length, rounded, median line slightly marked. Well defined but not exaggerated stop. **Faults:** Apple headed, distinct occipital crest, narrow or coarse. Stop heavily indented.

**Eyes**—Brown, in harmony with the coat, lively and expressive **Faults:** Too light, mean, or bird of prey eyes.

**Ears**—Set high, rather short, lightly fringed, though the ear ought to be well covered with hair. **Faults:** Low set, pendulous, too large, or with very curly hair.

**Neck**—Medium length, well set on the shoulders, without dewlap. **Faults:** Too long, too slender, too short and thick-set.

**Shoulders**—Oblique and well muscled. **Faults:** Too straight or too angulated.

**Forelegs**—Muscled and bony. **Faults:** Bone too heavy or too light.

**Chest**—Deep, descending to the level of the elbow, sides well rounded, deep as well as wide. **Faults:** Narrow, not deep enough, slab sided.

**Back**—Short, withers well defined, never sway-backed. **Faults:** Too long or sway.

**Loins**—Short and Strong. **Faults:** Long and weak.

**Hips**—Lower than the withers, set well into the loins.

**Croup**—Slightly falling. **Faults:** Too straight or too steep.

**Flanks**—Well rounded without excess. **Faults:** Fat and falling.

French Ch. Querou de Cornouaille is a contemporary example of the breeding from the famous Cournouaille Kennels that contributed so strongly to American fanciers when the breed was getting started in North America.

This dog is a famous show and field winner in France. He is Pipo and is owned by M. Jacques Piraux. This liver and white is considered to be of excellent type by continental authorities.

**Tail**—Level, docked if the dog does not have a natural short tail, always short, about 10 centimeters (3.9 inches), often with a little twist, and ending with a queue of hair. **Faults:** Long or bare.

**Forelegs**—Very straight, with pasterns slightly bent, clean and muscled. **Faults:** Pasterns too straight or falling radically, lack of feathering (elbow to pasterns).

**Hindlegs**—Strong thighs, stifles well bent, muscular, not cowhocked. Thighs well feathered half way to the hock. Hocks short, not too bent. **Faults:** Straight stifles, lack of feathering, too straight (hocks) or too bent.

**Feet**—Toes compact with a little hair between. **Faults:** Large, long, cat footed, splayed.

**Coat**—Flat, or slightly wavy, not excessively heavy. **Faults:** Curly or too soft.

**Color**—White and orange, white and liver, white and black, tricolor, or roan of any of these colors.

**Summary**—Thickset and strong backed. An elegant little dog, very vigorous in its movements, energetic, with an intelligent look, presenting the appearance of a full-blooded dog.

The judges should excuse, without prizes, all dogs under 46 centimeters or over 51 centimeters.

Lack of pigment is a fault on the nose. Lack of pigment on the eyelids eliminates the dog from receiving any prize. Lack of pigment is a serious fault and no dog having (a lack) of it should receive a rating of excellent. If the lack of pigment is very minor, the dog may receive a rating of very good.

Monorchids may not be shown in dog shows or compete in field trials.

The classes in a show will be in two divisions: (1) White and orange. (2) Other colors.

## Comment by the Author

The French Kennel Club is somewhat more realistic than is the American Kennel Club. Thus, it recognizes that if monorchidism (only one testicle descended) is a fault, it is equally a fault in show dogs and in field dogs. It is considered in most countries to be a transmissible fault. For that reason, the French Kennel Club bars monorchids in both shows and field trials. In the United States, the fault is ignored in dogs entered in field trials.

Judging systems vary in different countries. Some in Europe and elsewhere (Brazil is an example) "rate" the exhibits. Thus, depending upon its quality, a dog might win a rating of excellent, very good, good, or sufficient. In the Scandinavian countries, which have strong Brittany entries, dogs can get first, second, third, or 0, meaning "nil" or no award. France uses the system of excellent, very good, good, and sufficient.

Only a dog winning a rating of excellent gets a certificate toward its championship. And in case a number of dogs receive such a rating, then the judge picks the best of these for the championship rating. One dog of each sex is awarded this certificate.

A dog needs to win three of these to become a champion. But, in addition, one of these must be won at the annual Paris show. This limits the breed to two conformation champions a year. However, in the case of Brittany Spaniels, this is increased to four. The reason is that there can be two white and orange champions, male and female, and two in the other allowed colors.

In Europe and in South America and Mexico, it is possible for a dog to win an International Championship. This is one granted under the rules of the F.C.I., or Federation Cynologique Internationale, whose headquarters are in Belgium. An international beauty championship certificate (C.A.C.I.B.) can be awarded at any licensed F.C.I. show.

In Europe, to become an International Champion, the dog must win four C.A.C.I.B. certificates in three different countries, one at least of which must be won in the owner's country, or in the country of origin of the breed. In countries outside Europe, as for instance in Mexico, and in most of the South American countries, the rule is slightly different. The dog must win four C.A.C.I.Bs under four different judges, one of whom comes from another continent. Additionally, the dog will have to demonstrate some hunting ability, including freedom from gun shyness. Puppies cannot win C.A.C.I.Bs.

# 25

# French Field Trial Rules

In European countries, there are fewer specialist breeds than in the United States, Canada, and Mexico. On our side of the Atlantic, a Brittany Spaniel would normally be used on feathered game only. But in Europe, it might be required to prove itself on hares. It might also be required to retrieve on both land and water, and even to make "blind" retrieves.

In Europe, almost all hunting is done on foot. And so, field trials are conducted on foot. In our country, field trials for European breeds have inevitably felt the effect of our long established Pointer and Setter trials under American Field or Amateur Field Trial Clubs of America rules.

In our country, we would not dream of mixing a Springer Spaniel, a Labrador Retriever, and a Brittany Spaniel together in a licensed trial. But this is often done in Europe.

The rules of the French Kennel Club require two judges. Efforts are made to make all tests as nearly identical as possible. That is, in the same cover, with the same wind direction, and with similar retrieving tests. As a rule, the dogs are worked alone, that is, singly. However, if more than 18 dogs are entered, then the dogs work in braces.

The French penalize dogs which cast out so far as to disappear from sight. They expect that, in the woods, a dog will slow its pace so that it can keep in touch with its handler. Dogs are expected to cast back and forth in front of their handlers, and in crossing in front should not be farther than gun range, a maximum of about 60 yards, but with 40 being average.

Dogs are penalized for pottering. They may bump one bird, but if they bump a second, they are disqualified. When dogs are working in braces, they are required to back. Unproductive points are heavily penalized.

We require our dogs to "freeze" on point. The French follow a system which is used in England. The dog is expected to hold point until the arrival of its handler. Then, but only on command, it must drop into a crouching position.

The reason for this rule stems from the Middle Ages method of throwing a net over the covey. The crouching dog was out of the way. The rule survives from the belief that the standing dog might interfere with the shooting.

Readers of this book will remember that in the early trials in America, game was shot over the dogs. This was the procedure in France then, and it is still the same in most trials. Official gunners do the shooting.

An interesting, albeit unidentified, painting showing a Brittany Spaniel pointing a woodcock and an English Setter backing.

Steadiness to wing and shot is not required, provided that the dog marks the fall and makes the retrieve promptly. But if, in breaking, the dog interferes with the shooting, then it is penalized. Such interference, for example, might occur if the dog bolted after a started hare. In a somewhat contradictory rule, the dog is supposed to retrieve upon command of the handler. In part, this refers to the dog which has remained steady, and in part to special retrieving tests.

Field trial committees can vote to eliminate water tests, provided an announcement to this effect is made before the start of the trial. When a water test is given, it is "blind." That is, the dog is sent out to retrieve game it cannot see from shore.

Land retrieves of about 20 to 25 yards are often required. In such tests, the dead bird may be placed in a ditch or heavy thicket. Some obstacle, such as a low wall or fence is between the dog and the retrieve. The dog is expected to jump this barrier. Such retrieves are called "cold" retrieves. They are given when a dog has not had a chance to retrieve game which it pointed. Heavy penalties are made against dogs which carry their game sloppily.

Though the dog is not required to be steady to wing and shot, it must remain staunch until the handler comes up. And if the bird is not shot, it is expected to remain steady, that is, it should not make a useless chase.

A dog cannot win championship consideration unless it has been on point, and preferably on birds. However, if it has been repeatedly on point on hare, it can be awarded a C.A.C These initials stand for a certificate of ability. The dog must win four to be a champion.

# 26

# The Hall of Fame

IN 1965 the officers and directors of the American Brittany Club decided that it was time to recognize officially the great dogs of the past. There is an American Field Hall of Fame, a Beagle Hall of Fame, and even a Pigeon Hall of Fame. So it was voted to set up a Brittany Hall of Fame which would perpetuate the records of the breed's great dogs. The only condition for nominating a dog was that it be dead. It could be a male or a bitch.

Here are the names of those enshrined, with a brief outline of their records.

Kaer de Cornouaille. Imported from France by Alan Stuyvesant. First to make a name for himself in American field trials. Sire of three dual champions, all of which have been elected to the Hall of Fame.

Dual Ch. Allamuchy Valley Uno. A son of Kaer, an all around good dog, and the sire of many winners, bench and field. Owned by Alan Stuyvesant.

Dual Ch. Avono Happy. A son of Kaer, owned by Jack L. Whitworth. Won the national specialty twice, and won the "special" specialty under a French judge. He sired both field and bench winners.

Dual Ch. Britt of Bellows Falls. A son of Kaer, owned by Lucien J. Ufford. He was the first dual champion, and he was a great field winner, both in all-Brittany and in mixed breed trials.

175

Dual Ch. Angelique De Bretagne, owned by L. L. Tice.

French Ch. Gwennec de l'Argoat. He was brought from France by J. R. Joubert for Louis Thebaud. But he became immortal under the hands of René Joubert, who campaigned him in the Midwest. He sired the great Ch. Patrice de Sharvogue, another Hall of Fame dog.

Ch. Patrice de Sharvogue, owned by Dr. E. W. Averill. Patrice won the national specialty three times, and narrowly missed winning his field championship. Patrice did much to make the breed popular.

Dual Ch. Helgramite Howie d'Acajou, owned by W. E. Stevenson. His record of 61 placings was an all-time record at a time when there were fewer trials than today. He sired two dual champions.

Dual Ch. Pierrot de Fontaine Vallee, owned by Buck and Nicky Bissel. He is high on the list of sires of both bench and field winners.

Dual Ch. Pontac's Dingo, owned by Howard Crippen. He won the national championship twice and was the youngest dog ever to win a field championship under AKC rules. He sired two dual champions and many other winners.

Fld. Ch. Torchy of Lionheart, owned by Marion Baker. Torchy competed in both AKC and American Field field trials. His greatest record was made in trials under the latter. His performances, always flashy, made the sporting dog world take notice.

Dual Ch. Uno's Jet, owned by Dave Olund. This great son of Dual Ch. Allamuchy Valley Uno was brilliant in the field. He sired eight field champions and one dual champion, in addition to many winners both bench and field.

Dual Ch. Angelique de Bretagne, owned by Lester Tice. Angelique was a great winner, field and bench. In the field, her range, pace, and style won dozens of converts to the breed.

Dual Ch. Patsy of Edough, owned by Robert Buick. Patsy did her share of winning, bench and field, and then became an outstanding producer.

Dual Ch. Tex of Richmont. He was bred and owned by Dr. R. C. Busteed, but was later sold to N. O. Nielson. He was liver and white. He produced two dual champions, at least four field champions, and at least 41 winners from 19 different bitches.

Dual Ch. Towsey, owned by Thomas Black, and later by Jay Cahill. He won the national field championship three times and 21 first places in trials.

Dual Ch. Pacolet's Cheyenne, owned by N. O. Nielson. She was a daughter of Dual Ch. Tex of Richmont. Bred to Dual Ch. Albedo Valley Dingo, she produced 13 winners, including the first and second placings in the 1965 National Championship stake.

Allamuchy Valley Warrior, whelped in 1948 from a brother-sister mating (Ch. Tudor du Roc Hellou and Ch. Thais du Roc Hellou). He sired the famous liver and white Hall of Famer, Dual Ch. Tex of Richmont. He was rarely shown on the bench, but under the ownership of Clarence Goering, he produced nine bench champions.

Price's Sunflower Gal, bred by famed trainer, Lee Holman, owned by Gerald Price. She produced the great Fld. Ch. Way Kan Jill, and Am. and Can. Dual Ch. Way Kan Jeff.

French Ch. Dingo de Monts Noir, an early Brittany whose name appears in the pedigrees of many American dogs.

Dual Ch. Belloaks Ibby, owned and campaigned by Marcelle Bell. Her 56 placings were made between the ages of 2 and 11½ years. After she produced of Dual Ch. Belloaks King, she was spayed.

Dual Ch. Pacolet Sam, owned by Perry Mobley. He had 39 placings in field trials. He had 16 juvenile placings in puppy and derby stakes, and half of these, in each of the stakes, were firsts.

Fld. Ch. Way Kan Jill. She was whelped in 1958, by two Hall of Famers, Fld. Ch. Ferdinand of Leeway out of Price's Sunflower Gal. Jill won the U.S. Open in 1963 and 1966. She had 10 American Field placings and 22 in AKC trials. Among her progeny was National and Fld. Ch. Bazooka's Brandy. She is the breed's top producer with 22 field winners to her credit.

Dual Ch. Holley Haven Duchess, owned by Henry Holleyoak. She became a dual champion before her third birthday. She won the National Shooting Dog Stake at Carbondale in 1954, was fourth in 1955, and third in 1956. She was best of opposite sex to best of breed at the specialty that year and won the American Brittany Club dual award. She produced one dual champion, three bench champions, and one field champion.

Fld. Ch. Jeffrey of Argard, whelped in 1950, won the national championship stake in 1954. He had 10 placements, five of them firsts. Of his 21 winners sired, five were field champions. He also sired bench champions. He was owned by A. Leroy Magnuson.

Fld. Ch. Ferdinand of Leeway was owned by John and Ruth Lee of Indianapolis. He had 40 placements in field trials, and sired 42 winners. Of these, six were field champions, two were dual champions, and three were bench champions.

Dual Ch. Dingo's Little Mike, owned by George W. Wilson. Mike had 40 placings in trials. He was best of breed at the 16th national specialty show. He sired 24 winners, three of which were field champions, one a dual champion, and two bench champions.

# 27

# How to Name Your Brittany Spaniel

---

THE problem of naming dogs is often extremely puzzling to new-comers to the dog game and has no simple answers. This is because no two dogs can have the same name unless sufficient time has passed so that the first dog is dead. At this writing Brittany Spaniels are exceeding 15,000 registrations a year. Each of the 15,000 must have names not previously used, except as will be noted. Now if you add up the registrations for 15 years, you will have an idea of the problem.

In general, people want simple names for their dogs. Often they try to insist that the dog's call name be used. Yet the chances that the American Kennel Club would allow such names as Prince, Duke, Joe, Princess, Duchess, or Lady are zero. One Brittany Spaniel was, somewhat miraculously, allowed to be registered as Della. But with rare exceptions such as that, and those which follow, compound names must be used.

Because of their color, common Brittany names have been Rusty, Freckles, Ginger, and Sandy. You might be able to use one of these names alone. But you would have to expect that the American Kennel Club would add a numeral after the name. Thus, there have been at least 14 Brittany Spaniels named Ginger—Ginger II to Ginger 14.

And there is a Freckles VI. All these names, by the way, have been used for dogs of both sexes.

Popular names for female Brittany Spaniels have included Sue, Susie, Kate, Princess, Duchess, Bonnie, Lady Queen, Penny, and Nell. Most popular for males have been King, Prince, Duke, Joe, Buddy, Beau, and Ranger. They are excellent for call names because they can be spoken in a "command" tone of voice. But they must be combined with other name parts. For example, Sweet Sue of Valley Britt, Speedy Lady of Hayhurst Farm, and Dual Champion Doctor Joe of Kaymore.

The name combinations are worked out in many ways. Fred and Ann White developed the kennel name, Fredan. Edward and Dorothy Borger combined their nicknames to make Edandot. Henry Holleyoak used Holley Haven. Dr. Frank McHugh, the nutritionist, used Ultra-Mend, the name of the food supplement which he had developed. The pioneer, Walter B. Kleeman named his kennel, Klemanor. And John W. Lee made his, Leeway. John G. and Ellyn Lee made theirs, Joel.

Some have used their own names. Thomas Passamonte has used Passamonte. Elmer Flack used Flack's Tip Top Kennels. And E. and Gilda Lund use Lund, as in Dual Ch. Lund's Trooper. Kennels have used valleys, cities, states, and even streets. Examples of the former are Allamuchy Valley, Albedo Valley, Olentangy Valley, Vitchie Valley, and Fontaine Vallee. There are Spindle City Shorty, Jersey Jeff, and Kansas Kid. The pioneer breeder, Jack L. Whitworth, used Avono because he lived at Avon Lake, Ohio.

Years ago, the American Kennel Club would grant—and register—a kennel name for the life of the breeder. The Club felt then, as it does now, that when a person applies for a kennel name, he or she is intent upon becoming a serious breeder. But studies have shown that only a small number of people remain in the breeding field for longer than five years. In one case, the AKC protected a name, under the lifetime rule, even though its owner had been in an insane asylum for six years. It will now register for a fee a kennel name for five years, with renewal privileges. If, however, the owner of the name does not use it for six years, renewal might be refused, or the name might be granted to another kennel.

Many people make up a kennel name and do not bother to register it. They can use these names so long as they are not registered by others. In one case, a man had used an unregistered kennel name for 20 years. Then he was notified that he could no longer use it. A person in another breed had registered the name. It could happen that even

Ch. Copper Jill of Edwards, owned and handled by
R. H. Edwards.

```
                      Dual Ch. Tigre de Klemanor
          Ch. Tiger Joe de Triumph
                      Buckjet de Klemanor

     Ch. Ti War Roc de Triumph

                      Allamuchy Valley Warrior
          Ch. Warrior's Triumph Freckles
                      Toffee's Misty Freckles

  Ch. Ti War Chip de Triumph

                      Ch. Tudor du Roc Hellou
          Allamuchy Valley Warrior
                      Ch. Thais du Roc Hellou

     Ch. Penny's Penny de Triumph

                      Johnny's Pal
          Ch. Penelope de Evanston
                      Ch. K Haven's Daisy May

CH. COPPER JILL OF EDWARDS

                      Jud of Pasatrou
          Dual Ch. Jig of Kaymore
                      Lady Godiva de Basgard

     Ch. Flambeau's King of Kaymore

                      Ch. Flash de Malibeau
          Vickie's Beauty
                      Vickie

  Ch. Dee Dee Cricket of Edwards

                      Jet de Malibeau
          Dapper Danny
                      Dingo's Little Lassie

     Ch. Brentwood's Victory Song

                      Dapper Danny
          Ch. Brentwood's Jane of Hearts, C.D.
                      Ch. Flambeau's Birdy Britt
```

if you use your own name, it could be taken away from you by a person with the same name.

Half a century ago, if you imported a dog from another country, you could change the name in registering the dog with the American Kennel Club. This practice caused tremendous confusion in pedigree keeping, so the AKC banned the practice. If you have a kennel name, you can, under most circumstances, add this to the imported dog's name. For example, Premier De Callac of Pennbritt.

In naming your dog, several other factors should be observed. The first rule is to keep the name simple. Every dog is given a pet, or call name. If this is a name which carries authority when spoken sharply, so much the better. The authoritative voice and the sharply called name are major factors in dog control. If the call name fits into the full name, excellent. But remember, you are limited by the American Kennel Club to not more than 25 letters in the name.

Brittany Spaniel names which fit these suggestions and rules are given here as examples. Gunners Mate of Cyrus, whose call name could be Gunner, Mate, or even Cy or Gun. Jig of Kaymore is an example. So is Meadow Wink Buzz, whose call name could be either Wink or Buzz. There is another reason for using a simple name—it is less likely to be misspelled.

Many owners misspell names in registering their dogs. They then ask the AKC to correct this. But once registered, the name will not be changed by the AKC. You will have to use the misspelled name forever.

Newspaper writers unfamiliar with dog names often rebel at both their complexity and length. Newspapers have only limited space to give to reports of dog shows and field trials. Sometimes the complexity of the names has caused an entire field or bench report to be thrown into the waste basket.

In the early days, Brittany progress was seriously held up because of the unpronounceable and difficult to spell Breton names. Some of the names which have been the despair of newspaper and magazine writers are MacEochaidh, Aotrou, l'Argoat, Enqueue, and Ch. Count Guilliwime De Gwennec, C.D.

Some of these names were, of course, given to the dogs in France. When imported, they had to be used here. They have survived in part in the names of some of their descendents for an important reason. If part of the name of a sire can be used in your dog's name, then the line from which it comes is readily recognized by all in the breed.

This brings up another point. If a kennel name is registered, you cannot use the name without permission from the owner. The owner of the registered name may grant permission to use the kennel name. This may be done if the breeder feels the dog has a championship in its future. Permission to use the name must be written in by the registered breeder on space provided on the registration application.

There is an axiom among breeders of Thoroughbreds—the running race horses—that "No great horse has a bad name." This is only true most of the time. And many racing failures have great names. Yet the point is worth bearing in mind. In the names listed above, the dogs survived their names to become great. But, while Suzie Woozie may be a child's cute pet name for a pet, it is no name for a Brittany Spaniel champion.

Because of their supreme worth as field dogs, Brittany Spaniels offer many opportunities for attractive and appropriate names. Some particularly successful ones follow. Betty Briarhopper, Lady of Quail, Grouse Feathers, Zipp's Feather Merchant, Pacolet's Bushmaster, Prairie Ranger, Ultra-Mend Birdy Biddy, and Britt Afield Chummy. Thomas Melville used Fun Galore as a kennel name. It was a perfect title for promoting the breed.

Many a man registers his dogs in his wife's name. This is a courteous and gallant thing to do. But in one respect it is wrong. The report of a dog's victory in a magazine or local newspaper could mean the sale of both puppies and grown dogs. Often, however, the prospective buyer cannot reach the owner because the wife's name is not listed in the phone book.

This is, of course, also the problem with registered kennel names. But there are two possible solutions to this. One is to list one's name after the kennel name in parenthesis. Thus: Homewood Kennels, Reg. (J. R. Holmes). The other is to list the wife's name in the telephone directory, or to list the kennel in the advertising sections (yellow pages) of the phone book.

Dual Ch. Cindy's Chico Diable, owned by Charles Ayres and Joe Dahlheim.

# 28

# American Field Champions

THE American Field, and its *Field Dog Stud Book,* were the first to recognize the Brittany Spaniel when it came to North America. Later, the American Field was the first to recognize the American Brittany Club as the official American sponsoring club for the breed.

It has been said that the greatest single activity of the American Kennel Club is in field trials. Yet, if taken without explanation, this statement is misleading. Activity under American Kennel Club jurisdiction includes field trials for pointing dogs, flushing spaniels, retrievers, Beagles (the largest field trial group), Dachshunds, and Bassets.

The American Field conducts field trials for pointing breeds. Its trials are conducted under rules formulated by the Amateur Field Trial Clubs of America. These trials exceed 750 annually, with over 2,600 stakes. In 1969, more than 2300 Brittany Spaniels started in these trials. In numbers, they were third behind Pointers and English Setters.

In 1970, the last full year for which statistics were available, there were 3,032 Brittany Spaniel competitors in the trials. Here is a breakdown according to the 10 stakes which were run.

Open Puppy, 520 starters; Amateur Puppy, 27; Open Derby, 573;

Amateur Derby, 45; Open-All-Age, 932; Amateur All-Age, 272; Open Shooting Dog, 227; Amateur Shooting Dog, 364; Open Championship, 63; and Amateur Championship, 9. Open stakes therefore totalled 2,315 Brittany Spaniel starters, and amateur stakes, 717.

As mentioned earlier, dogs competing at trials under American Kennel Club rules can win points toward championships in various stakes. This is not the case in trials held under American Field jurisdiction. Under its rules, a dog can win a championship only by winning an officially designated championship stake. This means that winning an American Field championship is far more difficult than winning one under the AKC system.

Here are the dogs which have won field trial championships under American Field jurisdiction, together with their *Field Dog Stud Book* registration numbers, and their owners.

Bazooka's Brandy, 741884, Dan Huddleston
Benjji of LaRue, 534312, C. P. Plyler
Britt's Bazooka, 675519, A. H. Pillow
Carey's Freckles, 910152, J. J. Carey Jr.
Goldtone's Duke, 785111, Dr. George Pester
Gringo De Britt, 800744, Dr. and Mrs. Tim Poling
Gundy, 825737, Dr. C. T. Young
Holliday Britt, 800744, J. T. Cahill
Jac Pierre's Pride, 673210, J. E. Cohen
L'Etoile De Dingo, no number given, J. W. Freeman
Miller's Desert Dust, 616561, L. E. Miller
Pacolet Cheyenne Sam, 814923, Ken and Erin Jacobson
S'No Fun Mack, 833533, Dr. W. R. Heap
Sundown Sioux Land, 627176, E. L. Darby
Tess of Chippewa, 356121, Hilmer Peterson
Tigar's Jocko, 723756, John Munson
Towsey, 514892, J. T. Cahill
Way-Kan Jill, 596832, R. B. Leverich
Way-Kan Mandy, 693364, Harold Miller
Yankee Boy's Tommy, 531323, J. A. Costelow

There are two major events for Brittany Spaniels only which are held under American Field jurisdiction. These are the United States Open Championship and the International Brittany Field Trial Association Championship. Though a dog might be designated the winner, the title might be withheld. Here are the winners and their owners in each of the two events.

## United States Open Championship

1963. Way-Kan Jill, James Leverich.
1964. Bill's Buddy Boy, Dan Huddleston. Title withheld.
1965. Holliday Britt's Bazooka, A. H. Pillow.
1966. Way-Kan Jill, James Leverich.
1967. Way Kan Mandy, Harold Miller.
1968. Bazooka's Brandy, Dan Huddleston.
1969. Gringo De Britt, Dr. and Mrs. Tim Poling.
1970. Pacolet Cheyenne Sam, Ken and Erin Jacobson.
1971. Gundy, Dr. C. T. Young.

## International Brittany Field Trial Championship

1969. S'No Fun Mack, Dr. W. R. Heap.
1970. Jac Pierre's Pride, J. E. Cohen.
1971. Carey's Freckles, J. J. Carey Jr.

Dual Ch. Freck-O-Dee, owned by Stan Judd.

# 29

# The Dual Champions

PERHAPS the greatest glory of the Brittany Spaniel is its incomparable record in the earning of dual championships—in the shows and in the field. As of Jan. 1, 1972, some 100 Brittany Spaniels had won dual championships. Only the German Shorthaired Pointer has come close with—at this writing, some 95. Most other breeds have, at most, a couple of dozen. The English Springer Spaniel, which once could boast more dual champions than all the other breeds combined, has not had one in almost 30 years.

Before listing the Brittany Spaniels which have won dual championships, we should give the rather special accomplishments of a few. As pointed out earlier in this book, Lucien Ufford's Britt of Bellows Falls was the first Brittany Spaniel to win a dual championship. The year was 1946.

Dual Ch. Amos of Edough is the only dual champion ever to win the sporting group at a dog show. Many others have placed second, third, or fourth in the group.

Wippy De La Vallee Bourrault is the only French import ever to win a dual championship in the United States. Dual Ch. Tigar's Jocko, which is almost an American Field champion, was voted the "Dog of the Year" in the *Sports Afield* Magazine poll for 1965. He is the only dog, other than a Pointer, to win this award.

Dual Ch. Faulkner's Reddy, owned by Ejner and Gilda Lund.

Dual Ch. Lund's Trooper holds the record for producing the most dual champions—six. Since some of his sons and daughters are still competing, it is possible that he will increase this number. Dual Ch. Doctor Joe of Kaymore, now dead, produced four.

The concept of the dual dog is held so strongly by Brittany breeders and owners that competition for dual championships—and among dual champions—has been extraordinary.

The records of two dogs, both of the present day, and so susceptible to improvement, are given below.

Dual Ch. Faulkner's Reddy is owned, trained, and handled by Ejner Lund. At the time of writing he has won 60 best of breeds awards at shows, and has twice placed in the sporting group. He has 60 placements in AKC licensed trials, of which 27 are firsts. In addition, he has a first and second in American Field trials. His field competition has been entirely in adult stakes. He won the Oregon specialty show in 1967, 1968, and 1969, and the Washington specialty in 1970. He is sired by Dual Ch. Lund's Trooper, and his dam is Ch. Cindy of Beelflower.

Dual Ch. Pacolet Cheyenne Sam is owned by Ken and Erin Jacobson. He is the fourth generation of dual champions on his sire's side, and his sire's dam and grandsire were dual champions. He is a five time field champion and both an American and Canadian dual champion.

His record shows 61 total placements in field trials; 36 in AKC events; 15 in American Field trials; and four under Canadian Kennel Club jurisdiction. He was the 1971 national champion (American Brittany Club and AKC trial) and 1970 U.S. Open Champion. (American Field.)

His show record includes best of breed at the 1970 national specialty show. That year he was the top dual champion show winner in the country, with 22 best of breed wins, while also making the best show record of any Brittany in Canada.

Listed below are 120 dual champions of which we have record. Although we have searched the records carefully, it is possible we have missed one or more. Other dogs will become dual champions before this list can get into print.

Britt of Bellows Falls        Angelique De Bretagne
Aotrou Mac Eochaidh       Holley Haven Casey
Avono Happy                  Holley Haven Duchess
Allamuchy Valley Uno       Towsey

Ch. Covymoors Bomarc (Dual Ch. Trooper's Little Frenchman ex Dual Ch. Juchoir's Trooper Jill), owned by Al Langan and bred by Ted and Lois Hames. *Ritter photo.*

Dual Ch. Ultra-Mend Maisie (Ch. Ultra-Mend Ace High ex Ch. Goldstone Ultra-Mend Sioux), owned by Owen F. and Jeanne A. Mello and bred by Frank W. McHugh and Sharon L. Ulshoefer. *Norman photo.*

Dingo's Little Mike
Penny's Happy Pepi
Avono Hapte
Tex of Richmont
Helgramite Howie D'Acajou
Helgramite Chip
Helgramite Tarquinious
Helgramite Shamandre
Pierrot de Fontaine Vallee
Remarkable De Fontaine Vallee
Pacolet's Sam
Pacolet's Whist
Pacolet's Cheyenne
Doctor Joe of Kaymore
Kaymore's Megs
Jig De Kaymore
Detective Neal of Kaymore
Belloaks Ibby
Belloaks King
Belloaks Highflyer
Uno's Jet
Uno's Chief
Pontac's Dingo
Albedo Valley Dingo
Skippy Allamuchy Luke
Penelope De Evanston
Gallinacious Doc
Lamonte's Rebel
Shenango Valley Dingo
Amos of Edough
Patsy of Edough
Mandy of Edough
Wippy de la Vallee Bourault
Bonaire Doc
Britt of Blaisey Blas
Ch. Saxon of Fredan
Tigre de Klemanor
Evergray's Tic Toc Bobby
Paul's White Flash
Freckles VII
Ouragan Jerry's Bob
Penny's Happy Peppi
Sue's Jim Dandy Jigger
Grouse Feathers
Rusty of Beelflower

Way-Kan Jeff
Joel's Drole
Fredan's Buddy
Lund's Trooper
Trooper's Little Frenchman
Tigar's Jocko
Molko's Mike of Jacques
Sue City Sue
Appanoose Rust
Helgramite Howie
Juchoir's Shady Scamp
Lewis's Ringo
Tietjen's Red Raider
Birch Hill Tawny
Ultra-Mend Maisie
Faulkner's Reddy
Bernie's Butch
Begg's Royal Duke
Majestic Jake
Genii's Colorado Ladd
Foltz's Freckles
Spicks of Mugho Hill
Dusty's Shining Chevalier
Sir Robert of Beelflower
Skipper of Siouxland
Way-Kan Fritts
Eva's Trooper Jorinda
Suzabob's Humdinger
Mar-Ko Valkerie
Beau'Pere
Knox's Starbelle Broons
Chaplin's Golden Arrow
Kaymore Dapper Dan
Black Butte Ricochet Trooper
Early Times
Juchoir's Trooper Jill
Cindy's Chico Diablo
Dixie Du Blanche Happy
Destry
Pacolet Cheyenne Sam
Tipco's French Rebel
Holley Haven Heidi II
Faircrest Polyjet
The Circuit Contender

Brooks De Becque
Rusty of Highbrow
Mel's Red Rover
Jacques Des Rocheuses
Susabob's Hedgerow Happy
Freck O'Dee
Marmalade Sarah
Colorado's Yankee Timber
Pike's Peak Rambler
Tondee's Sandy Valley Duke
Char-Lee O'Dee

Suzabob's Gigolo
Jacque of Connie
Chipp Britt Jill
Mike Bazooka of Tejas
Shot Gun Liz
Gringo De Britt
The Little Joker
Coveymoore's Bomarc
Jock Scott of Big Meadow
Sodak Sandy Sioux
Rufus Rastus Johnson Brown

Dual Ch. Char-Lee O'Dee, owned by Francis Claser, was winner of the National Amateur Championships and was second in the National Open, both in 1971.

# 30

# The Dams of Champions

---

$E$VERY person who tries to campaign a dog to a championship, show or field, knows how difficult this is. How much more difficult it is then to be the dam or sire of a champion! The production of a champion by a bitch is, moreover, much more difficult than it is for a male. The opportunities for the male are perhaps four to 10 times as great as for the bitch.

The author once made studies of litter sizes at the American Kennel Club. Three English Setter dams have produced as many as 96 to 103 puppies during their lives. So far as can be determined these bitches far exceed the production records of all others in any breed.

As far as the American Kennel Club is concerned, a litter consists of the number of living puppies at the time of registration of the litter. If a litter consists of 15 puppies at birth, but eight die a few days later, then the litter would be registered as one of seven.

At least one litter of 15 Brittany Spaniels has been registered. This litter was carefully investigated before registration was approved. However, the author found the average of some 100 Brittany litters was six, that is, six living puppies per litter.

This means that if a Brittany brood bitch had 10 litters during her breeding life, she will have produced 60 puppies. Probably few of the great bitches have had that many. Many will not have been bred until

18 months old or older. Some may have been campaigned in field trials, and so may have had as much as two years taken out of their breeding life.

We may assume, therefore, that a dual champion bitch will produce fewer than 40 puppies. On the same basis of computation, a dual champion male might produce 180 puppies from 30 matings. With this in mind, the records of the leading dams are startling.

Pacolet's Somethin Special leads all dams in two respects. She produced 10 champions of which three were dual champions. Only nine males have produced as many or more champions. Only Dual Ch. Doctor Joe Of Kaymore and Dual Ch. Lund's Trooper have produced more dual champions, four and six respectively.

Dual champion bitches have shorter breeding lives than do others because of time out for show and field training and campaigning. Yet consider these records! Dual Ch. Holley Haven Duchess produced five champions, one of them a dual. Dual Ch. Kaymore's Megs produced four, two of them duals. Dual Ch. Pacolet's Cheyenne produced three, two of them duals. Ch. Suzanne De Beauch produced four champions, two of them duals. Ch. Joel's Drole produced two duals. Susitna Lady had two duals, as did Price's Sunflower Gal and Lady Godiva of Basgard.

Ch. Jule of Loufel ranks just behind Pacolet's Somethin Special in the production of champions, with nine. Eight of these were sired by Ch. Buck of Chippewa.

One cannot know how great the influence actually was of the sires when mated to these bitches. Dual Ch. Doctor Joe of Kaymore's record would be very great had Pacolet's Somethin Special not lived. But Ch. Buck of Chippewa sired only eight champions. Thus, his "nick" with Ch. Jule of Loufel almost certainly made his reputation.

Given below are the production records of those bitches which produced five or more champions. We have gone over the records a dozen times, and have eliminated many errors. If there should be others, we are sorry.

### Dam with 10 Champions

Pacolet's Somethin Special
   Ch. Kaymore's Golden Boy
   Ch. Kaymore's Dappled Desire
   Fld. Ch. Kaymore Joe of Weymouth
   Ch. Chisholm's Ogeechee

Dual Ch. Kaymore's Dapper Dan
Dual Ch. Kaymore's Megs
Dual Ch. Detective Neal of Kaymore
Ch. Belloaks Marcel Belle
Ch. Kaymore's Connecticut Yankee
Ch. Lincoln Skipper of Kaymore

## Dam with 9 Champions

Ch. Jule of Loufel
Dual Ch. Buckeye de Klemanor
Ch. Loufel's Handsome Harry
Ch. Peg B of Loufel
Ch. Busher of Klemanor
Ch. Buccaneer of Klemanor
Ch. Belloaks Ginger
Ch. Oxbow's Dandy Dan
Ch. Nancy A. of Loufel
Ch. Sue Special of Loufel

## Dams with 6 Champions

Holley Haven Bonnie
Ch. Holley Haven Suzette
Dual Ch. Holley Haven Duchess
Ch. Holley Haven Saddle Boy
Ch. Holley Haven Peppe Boy, C.D.
Ch. Holley Haven Salley
Ch. Aotrou's Pepin Jr.
Ch. Holley Haven Dixie
Ch. Holley Haven Banner
Ch. Holley Haven Sugar
Ch. Holley Haven Honey
Ch. Holley Haven Star
Ch. Holley Haven Brt
Ch. Suzabob's Bo-Jean
Ch. Chisholm's Ogeechee
Ch. Chisholm's Tondee
Ch. Chisholm's Knoxboro
Ch. Chisholm's Toccoa
Ch. Chisholm's Pocataligo
Ch. Chisholm's Combahee
Ch. Chisholm's Chief Tomo Chi Chi

Ch. Fun Galore Louella
  Ch. Anderson's Lady Louella
  Ch. Avono Corky
  Ch. Britt Afield Happy
  Ch. Britt Afield Jeanette
  Ch. Britt Afield Chummie
  Ch. Oxbow Dandy Dan
Dual Ch. Sue City Sue
  Ch. L'Moko's Brandy Sniffer
  Ch. Ja-Dor's Rum Ricky
  Ch. Ja-Dor's Little Dee Dee
  Ch. Ja-Dor's Martini
  Ch. Ja Dor's Hot Toddy
  Ch. J. J.'s Judd of Ja-Dor

## Dams with 5 Champions

Ch. Kay Haven's Daisy May
  Ch. Do-Car's Flashy Showman
  Ch. Skippy's Jezebel
  Fld. Ch. Dwight's Halloween Spook
  Ch. Penelope de Evanston
  Ch. Do-Car's Grand Prize
Fun Galore Jeanette
  Ch. Fun Galore Benedict

Dual Ch. Baron de Brentwood, C.D. (Fld. and Amateur Fld. Ch. Holliday Britt's Ed ex Ch. Nedbalek's Ginger), owned by Wayne Fessenden. *Petrulis photo.*

Ch. Fun Galore Suzette
Ch. Fun Galore Louella
Ch. Sports Afield Chummie
Ch. Cindie Of Bald Ridge
Dual Ch. Holley Haven Duchess
    Dual Ch. Holley Haven Casey
    Fld. Ch. Holley Haven Lucky
    Ch. Cle-Mar Holley Haven Contessa
    Ch. Holley Haven Dixie
    Ch. Holley Haven Tammy
Ch. Edandot Nanette
    Ch. Edandot Apache
    Ch. Edandot Abigail
    Ch. Edandot Gilly
    Ch. Edandot Buzzer
    Ch. Edandot Bonita
Ch. Nedbalek's Ginger
    Ch. Suzette De Brentwood
    Dual Ch. Baron De Brentwood
    Ch. Tuway's Kaymore Flash
    Ch. Senior Farms Tuway Joe
    Ch. Avalon's Chim Chim Cheree

Ch. Suzette De Brentwood, C.D. (Fld. & Amateur Fld. Ch. Holliday Britt's Ed ex Ch. Nedbalek's Ginger), owned and handled by Wayne Fessenden who is handling her to a win under the late Lee Murray. *Alexander photo.*

# 31

# The Great Sires
# of Champions

IN this chapter, the author has attempted to make a listing of all
the Brittany Spaniel dogs which have sired five or more champions.
The compiling of such a list is a nearly endless job. Each time one
goes over the tabulations, errors are found. So it is possible that some
still remain. If so, one can only apologize.

In compiling the list, the author has searched the records of the
American Kennel Club, starting with the earliest period in which
Brittany Spaniels were shown. This tabulation covers American champions only. However, some of these dogs have sired Canadian champions as well. If we were to count these Canadian champions as
well, then Ch. Fun Galore Chummie would move up from six to
eight; Fld. Ch. Mark of Passamonte would jump from four to seven;
Dual Ch. Avono Happy would be credited with 12 instead of 11;
Dual Ch. Holley Haven Casey would add three to make a total of
six. And Dual Ch. Lund's Trooper would jump to 24.

It will be noted that, on the whole, champions have sired champions. The two greatest non-champion sires are Kaer de Cornouaille
and Allamuchy Valley Warrior. It will be noted that show champions
have sired field champions and the latter, show champions. This must

be a source of great pride for all owners of Brittany Spaniels. It proves that the qualities of the breed have in no sense been weakened either by show or by field competition.

Two dogs stand far above all the others. They are Dual Ch. Doctor Joe of Kaymore, with 23 champions to his credit, and Dual Ch. Lund's Trooper, with 22. Since the latter is still living, he has a chance to take the lead.

The following table lists the sires together with the champions which, according to our search of the records, should be credited to them.

### Sire of 23 Champions

Dual Ch. Doctor Joe of Kaymore
    Ch. Brit de Fontaine Vallee
    Ch. Kaymore's Connecticut Yankee
    Ch. Sequani's Sam Son of Kaymore
    Fld. Ch. Kaymore's Chipper
    Ch. Sequani's Tortuga
    Ch. Lincoln Skipper of Kaymore
    Ch. Flying Dutchman Nitro
    Ch. Kaymore's Dappled Desire
    Ch. Kaymore Garcon d'Amour
    Fld. Ch. Kaymore Joe of Weymouth
    Ch. Tina of Kaymore
    Ch. Torchy Jeff of Kaymore
    Ch. Kaymore's Quail Rustler
    Fld. Ch. Ashurst Torchy
    Dual Ch. Birch Hill Tawny
    Ch. Kick of Kaymore
    Ch. Belloaks Marcelle Belle
    Dual Ch. Detective Neal of Kaymore
    Ch. Kaymore's Cinderella
    Dual Ch. Kaymore's Megs
    Dual Ch. Kaymore's Dapper Dan
    Ch. Chisholm's Ogeechee

### Sire of 22 Champions

Dual Ch. Lund's Trooper
    Ch. Kaer La Belgae
    Dual Ch. Juchoir's Trooper Jill
    Dual Ch. Faulkner's Reddy
    Dual Ch. Early Times

Dual Ch. Trooper's Little Frenchman
Ch. Tuppence Halfpenny
Ch. Bi-Mar Ranging Trooper
Ch. Trooper's Boots And Saddle
Ch. Trooper's Mona Lisa
Ch. Lewis's Lady Trooper
Ch. Britt of Bernardo
Ch. Embrheight's Lady Foltz
Ch. Trooper's Tiger Lily
Ch. Beau De Trooper
Ch. Windy Hills Sweet Bippy
Dual Ch. Eva's Trooper Jorinda
Dual Ch. Black Butte Ricochet Trooper
Ch. Trooper's Northwest Buddy
Windy Hills Trooper's Tuffy
Ch. Idabritt's Freddie
Ch. Black Butte Starlight Trooper
Ch. Scott's Trooper Jim Brandy

### Sire of 13 Champions

Ch. Bonnie Kay's Duke of Sequani
Ch. Sequani's Dana MacDuff
Ch. Sequani's High Hopes
Ch. Sequani's Dana O'Teed
Ch. Harmony Lane Rattlesnake Bob
Ch. Harmony Lane's Bird's Eye Mabel
Ch. Harmony Lane's China Polly
Ch. Harmony Lane Freck's Bad Boy
Ch. Harmony Lane Laughing Sam
Ch. Harmony Lane Canada Bill
Ch. Windy Pine's Bold Bobby
Ch. Dana's High Spirits
Ch. Dana's Aimee of Winfield
Ch. Le Marquise De Burgundy.

### Sires of 12 Champions

Dual Ch. Tex of Richmont
Ch. Suzette of Richmont
Dual Ch. Pacolet's Cheyenne
Dual Ch. Pacolet's Whist
Fld. Ch. Sooner Ranger

Fld. Ch. Riviere Valley Suzette
Fld. Ch. Pacolet's Genii
Ch. Kaymore Tex of Edandot
Fld. Ch. Tawney of Clermont
Fld. Ch. Tex's Little Luke
Dual Champion Uno's Chief
Ch. Chisholm's Toccoa
Ch. Chisholm's Knoxboro
Ch. Chisholm's Kombahee
Ch. Chisholm's Pocataligo
Ch. Chief Tomo Chu Chi
Ch. Liza's Uno Bouncer
Ch. Suzabob's Desert Rose
Dual. Ch. Suzabob's Humdinger
Ch. Suzabob's Tomahawk
Ch. Suzabob's Lady Golden Rod
Ch. Francis's Muchy
Ch. Joel's Copper Cricket

### Sires of 11 Champions

Dual Ch. Pierrot de Fontaine Vallee
Ch. Be Kay Jacques
Ch. Juchoir's Marvelous Mauser
Ch. Juchoir's Cotton Candy
Ch. Juchoir's Some Shoveller
Ch. Juchoir's Restless Gun
Ch. Juchoir's Military Might
Ch. Juchoir's Jee Whiz
Ch. Juchoir's Shady Scamp
Fld. Ch. Juchoir's Chocolate Candy
Fld. Ch. Juchoir's Bronze Bigwig
Fld. Ch. Juchoir's Fleck O' Bonanza
Dual Ch. Avono Happy
Ch. Duffy of Belle Brit
Dual Ch. Avono Hapte
Ch. Avono Jack
Ch. Avono Corky
Ch. Britt Afield Happy
Fld. Ch. Ronile Avant Courer
Ch. Avono Retta
Ch. Valfont Lorelei
Ch. Ashurst Jerry

Although showing dogs is an absorbing pastime, it is also a demanding one. Here Bob Reimers and his Ch. IdaBritt's Freddie catch up on their rest before ring-time. *Betty Jane Nevis photo.*

Ch. IdaBritt's Freddie, this time in a more formal moment. He is pictured completing his championship at the Northern California specialty under judge Rutledge Gilliland, handler Frank Houska. He is owned by Bob and Joann Reimers. *Bennett Associates photo.*

   Ch. Suntan's Happy Hi Tone, C.D.
   Ch. Milady Patrice Avono
Kaer de Cornouaille
   Ch. Allamuchy Valley Luke
   Ch. Allamuchy Valley Addie
   Ch. Allamuchy Valley Joe
   Dual Ch. Allamuchy Valley Uno
   Fld. Ch. Allamuchy Valley Omar
   Ch. Jan of Loufel
   Ch. Kaerson of Loufel
   Ch. Jule of Loufel
   Ch. Avono Jake
   Dual Ch. Britt of Bellows Falls
   Dual Ch. Avono Happy

### Sire of 10 Champions

Allamuchy Valley Warrior
   Ch. Warrior's Triumph Freckles
   Ch. Warrior's Duke De Triumph
   Ch. Warrior's Jake The Joker
   Ch. Warrior's Vicki De Triumph
   Ch. Warrior's Wendy De Triumph
   Dual Ch. Tex of Richmont
   Ch. Penny's Penny De Triumph
   Ch. Penny's Cactus Kate
   Ch. Hel's Oklahoma Chink
   Ch. Bo Bo Lot

### Sires of 9 Champions

Dual Ch. Uno's Jet
   Ch. Uno's Rex of Paradise
   Dual Ch. Uno's Chief
   Fld. Ch. Pacolet's Hellou Jet
   Fld. Ch. Gagel's Dutchman
   Ch. Holley Haven Dixie
   Fld. Ch. Passamonte's Jet Commander
   Fld. Ch. Pinoak Guy
   Ch. Holley Haven Tammy
   Fld. Ch. Evergray's Tic Toc Tommy II
Ch. Holley Haven Banner
   Ch. Nys-Britt's Corker
   Ch. Steele's High Jinks
   Ch. Bonnie Lassie II

Ch. Ultra-Mend Ace High, owned and bred by Frank W. McHugh. He is shown making a win under the late Major B. Godsol and is being handled by his owner.

Ch. Ultra-Mend Jacques (Ch. Ultra-Mend Ace High ex Ultra-Mend Birdie Biddie), owned and bred by Frank W. McHugh, boasts a show record that places him in the front rank of show winners. He has won 86 bests of breed and ten Sporting group placings. *Norman photo.*

Ch. Holley Haven Britt
Ch. Hire's Little Tania
Ch. Holley Haven Kelley Girl
Fld. Ch. Go Jack II
Ch. Holley Haven Yvette
Ch. Twin Oaks Sun Spinner
Ch. Ultra-Men Ace High
   Ch. Ultra-Mend Jacques
   Ch. Ultra-Mend Seour
   Ch. Ultra-Mend Hi Hope
   Ch. Ultra-Mend Ace High Too
   Ch. Ultra-Mend Rusty
   Dual Ch. Ultra-Mend Maisie
   Ch. Highland Ultra-Mend Lacey
   Ch. Doctor Frank W. McHugh
   Ch. El Capitan Happy Sis
Fld. Ch. Ferdinand of Leeway
   Fld. Ch. Belloak's Leo
   Ch. Juc-O-Lee Missy
   Fld. Ch. Way-Kan Jill
   Fld. Ch. The Ridgerunner
   Ch. Meg's Bunko Belle
   Fld. Ch. La Petite Blanche
   Dual Ch. Joel's Copper Jacques
   Dual Ch. Joel's Drole
   Ch. Bellewood Sue
Fld. Ch. Chip's Get
   Ch. Cherie Beaver Dam Misty
   Fld. Ch. Ffynant's Double Trouble
   Fld. Ch. Storm Duke
   Ch. Beaver Dam's Hey You Bob
   Ch. Sassy Sue of Beaver Dam
   Ch. Chip's Lucky of Beaver Dam
   Ch. Suzabob's Seminole Sadie
   Ch. Suzabob's Diamond Chip
   Ch. Beaver Dam's Rusty

## Sires of 8 Champions

Ch. Buck of Chippewa
   Ch. Peg B. of Loufel
   Ch. Buckeye De Klemanor

Ch. Loufel's Handsome Harry
Ch. Buccaneer of Klemanor
Ch. Belloaks Ginger
Ch. Oxbow's Dandy Dan
Ch. Busher of Klemanor
Ch. Sue Special of Loufel
Ch. Holley Haven Beau
   Ch. Holley Haven Sugar
   Ch. Holley Haven Marty Star
   Ch. Holley Haven Honey
   Ch. Holley Haven Valerie
   Ch. Holley Haven Nastra
   Ch. Holley Haven Beaucin's Tiger
   Ch. Edgewater American Beauty
   Ch. Suzabob's Bo-Jean
Ch. Suzabob's Bobo C.D.
   Ch. Suzabob's Pride of Gayterry
   Ch. Suzabob's El Capitan
   Ch. Suzabob's Honey Boy
   Ch. Suzabob's L'Andre De Mergol
   Fld. Ch. Errol of Flynn
   Ch. Suzabob's Freckled Miss
   Ch. Suzabob's Gigolo
   Ch. Bebo Britt
Fld. Ch. Jeffery of Argard
   Ch. Flash De Malibeau
   Ch. Buck De Malibeau
   Ch. Storm of Malibeau
   Ch. Sunka of Minnehaha
   Fld. Ch. Burk's Chip of Argard
   Ch. Jerse Bell
   Fld. Ch. Major Valley Forge
   Fld. Ch. Jeffery D'Or

### Sires of 7 Champions

Ch. Bonnie Kay's Ricki's Image
   Ch. Havre Des Bois Seigneur
   Ch. Hazeldell's Jubilee
   Ch. Miss Sue's Gad-A-Bout C.D.
   Ch. Bonnie Kay's Duke of Sequani
   Ch. Havre Des Bois Dotty

Ch. Sequani's Queenie Too
Ch. May Gem's Mimi Moneque
Fld. Ch. Miller's Desert Dust
    Ch. Crab Orchard's Dusty Hi Flyer
    Ch. Dusty's Shining Chevalier
    Fld. Ch. Dusty's Little Tex
    Fld. Ch. Jane De Carlo
    Ch. Appanoose Desert King
    Ch. Mo-Valley's Desert Sand
    Dual Ch. Chaplin's Golden Arrow
Dual Ch. Lamonte's Rebel
    Bi-Mar's High Hopes
    Marquette De Becque
    Kadon's Pippa
    Ches-Val's Sparky
    Chantilly Be Becque
    Hunterlane's Bonnie Delight
    Fld. Ch. Sky Spear
Fld. Ch. Reno Diablo
    Dual Ch. Cindy's Chico Diablo
    Ch. Shot Gun Liz
    Ch. Star's Miss Diablo
    Ch. El Diablo Blanco
    Ch. Hot Shot Reno
    Ch. Apache Diablo
    Ch. Reno's Jet
Ch. Flambeau's King of Kaymore
    Ch. Sizette Encore of Hunterlane
    Ch. Copper Trey
    Ch. Dee Dee Cricket of Edwards
    Ch. Hunterlane's Painted Lady
    Ch. Hunterlane's King's Hi-Wind
    Ch. Sandy of Edwards
    Fld. Ch. Cracker Jack of Bay
Dual Ch. Helgramite Howie D'Acajou
    Ch. Ross's Chico Topper D'Acajou
    Ch. Meadow Ridge Trash Man
    Dual Ch. Helgramite Tarquinius
    Fld. Ch. Helderberg Misty
    Ch. Hobson's Choice of Helderberg
    Ch. Helgramite Tinker

Dual Ch. Helgramite Shamandre
Champion Ti-War Chip De Triumph
    Ch. Jo No's Rocky Boy
    Ch. Richard's King Henry
    Ch. Jandy's Tuff Girl
    Ch. Bridget of Edwards
    Ch. Sposaro's Miss Chievous Amber
    Ch. Vickey of Edwards
    Ch. Copper Jill of Edwards

### Sires of 6 Champions

Champion Fun Galore Chummie
    Ch. Fun Galore Benedict
    Ch. Fun Galore Suzette
    Ch. Fun Galore Louella
    Ch. Sports Afired Chummie
    Ch. Wild Haven Chummie
    Ch. Scott's Fun Chum
Champion Bonnie Kay's Ricki
    Ch. Bonnie Kay's Lady
    Ch. Bonnie Kay of Woodworth
    Ch. La Fran Cookie
    Ch. Billy Boy Sport
    Ch. Happy Hunter's Belle Amie
    Ch. Miste Mona May Jeanette
Champion Lakeside Secret Threat
    Ch. Lakeside Secret Joy
    Ch. Lakeside Secret Royal Queen
    Ch. Lakeside Secret Foxette
    Ch. Lakeside Secret Fair Play
    Ch. Lakeside Secret King Pin
    Ch. Che-Mar Sasigal
Dual Ch. Albedo Valley Dingo
    Ch. Meg of Kaymore
    Ch. Pacolet's Dingo's Rusty
    Dual Ch. Pacolet's Sam
    Ch. L'Etoile De Dingo
    Dual Ch. Shenango Valley Dingo
    Ch. Kazan's Little White Dove
Dual Ch. Towsey
    Amateur and Fld. Ch. Towsey's Bub

Ch. Tom's Zipper King
Ch. Kruger's Captain Thrape
Dual Ch. Dixie Du Blanche Happy
Ch. New K. Candy
Fld. Ch. Kruger's Soldier Boy
Ch. Randy's Ranger
　Ch. Penny Halfpenny C.D.
　Ch. Moore's Brother Bart
　Ch. Ranger's Johnny Ringo
　Ch. Evergreen's Autumn Gold
　Ch. Ranger's Lady Valerie
　Dual Ch. Tietjen's Red Ranger
Ch. Zipp's Feather Merchant
　Ch. Greenfield Thunderbird
　Ch. Greenfield Chickasan
　Ch. Greenfield Golden Girl
　Ch. Greenfield's Sir Lancelot
　Fld. Ch. Greenfield Ramblin Rose
　Fld. Ch. Greenfield Annie's Ace of Hearts
Ch. Juchoir's Tuffy
　Ch. Juc-O-Tupness Junior
　Ch. Juchoir's Sunsport
　Ch. Black Butte Sunsport Touche
　Ch. Black Butte Ace Wild
　Ch. Rufus Rastus Johnson Brown
　Ch. Jeu Chasseur Blaizer
Ch. Bourbon De Colauzer
　Ch. Pipermint De Colauzer
　Ch. Cognac De Colauzer
　Ch. Armagnac De Colauzer
　Ch. Coquette Celu De Colauzer
　Ch. Sir Freckles De Colauzer
　Ch. Bee Bee
Ch. Tigre De Klemanor
　Ch. Tigre Joe De Triumph
　Ch. Tigre Par Le Tigre De L'Argoat
　Ch. Magre Par Le Tigre De L'Argoat
　Ch. Edandot Apache
　Ch. Edandot Abigail
Ch. Avono Jake
　Ch. Blondie Rigolo

Ch. Toni de Fontaine Vallee
Dual Ch. Pierrot de Fontaine Vallee
Ch. Laure de Fontaine Vallee
Ch. Pierette de Fontaine Vallee
Dual Ch. Remarkable de Fontaine Vallee

## Sires of 5 Champions

Dual Ch. Britt of Bellows Falls
  Ch. Basbleu's Sandy of Loufel
  Ch. Morrie's Brit of Redding
  Ch. Spindle City Shorty
  Ch. Spindle City Rusty
  Dual Ch. Evergray's Tic Toc Bobby
Aotrou's Pepin
  Ch. Aotrou's Pepin Jr.
  Ch. Holley Haven Suzette
  Dual Ch. Holley Haven Duchess
  Ch. Holley Haven Saddle Boy
  Ch. Holley Haven Peppi Boy
Dual Ch. Trooper's Little Frenchman
  Ch. Frenchman's Yankee Nickel
  Ch. Threepence Halfpenny
  Ch. Coveymoore's Bomarc
  Ch. Killey
  Ch. Trooper Jill's Frenchman
Ch. Big Boy Bales
  Ch. Lady Bird Bales
  Ch. Baby Doll Bales
  Ch. Minni Mor Bales
  Ch. Bales Sam Boy
  Ch. Bales Suzi's Merry Christmas
Dual Ch. Shenango Valley Dingo
  Dual Ch. Suzabob's Hedgerow Happy
  Ch. Holley Haven Flint
  Ch. Holley Haven Dust Girl
  Ch. Penny Des Collines
  Ch. Twin Oaks Stacy of Phes-Phar
Johnnie's Pal
  Ch. Do-Car's Flashy Showman
  Ch. Happy Jill of Do-Car
  Ch. Ray-Vi's Tinker Belle

    Dual Ch. Penelope de Evanston
    Ch. Do-Car's Grand Prize
Dual Ch. Pontac's Dingo
    Dual Ch. Albedo Valley Dingo
    Dual Ch. Dingo's Little Mike
    Fld. Ch. Joey of Hunterhaven
    Ch. Britt Afield Jeanette
    Fld. Ch. Gladjoe's Pride
Dual Ch. Avono Hapte
    Dual Ch. Belloaks Gunner
    Fld. Ch. Avono Commanche
    Ch. Belloaks High Flyer
    Ch. Edandot Bonita
    Ch. Edandot Buzzer
Ch. Kaymore Tex of Edandot
    Ch. Edandot Gilley
    Ch. Edandot Halo
    Ch. Edandot Iane
    Ch. Candilane's Jack of Hearts
    Ch. Ju-Di's Peggy Sioux
Ch. S-M Sam De Triumph
    Ch. Shaynu's S-J Jake De Leonne
    Ch. Katie De Triumph
    Ch. Crestwood's Rambling Belle
    Ch. Ruddy Of Jo-Jo
    Ch. Orange Marmalade De Triumph
Dual Ch. Tigar's Jocko
    Ch. Coveymoor's Tigar Belle
    Ch. Hilltop Traveller
    Ch. Pete's Gimlet C.D.
    Ch. Myska
    Ch. Jocko's Fordot
Amateur & Dual Ch. Towsey's Bub
    Dual Ch. Destry
    Ch. Bi-Mar Sweet Joy
    Ch. Wesmer's Wayward Meg
    Ch. De Leonne Red-Bud
    Ch. Bub's Debbie
Ch. Sun Tan's Happy Hy-Tone C.D.
    Ch. Lakeside Secret Threat
    Ch. Cle-Mar's Jolie Gae

    Dual Ch. Penny's Happy Pepi
    Ch. Ginger Lady Coquette
    Ch. Bell-Tone of Larry
Fld. Ch. Dingo's Little Mike
    Ch. Gladwyn's Smokey
    Ch. Dingo's Dusty De Triumph
    Dual Ch. Holley Haven Casey
    Ch. Holley Haven Banner
    Fld. Ch. Mike's Little Patrick Boy
Fld. Ch. Teka of Sioux Land
    Dual Ch. Mar-Ko Valkerie
    Fld. Ch. Rendezvous Skipper
    Fld. Ch. Epper of Sioux Land
    Fld. Ch. Tearaway Broccho
    Ch. Sioux's Terlmaed Hilltop Jill
Dual Ch. Pacolet's Sam
    Dual Ch. Pacolet Cheyenne Sam
    Fld. Ch. Woody's Pontiac Dingo
    Fld. Ch. Bellewood Polly Ann
    Ch. S-M Sally De Triumph
    Ch. S-M Sam De Triumph
Ch. Ches-Val's Sparky
    Ch. Cageo's Perkiomen Valley Zipp
    Ch. Cageo's Perkiomen Valley Jock
    Ch. Surgenpride Duke D'Orange
    Ch. Cageo's Chatty Kathy
    Ch. Cageo's Little Rascal

# 32

# How to Prepare Your Dog
# for the Shows

WHEN the American standard was written, those who took part in constructing it had in mind a dog which could leave the field and be shown on the bench. They visioned a dual purpose dog, as the Brittany Spaniel then was. And they intended to keep it one. That their judgment was correct is proven by the astonishing number of Britts which have won both in the field and at the shows.

Most sporting dogs cannot compete successfully in both branches of the sport. For example, the standard for the American Cocker Spaniel says: "The ears, chest, abdomen, and posterior sides of the legs should be well feathered, but not so excessively as to hide the Cocker Spaniel's true lines and movement or affect his appearance and function as a sporting dog."

One who sees the modern Cocker Spaniel in the ring will recognize that the appearance and function of the animal as a sporting dog have been destroyed. The American Cocker Spaniel has, therefore, disappeared from the sporting scene. The English Springer Spaniel is popular both as a show dog and as a pheasant dog. Yet one who studies the show dogs and those which compete in field trials must believe that he is looking at two different breeds.

214

Ch. Frenchman's Yankee Nickel, owned by Dorothy MacDonald, has built a fine show record and is a Specialty winner. This appealing head study by Joan Ludwig was made for the cover of *Pure-Bred Dogs—American Kennel Gazette. Ludwig photo.*

It was to avoid this divergence of type, and the formation of two radically different breeds, that the Brittany standard was drawn. But standards are useful only so long as breeders and competitors adhere to them. It is often said that the judge is the custodian of the standard. If, in judging Cocker Spaniels, the judge applied the standard, he would withhold all awards. Yet judges know that Cocker Spaniel show dog people want their dogs the way they are being prepared and shown. So in the long run, it is the breeders and exhibitors who must protect their dogs by breeding to the standard.

Before showing a dog in the ring, each Brittany owner should check it against the standard. This is difficult to do. Hundreds of people read standards, look at their dogs, and then say: "He fits the standard perfectly." Yet the dog may be a pathetic specimen. Still, there are three points that the owner can check. The first is height. Is your dog too tall or too small? The second concerns color. Does it have black in its coat, or a nose so dark as to appear black? Is it the tri-color—liver, white, and tan? And does it have excessively long and heavily feathered coat? To ask it differently, does it have so much coat that it will require excessive trimming to make it presentable?

Measuring the height of a dog is quite difficult. Not one owner in a thousand has the standard measuring equipment required by the American Kennel Club for making official measurements. Moreover, two persons skilled at measuring dogs, can come up with two different heights. And finally, owners are always inclined to give their dogs the benefit of a half inch or so. But an exact measurement is not usually required. That is, it is important to know only that the dog is neither over 20½ inches at the withers, nor under 17.

A very simple device can be made to determine this. Most hardware stores and building supply houses have soft iron dowel rods. One should get a 48 inch or longer piece with a diameter of three-sixteenths of an inch. This can be put into a vice and can be lightly pounded and bent to form a three sided wicket, such as is used in croquet. The wicket should be 20½ inches tall. If a 48 inch dowel rod is used, then its width will be seven inches. If a longer rod is used, the width can be seven or eight inches, not wider. The ends are then cut off to make the height exactly 20½ inches.

Place your dog in a show position. It should be standing with its forelegs perpendicular to the ground, and parallel to each other when viewed from the front. The head should be held up in its normally alert position. The wicket is then set under the hair at

Ch. Windy Hills King of Hearts (American and Canadian Ch. Windy Hills Spike ex Watch-A-Kee Geronimo's Dream), owned and handled by Robert Eldridge and bred by Al Langan. He is shown going best of winners at the International Kennel Club of Chicago under judge Dale McMackin. *Gilbert photo.*

Pix-O-Dee Sioux and Ch. Evansport's Star of David, owned by Joel K. Evans and Douglas Birchfield, were best brace in the Sporting group at the Chain O' Lakes Kennel Club under the late Nelson Groh. Mr. Evans handled the pair to the win. *Ritter photo.*

the highest point of the shoulders, where they join the neck. If the wicket does not touch the ground, then the dog is over 20½ inches tall, and so has a disqualifying height. A similar wicket can be made for determining whether or not a small dog is too small to qualify. But in this case, if there is space between the cross bar of the wicket and the shoulders, then the dog is too small.

There are judges who are afraid to ask to have dogs measured in the ring. Some judges feel that the measuring committees will not do a proper job. So they refuse to call the committee. An exhibitor who is competing in the ring can ask that any other dog in the ring be measured, but most exhibitors feel it is unsporting to demand this. Others delay asking, hoping that the questionable dog will not win anyway. But once the awards have been made, it is too late. It should be said here that each exhibitor has a share and a responsibility in the sport. If the exhibitors in the ring allow over- or undersized dogs to win, they are all equally responsible for harming the breed. Finally, the owner who tries to win a championship with an over- or undersized dog is only fooling himself as well as harming the breed.

The question of proper color is more easily handled. Any person who is not sure of the color of the dog's nose, for example, can take it outside into the bright sunlight and get an exact answer. But here again, owners are apt to give their dogs the benefit of a doubt which the judge will not do. And here again, the owner who tries to claim that this black is really only a very dark brown is merely being dishonest with himself.

There is a final physical test which each person who intends to show a dog should make. This is to discover whether the dog has both testicles. The American Kennel Club rule is that a dog must have two normal testicles normally placed in the scrotum. If he does not, then the judge must disqualify him. The owner can save a lot of future embarrassment if this check is made before the dog is taken into the ring.

Many an embarrassed and startled owner will tell the judge: "Well, he had two when we checked him yesterday." What has happened is this. The dog is inexperienced. He is a house dog. This is the first time he has been around a thousand dogs. He has never known the strange noises, the strange surroundings, and all the strange people. In fright, he tends to draw the testicles up the scrotum and close to the body. He may even draw them into the body, assuming that the inguinal canals are large enough to permit this. So something

Ch. Spot of Edwards, a liver and white, bred, owned and handled by R. B. Edwards.

more than a check is necessary. Before taking a dog to a dog show, the owner should accustom him to strange noises, strange places, and dozens of people who will want to reach down and pet him.

There is a tendency to "over prepare" a Brittany Spaniel for the show ring. Owners should always remember that excessive trimming destroys breed character. The Brittany Spaniel is not a "pretty dog." He is one of the greatest of all working dogs, and he should look the part. Owners should remember that the standard was drawn by sportsmen who wanted to insure that a great field dog could leave the trial course and enter the show ring the same day.

Overtrimming is probably practiced by the professional handlers more than by those who handle their own dogs at shows. The professional handlers recognize that, for most breeds, a dog show is simply a beauty contest. So they try to make their dogs beautiful. Judges

admire beauty, too. But there are some who recognize that beauty
in a Brittany Spaniel consists of soundness, conformation to type,
and of the marvelously muscled body which the Brittany Spaniel
has, or should have.

The tendency is to use clippers on the neck and shoulders, and
even on the back and on the rib cage. The reason for doing this
is to accentuate the length of neck and the layback of the shoulders.
Clipping the top of the back may accentuate the top line. But it
also robs the Brittany Spaniel of its tight, beautifully weather-resistant
coat. For 25 years it has been said that, if Brittany Spaniels were
to win groups and bests in show awards, then they would have to
be trimmed in this way. Yet Brittany owners should be more interested
in breed competition, in making champions, and in displaying their
dogs as they should be shown, than in winning groups. And, it follows
that they should be teaching judges to know that the over-trimmed
Brittany should be penalized, not rewarded.

This is not to say that all trimming should be avoided. The hair
on the neck and shoulders may become unkempt. A heavy neck and
shoulders ruff does make it appear that the neck is too short and
the shoulders too straight or upright. Some thinning and smoothing
can be done, but clipping, never. The groomer must always keep
in mind Brittany breed character.

Brittany Spaniels differ from other spaniels in not being excessively
hairy about the feet. An occasional dog, however, will show this characteristic. In such cases, hair should be shoved upwards between the
toes, and then cut off. Hair on the top of the foot tends to make
the foot appear flat. The nails should be trimmed. Long nails tend
to flatten out the foot. They are a hindrance in the field, since they
catch on brush and slow forward motion. And they prevent normal
action of the toe and foot muscles. They should be clipped back
to, but not into, the quick. This is easily visible in the Brittany foot,
being a pinkish area fed by a blood vessel.

If toe nails have been allowed to grow too long for too long a
time, it might not be possible for the owner to cut them back far
enough without causing both pain and bleeding. In such cases, consult
a veterinarian. He may anesthetize the dog, cut the nails deeply back,
and then stop the bleeding. The nails and quick will then adjust
back to normal. After that, the owner can cut the nails him, or herself.
There are several types of nail clippers. One has very heavy blades
which simply meet. The other has a sort of guillotine blade which
is enclosed in a track. This is probably easier to use for most people.

Unless the dog has just come off a field trial course, as would be the case when field trials and bench shows are held together, it should be clean. A bath is best given two days before the show. If the dog is bathed just before the event, the hair is apt to be soft, fluffy, and ruffed up. Professional handlers prevent this by pinning a bath towel about the dog after it has been partially dried out. The hair will then lie flat or will be slightly wavy, as a Brittany coat should be.

Most professionals "chalk" the white on their dogs. This imparts a brighter white, and makes the dog look cleaner. It can be done with the Brittany Spaniel in those areas where the white is pure. That is, in non-ticked or non-roaned areas. But the owner should remember that there are rules about the preparation of a dog for the show ring.

Chalk, or any other cleaning substance, must be brushed out before the dog enters the ring. If the judge pats the dog and a cloud of dust rises, he must immediately dismiss the dog. Coloring matter is not permitted. You cannot use color materials to make the orange brighter or the liver darker. If the judge finds coloring on his hands as he examines the dog, it will be dismissed immediately. And if he suspects dye, more serious consequences may result.

The teeth should be checked for tartar. Of course, this should be done occasionally whether or not the dog is to be shown. But no dog should be taken into the ring with heavy tartar deposits on its teeth. A veterinarian can remove the tartar. Many are willing to show the owner how to split it away, so that later trips to the veterinary hospital are not necessary.

Unkempt hair which destroys the appearance of the ears, where they join the skull, can be trimmed off. The eyes should be checked for matter. The dog is given a final brushing. And he is ready to enter the ring.

# 33

# How to Show Your Brittany Spaniel

---

SHOWING dogs is an art. That is why professional handlers are so successful. But the pros work at it. If owners worked just as hard to prepare their dogs—and themselves—they could be as successful as the handlers are. In fact, many owner-handlers can beat the professionals. They can and they do.

Early training to pose and to walk properly on leash are sometimes unpleasant for the dog. So it is wise to do this training when the dog is hungry—for instance, just before mealtime. The dog quickly understands that following training it will get a meal. So it pays attention to you and works enthusiastically. This is all the more true if the dog is fed once a day.

The first step is to teach your Brittany Spaniel to pose. Common expressions for this are: "Stack your dog," and "Set up your dog." To learn how a dog should pose, study magazine pictures of Brittany Spaniels being posed, and also those of other sporting dogs. Also, study the pictures in this book. You might take as an example the picture of Fenntus du Cosquerou, one of the first of the breed to come to this country. Do not study the pictures of Cocker Spaniels. They are posed far differently than are other sporting dogs. What may be right for them is incorrect for Brittany Spaniels.

Ch. Ultra-Mend Valgo Cracker (Pierre de Bayard ex Tora de Cotignac), owned by Frank W. McHugh and bred by Harriet Belcher. *Ludwig photo.*

Ch. Tippi of Calindore, was winners bitch for five points at the Northern California Specialty under judge Everett Metzger enroute to her championship. James S. Everett is the handler.

After you have gotten a fairly good concept from studying pictures, try setting up your dog. At this point, many handlers lift the front end of their dogs, either by a hand under the rib cage just behind the legs, or by the neck. They then let down the front so that the forelegs are perpendicular to the ground. If, then, the front legs are not quite true, they will take each leg by the elbow and set it properly. Do not lift the leg at the foot or pastern since you can never quite get the leg into true position in that way. A true position is one in which the legs are perpendicular to the floor or ground, when viewed from the side, and parallel to each other when seen from the front.

They then turn their own bodies slightly and attend to the rear end. While the left hand holds the dog in position by the collar or leash, the right hand is placed at the stifle joint. The leg is lifted and placed into proper position. The same procedure is used to set the other leg. Often, when the second hind leg is set, the dog will try to move the other forward. You say "no" sharply, and then reset the legs.

When the hind end is true, the back pasterns, often called the hocks though the hock is really the joint, are perpendicular to the ground when viewed from the side, and parallel to each other when seen from behind. Now a Brittany Spaniel should have some angulation at the stifle and hock joints. In particular, it is the angulation at the stifle joint, formed by the upper and lower leg bones, which provides the drive needed by a great field dog. So try to set the hind legs to indicate as much drive as possible.

If you have set the feet too far back, the foot pads will not touch the floor. The dog may begin to slip, since it cannot get safe footing. Also, if set too far back, the hock joints will be pulled inward, and the feet will tend to toe out. You will then have set the dog into a cow hocked, and very faulty, position. If the legs are set too far under, the dog will appear to be too straight in stifles (insufficient angulation) and there will be a tendency to roach back.

When one first starts to pose a dog, the dog will try to put its head down. Lift the head, give a sharp command, and if necessary, slap the dog lightly and upward under the chin. The dog's second reaction will be to roach its back and pull its hind legs under it. But once again you scold the dog and reset the hind legs. Once the dog is in position, compliment it, and stroke it along the back until it relaxes. Sometimes it helps to stroke gently under the chin. After your dog has held the position for a minute or two, compliment it, walk it around on the leash for a minute or so, and then repeat the entire exercise.

If you watch Doberman Pinscher handlers, you will notice that they scratch or tickle their dogs on the undersides of their tails. Doberman Pinschers have about as much tail as does a Brittany Spaniel. The purpose is to get the Doberman to raise the stump, or tail stub. This creates an illusion. It makes the back appear short, since the back line is broken at the tail.

Now a Springer Spaniel is supposed to be square when measured from the ground to the highest point of the withers, and from there to the root of the tail. But a Brittany Spaniel should be square when measured from the ground to the highest point of the withers, and from the breast bone to the back side of the thighs just under the tail. This means that the Brittany is a tall, leggy spaniel. So getting it to raise its tail stub will help to show the judge that this is exactly what it is. But you must study your dog. If the dog's chest is slightly shallow, or if it appears to be because all the hair on the underside of the chest has been pulled off during field work, your dog may appear to be too leggy. In that case, you won't want to get the tail stub elevated.

You should practice all this in front of a knowledgeable show dog person. Or you can practice in front of a full length mirror. In the latter case, you may not be able to get the entire dog's reflection from the mirror at one time. Then first set up the dog so that you can see the front half with a side view. When you are satisfied that you have set the legs properly, lift the dog around so that the reflection is of the front. Check to be sure that the legs are parallel to each other. Then look down to be certain that they are also perpendicular to the floor. Repeat this with the hind half of the dog. Again view it from the side and from the rear, and check particularly to see that you have not made the dog cow hocked.

So far, we have said nothing about the head except that you should keep it elevated. Now you want to show the neck in a lovely, convex arch. So do not elevate the head until the nose points toward the ceiling. To do so may force the neck into a concave, or ewe-necked, position. Try to keep the head in a more natural position, its top line parallel to the floor, or only slightly tipped above parallel. Sometimes you can shove the head backward just slightly to give the neck a convex arch. But if you shove it back too far, you will make the neck look too short, and the shoulders too upright, or straight.

Having set their dogs into proper show position, most handlers try to keep them alert by "baiting" them. Some use a squeaker, or a toy, such as a toy mouse. These are fine for terriers and toy dogs.

Others use a bit of dog biscuit. But the most successful baiting material is a chunk of liver fried hard. Some handlers will even allow their dogs an occasional nibble. But successful baiting, too, requires practice. For you must teach the dog to maintain its position while being alert to the fried liver.

Once you have taught your dog to pose, to allow you to set it up in show position, and to hold that position, you take the next step. The dog must learn to hold its position in the presence of other dogs. And it must learn to allow strangers to handle it, as judges will. These people should handle the muzzle, look at the ears, touch the shoulders, lift a front foot, put slight pressure on the back, check the hip sockets, perhaps lift a hind leg and, if the dog is a male, check its testicles.

You must teach your dog to permit examination by both men and women. A judge hears something like this a hundred times a year: "My dog doesn't like men." Or: "He isn't used to men." Or: "He's afraid of women. I think their skirts frighten him." The judge, however, cannot accept such excuses. He can only tab the dog as being shy, or as having some other personality problem. He will penalize the dog accordingly.

Similarly, it is necessary for the dog to learn that it must pose quietly in the presence of other dogs. This is not difficult if you have other dogs. If you haven't, then ask neighbors to come over to your yard, with their dogs on leash, while you pose yours. This will require only a few lessons, but they will be valuable. Also, pose the dog along the street, so that it gets used to standing quietly while cars, trucks, children on bicycles and tricycles, and running children, are passing by.

The next step is to teach the dog to walk, or to trot, on leash. For this, it is best to use a show lead—one that is both a collar and a leash. Fasten the leash so that it is directly under the chin. You do this in order to teach your dog to move with its head up. Only in this way can the judge check the dog's movement when it is coming toward him.

At first, the dog will fight the lead and will try to force its head down as it moves. Usually, a few gentle jerks upward are sufficient to correct this. When the leash is too tight, or when the dog fights it, gagging or light vomiting may occur. This is a natural reaction. But when it happens in the ring, the judge can only register the thought that, either the dog has been badly trained, or it has a personality defect. Either way, it can be a mark against your dog.

Ch. Tuway's Jolli Judi (Ch. Tuway's Kaymore Flash, C.D. ex Ch. Suzette De Brentwood, C.D.), owned and bred by Wayne Fessenden, was the winner of the 1969 Dual Futurity. She is shown here being owner handled to a win under judge Phil Marsh. *Petrulis photo.*

International (FCI) and Mexican Ch. Tuway's Holliday Marc (Fld. & Amateur Fld. Ch. Holliday Britt's Ed ex Ch. Tuway's Jolli Judi), owned by Wayne Fessenden, is the first American-bred international champion of the breed. Here he is making a Win under the author at Mexico City.

Ch. Tuway's Carla (Dual Ch. Baron De Brentwood, C.D. ex Perry's Jill Marlene), was best of opposite sex at the 1970 ABC Bench Futurity under judge Maidza Van Deusen. *Petrulis photo.*

Ch. Richard's King Henry (Ch. Ti War Chip de Triumph ex Jo-No's Mike's Springtime Sandy), owned and handled by R. B. Edwards, was the #2 Brittany in America on the Phillips ratings in 1970. He is shown making a best of breed win under judge Theodore Gunderson. *Booth photo.*

Ch. Ju-Di's Peggy Sioux, owned and handled by Richard Pocock, was best of breed at the Western Pennsylvania Kennel Association under the late Virgil Johnson. *E. H. Frank photo.*

When the dog's legs propel it along in a straight line, the animal is said to be true in movement. If the body is slightly turned so that the dog is moving forward at an angle, the dog is said to be crabbing or sidewinding, that is, the hind end is slightly to the right or left of the front end. You will get the idea if you first move a ruler lengthwise in a straight line, then turn it slightly but move it along the same line.

Often, crabbing is due to lack of training, or simply to sloppy gaiting. This may sometimes be corrected by gaiting with a tighter leash. But ideally, you want the dog to move truly while on a loose leash. So a better method is to gait the dog along a sidewalk. If the dog crabs to the left, then walk with the dog between you and the outside edge of the sidewalk. He must then move truly, or his hind legs will keep falling off the walk. You can do the same thing by putting the dog between you and the curb.

Sometimes an owner will gait his dog so slowly and with the leash holding the head so high that proper movement is impossible. When viewed from the side, the dog's action may appear to be a hackney type, with the front legs being lifted too high. In such cases much forward motion is lost. Or the dog may be held back so that all four legs move forward with very short, mincing steps. Practice until your dog will move forward at its fastest stride, without breaking into a gallop, and without getting out of a true forward line. Your dog cannot move truly unless you adjust your own movement to its best gait. So learn to rate yourself with your dog. Have people watch and criticize as you move together.

Gaiting, too, should be done along busy streets so that your dog will become used to the rumble of trucks, the shouting and passing of children, and the presence of other dogs. Take it to shopping centers. Let people bend down to pet it. Make it gait and pose in parks, in auto repair shops, or wherever there will be unusual noises. The judge simply cannot accept such excuses as: "He does this beautifully at home." Or: "He doesn't like to show in buildings." Or: "These strange noises scare him."

Before you take your dog into the show ring, study the breeds and classes that are judged before your class. Be present at least an hour before the hour scheduled for judging your breed. This will help to get the dog used to the show. It will also give you an opportunity to study the way the judge conducts his ring. For example, if the judge has the dogs set up, and then examines them before gaiting them, then be prepared to set your dog up after the first ring go-round. If he gaits them straight out and back on a narrow mat, be prepared to do that, and that only. Don't stupidly ask him if you should gait straight out and back when that is the way he has gaited a dozen dogs before you. If he wants you to move your dog in a triangle fashion, or out and then back and forth across the ring in a "T" pattern, he will tell you to do so.

There is another reason for being at least an hour ahead in reaching the show. Let us suppose that the judge's 10 o'clock assignment shows six Chesapeake Bay Retrievers, then seven Pointers, and then 10 Brittany Spaniels. If the judge judges at a normal rate of speed of 20 to 25 dogs an hour, you could expect that Brittany Spaniels will be judged at or after 10:30. But some of these dogs may be absent. In that case, you will be judged earlier—at 10:15 a.m. if half the others are absent. Finally, you should report to the ring steward and get your arm band at least 20 minutes before actually judging of your breed starts. In this way, the judge will not be held up.

Most judges do not care whether dogs are lined up in catalog order or not. If one does, he will ask his steward to bring them in in that order. This usually facilitates checking the entries in a big class. But what the judge does want to see is your arm band number. Be sure that you turn your arm band so that the judge can see it easily. He is not interested in the dog food advertising on it. But in hundreds of cases that is about all he can see. The judge who must ask to see a number 100 times, or who must take 500 extra steps, and lean around 100 arms, is likely to get irritated before the day is over.

When the judge lines up the dogs and asks exhibitors to pose them, allow plenty of room between the dog in front of you and the dog behind. Only in that way can you set up your dog without cramping it, or yourself and the judge. Do not allow yourself to get stuck at the end of the line, and in a corner where you will be partially hidden from the judge. If the entry is large enough to require two sides of the ring, and you are at the end of the long side of the "L", turn your dog to round off the corner. In this way, the judge will get a perfect look at your dog.

It is customary to set the dog in show position, and then to remove the leash. This is to prevent the leash from breaking the flowing lines of the dog. If your dog has been well trained you can do this safely. But practice this a dozen times before you attend the show.

If you are fortunate enough to get winners dog or winners bitch, then you must compete for best of breed. (In Canada, winners dog

American and Mexican Ch. Tuppence Halfpenny, owned, bred and handled by Dorothy Macdonald, is the first Brittany to hold championships in both Mexico and the United States. *Ludwig photo.*

Ch. Ma Chere Clementine, owned by Al Langan and bred by Walter S. Oberlin who was one of the very early Brittany breeders. She is being handled to a win under judge Derek Rayne by Robert Eldridge. *Frank photo.*

and winners bitch compete, and then the best of winners only enters to compete with the champions for best of breed. But in the United States both winners dog and winners bitch compete with the champions for best of breed.)

The best handlers make a careful study of judges. They watch them constantly. In this way, they learn that judges have certain guide lines. They are tough on dogs with bad feet; they like great angulation of the hind legs; they are "head hunters." You, too, should study judges. By watching the judge as the passes on the breeds ahead of yours, and in your own, you may get some valuable tips on how to present your dog.

There are some "dont's" which you should make a part of your dog showing bible. Don't enter the ring and say: "Hello judge, it is nice to see you out our way again." Or "Glad to see you back again." Or: "It's good to have a competent man on our breed for once." Dozens of exhibitors make this mistake. The judge is bound to think that you are simply buttering him up, currying favor. And all the other exhibitors will be sure of it.

If you know the judge, don't rush up to talk to him before the judging. And don't take him out to dinner the night before, nor invite him for the night after. Other exhibitors will be sure that both you and the judge are dishonest. Wait until the judging is over, then talk to him; then invite him out to dinner, even if you have lost. A famous judge once said: "A judge is the most popular man in the world before a show, and the loneliest afterward."

Don't ask the judge what he didn't like about your dog. He might have liked it very well. Any faults in it may have been very minor. He may simply have liked another dog better, and upon a matter of viewing which is impossible to explain—overall balance. You can ask an opinion on young puppies. Many people take puppies to the show just to get outside opinions on the prospects—opinions from other exhibitors and from the judges.

If you lose, don't get mad at the judge, or at your dog. If it is a good dog, there will be other shows and other judges. Two very competent judges may differ in the way they total the merits and faults of two dogs. In a very important sense, both of them may have sound judgment. So you thank the judge for doing a good job, and decide that tomorrow will be another day, and a winning one.

Ch. Sir Duke De Art, C.D., owned by Charles E. Waters, was best of breed at the International Kennel Club of Chicago under judge Dale McMackin. *Gilbert photo.*

Ch. J.J.'s Judd of Ja-Dor, owned by John Chokran, is the sixth champion out of Dual Ch. Sue City Sue. He is shown making a win under Judge Heywood R. Hartley. *Gilbert photo.*

# 34

# Early Field Training for a Brittany Spaniel Puppy

UNTIL recently, it was a rule in field dog training that no dog should be given formal training until it was eight months to a year old. The key word in the rule is "formal," or precise and severe training. It was felt that precise, steady training would ruin a puppy's spirit, shorten its range, and perhaps make it bird shy. The rule still holds, as far as severe training goes. But the careful, and detailed study of puppies now indicates that a six to 12 weeks old puppy can be given some basic training that may make it possible for the puppy to develop into a great field dog.

Studies at the Jackson Memorial Laboratory at Bar Harbor, Maine, and elsewhere since, have shown that the period from six to 12 weeks is the most critical in a puppy's life. During it, the puppy's mind is most receptive. The puppy is trying very hard to adapt itself to its environment. Lessons learned during this period are normally learned for life. Bad habits learned at this time will be difficult to break; good habits become the springboard upon which good adult behavior is launched.

Every person has seen a seven weeks old puppy happily waddling along on a string held by a child. The puppy has already learned

An eight-week-old litter of Brittany puppies—future masters of the bird field.

to walk on a leash. This is an important first step. The puppy has taken it without the shock that it would get if leash broken at six months. It is important for a field dog because it means that the puppy can be taught to stop and point, and to hold that point during a flush. If taught during this period, the puppy may never later break a point.

Once the puppy has been taught to walk on leash, a game bird wing can be put in the grass ahead of it. As the puppy moves along, every cell in its nose is gathering in odors. As the new, and strange odor reaches its nose, the puppy stops to savor it. Now instinct awakens in all the other cells of the puppy's body. "This," they will whisper to the brain, "is the odor which a thousand generations of bird dogs ahead of me were taught to find. This is the reason that I was bred."

The puppy is on leash. It stops momentarily to get the meaning

Ch. Suzabob's Bobo, C.D. on point and being backed by his liver and white son Suzabob's Five O'Clock Shadow. Both dogs are owned by R. E. Young.

Winners at the 1963 Quail Classic included (l. to r.) first—Kaymore's Joe of Weymouth, owned by James B. Bell, Jr. and handled by Phil Morehouse; second—Wood's Pontiac Dingo, owned by John St. Paul, III and handled by Jane Thompson; third—Rusty of Highbrow, owned and handled by Ernest Facer; fourth—Dual Ch. Belloaks King, owned by James B. Bell, Jr. and handled by Phil Morehouse. He is posed here with Martin Best. *Hemmer photo.*

of the odor. The owner can now apply light leash pressure, and can steady the puppy by voice while also assuring it that the odor is a proper one for puppy to savor. After a few lessons, the puppy will stop automatically.

The next step is to fasten the wing to a fishing line at the end of a fishing pole or fly rod. The owner can restrain the puppy in a point while "flushing" the wing. It sounds simple, and it is. The puppy is pointing, and is being held steady by light leash pressure, while something exciting is being "flushed" in front of its nose. A conditioned reflex is being set up to point, and to remain steady to flush.

During this period, one must use great caution. No lesson should last longer than two minutes. Any long lesson will tire the puppy and make it hate all training. But a series of one or two minute lessons, repeated half a dozen times a day can be permanently learned while remaining fun. The owner must constantly restrain himself from making the lesson too long. Too short a lesson is still better learned than one too long. Every lesson must be accompanied by plenty of compliments and voice assurances, and plenty of petting. And there must be adequate rest and play periods in between.

Every puppy loves to rush out to retrieve things. But they don't always want to bring them back. Instead, they would prefer to romp off with them. Formal retrieving lessons can come later. But "fun retrieving" can be taught at this time. The puppy is kept on a light cord line. The object to be retrieved is thrown out a few feet ahead of the puppy. It rushes out and grabs the object. The owner simply draws the puppy to him while complimenting it. This lesson can be repeated three times. It is play, but even play can be tiring if repeated too often. The lessons can be repeated at intervals every day. The object at this time is simply to condition a reflex action in the puppy to rush out to retrieve, and to return it to its owner's hand.

Probably every owner of a prospective field dog worries about the possibility that his dog will be gun shy. The causes of gun shyness, noise shyness, or storm shyness are not known. Sometimes all three occur in the same dog. But this is not always true. A Brittany Spaniel owned by the author would be sent into epileptic convulsions during an electrical storm. But he was not gun shy. And a gun shy Springer Spaniel was not afraid of other noises.

It must be your aim to make gun fire a part of your dog's life. In a six to 12 weeks old puppy this is easily done, though only if

Fld. Ch. Heady's Skip Britt, owned by P. A. Pittman, has won six open stakes and is the sire of nine winners.

the dog does not have some pathological fault in respect to noise. The owners of puppies sometimes fire cap pistols just before feeding. They wait until the attention of the puppies is diverted at the far end of the run. They then fire the pistol, and call the puppies to their meals. The puppies come to associate the firing with the pleasures of eating. The puppies also learn to rush to the sound of gun fire. A shot fired into the air has helped many an inexperienced and lost dog to find its owner.

Sometimes an owner holds a puppy in his arms while another dog points. He then flushes the bird, and puts the puppy into the warm scent left by it. Later, he can hold the puppy, either in his arms or in the scent while someone at a distance fires. It is not necessary to kill the bird. For example, it can be a pigeon tied to the end of a fishing line and "planted" in light cover. As the pigeon reaches the end of the line, it is brought down and the gun is fired. The trained dog is then sent out to make the retrieve while the puppy watches. Here the puppy is learning the excitement of hunting. It picks up this excitement from the scent, the flush and shot, and the excitement shown by the other dog as it rushes out to make the retrieve.

Every dog must gain field wisdom. It can gain a part of this during the six to 12 weeks old period. It must learn to climb banks, to search for holes under fences, or to jump through holes in the fences, or over the tops. It must learn to cross streams, either by searching for a shallow place or by swimming. As it gains field wisdom, it will also gain the confidence to cast out and away in searches of birdy cover.

You must remember not to tire your dog by too long walks or running while still so young. If you tire it too much, it may lose interest. And too much running may injure bones before they have had a chance to change from cartilage into hard, strong bone. So make your field walks short, but with a purpose. One trainer used to take six weeks old puppies in his hunting coat while training other dogs. He would set the puppy down into a warm scent, then let it work out the area, then pocket it again.

The owner can take a puppy to a creek bank. He can set the puppy down along the water's edge, or he can let the puppy find its own way down the bank. Puppy wants to be with master, so if the owner simply walks over the bank, the puppy will find its own way down. If then, the owner walks across the creek at a shallow spot, the puppy will follow. There can then be lessons where the puppy must swim or get left behind. The same procedure can be followed in going up a bank. The owner selects one which will not be too hard. If the puppy cannot climb it, the owner simply walks along the bank to a spot where the puppy can climb up.

The same procedure is followed at fences. At first, the puppy will not know how to search for a hole under the fence. So the owner climbs the fence, then walks along until there is an opening. He may have to show the opening to the puppy the first time. After that, the puppy will conduct its own searches.

Jumping through holes is more difficult to teach. The owner may have to pull a leash through the hole, then tug upward gently until the puppy gets the idea. A simple method is to teach the puppy to jump over low objects. The owner puts puppy on a leash, walks to the barrier and, though it is not so high that he must jump, he pretends to jump over. The puppy will get the idea quickly. Jumping through holes then is simple to teach. Of course, you deliberately make your walks include things which puppy can, and will have to jump.

In all these lessons, it is important not to help the puppy unless it is absolutely necessary. Do not help it up, or down a bank. It may come to depend upon you always to help it. Once you've shown it how to jump, never help it again.

People sometimes speak of a dog's homing instinct, that is, the ability of a dog to find its way home. This may indeed be an instinct. But much of it is training and acquired knowledge. We know a man who deliberately tries to lose his puppies. He takes them to an area of woods and flat lands and ravines. While the puppies are busily exploring, he slips away, and returns to the point from which the walk began.

The puppies, suddenly finding themselves without a guiding master, become panicked. But only for a minute. They quickly get to work to back track. The owner helps very young puppies by trying to leave extra deep footprints in spongy turf. In his first lessons, he is not more than 25 yards away. He then gradually lengthens the distance. At first, he may help with a couple of voice calls, but not afterward. Puppies taught in this way can never be lost in the field, and they quickly acquire great boldness and field sense.

Most Brittany Spaniels, even though working to a man on foot, hunt at some distance away. They learn the position of their master by his occasional voice calls. These are no more than unintelligible cries, but the dogs recognize their masters' voices and position themselves accordingly as they hunt.

Yet there are times when the dog must respond, must quit hunting, and must come to heel. This can be taught to very young puppies. You can use your own vocal whistle, or a wind whistle. You may have taught the puppy to come to the feed dish when a cap pistol is fired. You can fire your gun in the field to make the puppy respond. Or you can teach it to come to its meals when you whistle. Of course, you have to use imagination.

For instance, you might have someone take the dog a short distance away just at feeding time. Then you blow your whistle, and set down the food dish. Or you wait until the puppy is around the corner of the house, then blow the whistle. What you are doing is imprinting in the dog a reflex action to come instantly upon that whistle call.

Another method is to put the dog upon a light long cord. Then when the puppy is going away from you, you whistle, snub the dog short, and then begin to draw it in to you. Puppy may put on the brakes. But you continue to draw it in, and you praise it as you do so. When it reaches you, you pet and compliment it. This lesson must be repeated again and again until the puppy automatically turns and comes to you when you blow that particular whistle.

In this chapter, we have been writing solely of early field training. Yet field dogs should be bold and confident under all circumstances. So they have to gain experience under many and varying conditions.

During this period, you should be taking your puppy into the home. It needs to know about hardwood floors and waxed composition floors, about rugs and home noises. And it must meet a lot of strangers.

Among these strangers should be cats and chickens. A cat or a kitten will quickly teach a small puppy to respect it. One scratch on the nose and puppy learns its lesson permanently. A grown dog, however, might become a cat killer once one has scratched it. Nothing can be more embarrassing than to have your fine hunting dog rush into a farmer's yard and chase and kill his cat, or his chickens. If you have a cat in your home, the lesson will be learned at six weeks of age. If you haven't, then take your puppy to visit a cat, or preferably, a kitten.

And take it to a farmer's chicken yard. Here use a training rope; for instance, a builder's chalk line. Tie one end to puppy's collar. Let it drag the rope. If it starts to chase a chicken, say "no" sharply, and at the same time upset the puppy. Remember that a sharp upset is much better than a few weak jerks. Be stern enough so that only one or two lessons are sufficient. But after such lessons, work with your pheasant wing, so that puppy quickly learns that one is forbidden, and the other is its way of life.

If at the 12th or 14th week, these lessons are mostly stopped, the puppy will still not forget them. The puppy can then be taken out of training, so to speak, and just allowed to grow. But field romps, in all sorts of cover, should be continued, so that the puppy continues to grow in field wisdom. Then when formal training begins, puppy will be bold and confident. He'll quickly return to the responses you taught him as a baby, and he will become an easily trained and experienced field dog.

# 35

# Yard Breaking the Brittany Spaniel

---

Y ARD breaking is that part of field training which can be done in your back yard. But it is more than that. It is obedience training. It can, and should be, given to all puppies whether or not they are ever going to compete in field trials or in dog shows or obedience trials. It is the basic obedience which makes a better companion of every dog.

You should teach your dog to heel both while on a leash and when free of it; to sit when you stop; to sit and to lie down upon command; to come when called; and to carry and to retrieve. All these things can be taught in your backyard, on the sidewalks in front of your house, and in special trips to shopping centers, or to places where there are people and animals which will tend to divert your dog's attention.

Heel and sit can be taught in one lesson. The dog should heel on your left side. The reason is that most people are right handed. So they carry things in the right hand. They also carry their gun on the right side. But, if you are left handed, you could teach the dog to heel on the right side. Here we assume you will have the dog walk at heel on your left side.

Start walking. Say the dog's name and a stern "heel." Jerk on the leash to pull the dog up to your heel. If it tries to go ahead, jerk lightly to bring it back, and again command "heel."

After you have walked 20 to 30 steps, stop and command "sit." Instantly grasp the dog's collar with your right hand, and the skin of the rump with your left. Pull backward with both hands, and downward with the left. The dog is thus forced to sit. Make it hold this position for a minute or so. If it tries to get up, restrain it, and repeat the command "sit." Now start forward and command "heel." Walk 20 to 30 steps, and then stop and repeat the "sit" exercise.

As in most training exercises, do not make the mistake of making lessons too long. Work with the dog for five minutes. Then allow a rest period of half an hour. Follow with another 10 minute lesson. Give four or five such lessons a day.

Sometimes the dog will pull ahead so hard that the pressure on the neck made by the collar makes the dog choke. If fairly severe jerks and the "heel" command do not bring the dog back to heel, there is a simple method for correcting the error. Use an umbrella, a cane, or just a long stick. If the dog pulls ahead, tap it lightly 'on the nose. This will cause it to back up. After a few times, the stick can simply be used as a guide. It can be held ahead of the dog, and it will not pull ahead. Sometimes, a cane or umbrella can be swung back and forth as a pendulum.

If the dog is being trained for the field, or for simple home obedience, it is not necessary to have it walk close to your side. If it is to compete in obedience trials, then close heeling is required. A simple method of teaching close heeling is to do the exercises along the edge of a sidewalk, or along a street curb. If along a sidewalk, then walk close enough to the left edge so that the dog must stay close to your side or get off the sidewalk. If on the street, walk along the left side, with the dog between you and the curb. This method is particularly good for dogs which tend to walk with the forelegs near you, but with the hind end pointing away. That is, the dog is walking crab-wise.

Different dogs require different lengths of training for any given exercise. But an important factor in training is attention. The dog which will not give you its attention is difficult, or even impossible, to train. Most Brittany Spaniels given you their attention and they learn quickly. So for most of them, the heel and sit lessons should be well learned within three days. But if you are training your first dog, remember that you are also training yourself. So, since you are not an expert, a somewhat longer period may be required.

The next step is to teach the dog to heel and sit "free." That is, to work free of the leash. Always start each lesson by repeating first those previously learned. So give your dog two minutes of work on leash. Now, with the dog sitting at your left heel, take off the lead, while cautioning it with your voice to remain sitting. Now command "heel" and start walking forward. But be prepared to grab the collar and give a slight jerk if the dog does not instantly respond. Be preppared also to grab the collar and jerk the dog back if it tries to go ahead. Here again, the cane, umbrella, or long stick can help to guide the dog.

If your dog has learned its first lessons well, it should learn to heel and sit free within a maximum of three days. But again, remember to start each day with heeling and sitting while on the leash. You will be really amazed at how quickly your dog learns to obey while off the leash. Yet the lesson will not be fully learned until you have worked the dog under all sorts of conditions, such as while other dogs are in the yard, while children are running and playing nearby, and where there are many people, as at a shopping center.

"Sit and stay" is the next lesson. If your puppy lives in the house, this can be simply—and quickly—taught at feeding time. Mix up the dog's food. Then have your dog sit in a corner. Command it repeatedly to sit and stay while someone else puts down the food dish in a far corner of the room. Be prepared to grab the dog if it starts to rush for its food. Make it sit again. And then place the palm of your hand in front of its nose as a warning. If it ignores the command and hand, grab it again, and again force it to sit. After a moment, remove your hand and say "okay" or some other signal which will tell the puppy it can go to its food.

If you are feeding twice a day, the lesson can be repeated twice a day. But you can also practice using dog biscuits. Your next step is to make the dog sit in the corner while you put down the food dish. Put the dog in the corner as usual, then caution it to sit, and keep the palm of your hand out toward the dog. Then get the food dish, back away from the dog and carefully set down the dish. If the dog "breaks" and rushes toward the food dish, catch it on the way. Carry or drag it back to its corner, and then make it sit for a moment before letting it go.

Carrying it back can be both a correction and a mild form of punishment. The best way to carry it is to grab the puppy by the scruff of the neck and by the skin on the rump. No dog likes to be carried in this way. But in dogs as lightly made as the Brittany Spaniel, the method is harmless but very effective.

The next step is to practice outside. Take the dog into the yard. Practice your heeling on and off a leash. Now command the dog to sit. Step carefully in front of it. Keep repeating the command "sit," and use the palm of your right hand as a restraining signal. Now back slowly away. If the dog "breaks" catch it and carry it back to the spot from which it broke. Repeat again and again, always backing away.

When the dog will remain sitting until you say "okay" or give it a hand signal by dropping your hand, or both, you are ready for the next step. Back away as before. Now turn around. The dog may break. If it does start over again. Once it will stay when your back is turned, try something new. With the puppy sitting, stand in front of it, command it to sit and stay. Turn your back and begin to walk away. If the puppy breaks, carry it back to the spot from which it broke, and start over again. At first, walk slowly away. Later move away rapidly.

Now you are ready for the next lesson. This is to teach the puppy to sit and stay while you are out of sight. You can sit the puppy at one end of the yard, then walk into the garage, or around the corner of the house or barn. If puppy breaks, try to catch it before it reaches you, scold it, and return it to its spot. You can figure that the puppy has not learned the lesson thoroughly until you can stay out of sight for several minutes.

At first, you will want the puppy to sit in its position until you have returned to it, and have placed yourself so that the puppy is at your left heel. Later, you can let it come to you when you call. But, if you start to let it do this too soon, you may be teaching it to break and not to wait until the command to "come."

This lesson must be practiced under all sorts of conditions. If your puppy is a house dog, then you should practice making it sit in one room while you are in another. Later, you must practice where there are other people and other dogs to distract it. One of the lamest of excuses is: "Well, he does this perfectly at home . . . ."

You must also teach your dog to lie down, and to stay there until told it can get up. An occasional dog cannot be taught this. It is the author's experience that such dogs have some degree of inherited shyness. When lying down, they feel defenseless and become frightened. If you cannot teach your Brittany Spaniel to lie down, and to stay there while you are out of sight, then it might be wise not to use the dog for breeding. A further such test is to make the dog lie down in the dark and to stay there while you move some distance away.

There are various ways to teach a dog to lie down. One is to make it sit. Then grab its front legs and upset it, while commanding "lie down." Restrain it in the lying down position while complimenting and soothing it. Another method is used with a leash. Have the puppy sit. Place the leash under the arch of one shoe. Now pull up on it while commanding "lie down." As you pull up, the puppy's head and neck are forced down. When puppy is squatting on both hind and front legs, shove it over onto its side.

However you do it, compliment the puppy but restrain it from getting up. Finally, you can tell it to sit and allow it to take that position. It is important to teach it the difference between sitting and lying down. Remember also to practice this lesson under all sorts of conditions. To do so is to give the puppy confidence in both you and in the world about it. And this is important whether you are to train the dog for field or obedience work.

Jumping, if properly taught, is one of the fun lessons for dogs. A simple way is to put the dog on leash, then to approach and to walk over a low barrier. If the puppy balks, step back to its side. Walk back a few steps, turn and again approach the barrier. As you step over, command "jump" and lift upward on the leash. Forced in this way, the puppy will try to jump the rest of the way. Compliment it with petting and by voice. Repeat again and again and as the dog learns to make the jump, begin raising the barrier.

Also, take the dog off leash and walk over. As you raise the barrier, begin running to it, and jump over yourself. Then as you continue to raise it, run along side while the dog jumps over.

The dog is not well trained until it will jump over at your command. First, sit the dog a few steps away, then stand a few steps away on the far side. Face the dog, call it and command "jump." Be prepared to rush forward and to stop it if it tries to run around. Set it directly in front of a very low barrier, step over, and then command "jump." Eventually, the dog will get the idea and will jump over at command, even when you are some distance away, and order it to go forward and to jump.

Also, the dog is not well trained until it will jump over a variety of barriers or objects. The author once knew an obedience trained Standard Poodle which could get perfect scores in utility work. It was a perfect jumper over the standard jumps which are used in obedience work. But this dog would balk at a low field fence, and would refuse to jump over an overturned chair or other object. So practice with your dog. You might even practice having it jump over a kneeling youngster.

In similar fashion, teach it to broad jump. Standard broad jump hurdles, as used in obedience trials, are easily made. These are boards four feet six inches to five feet long. They are supported by end pieces which are six inches high at the forward edge, and four inches at the near edge. This gives them an upward and forward slope. You can make two or three of these, with four being ideal. One can be five feet long; the second, four feet 10 inches; the third, four feet eight inches, and the fourth, four feet six inches. In this way, they can be nestled together so as to take up the space of only one when not in use. They should be painted flat white. Practice with these, until the dog will race to them and leap over three or four when well spaced.

In obedience trials, a Brittany Spaniel would be required to jump over a barrier one and a half times its height. Thus a Brittany 20 inches tall would have to jump a 30 inches tall barrier, and clear it without touching it. In the broad jump it would be required to jump 60 inches clear. So you should practice until the dog will leap such a distance. But also practice having it jump over brooks or ditches. Rember that you are teaching the dog to do the unusual as well as the usual. If you practice making it do unusual things, you will be giving it the confidence to do things at your bidding which it has not done before.

Retrieving should also be taught during yard breaking. As written earlier, retrieving comes naturally to very young puppies. But it is play, not work. The difference is that you must teach your dog MUST. When you order it to retrieve it must do so. Also, during play retrieving, the puppy will tend to chew on the object, it will want to take it in the opposite direction, and it will not want to give it up.

It is the author's belief that a dog should be taught to carry before it is taught to retrieve. If it is taught to carry first, then it will always retrieve with style later on. There will also be less danger of hard mouth—the condition in which the dog either chews the game or crushes it in its mouth.

Teaching the dog to carry is done in two steps. The first is simply teaching the dog to hold something in its mouth until told it can give the object to you, that is, can put it into your hand. This lesson can be taught in the home or in the back yard. The object can be anything. A newspaper rolled up and tied is excellent. A block of wood can be used. You may even use a block of wood to which a pheasant or pigeon wing has been nailed.

Have the dog sit. Kneel beside it. Command "hold" or "carry," though the former is to be preferred. Place your left hand over the dog's muzzle and squeeeze between the teeth. The dog is then forced to open its mouth. Place the object to be held—dummy is a good word for it—in the dog's mouth. Command "hold it." The dog will try to spit out the dummy. But prevent this with your right hand. At the command "okay" take the dummy. Repeat this four or five times. You may have to slap upward under the chin to get the dog to hold the dummy. If so, do it lightly, while using a commanding tone of voice.

As soon as the dog understands, and will hold the dummy until told to release it into your hand, you are ready for the next step. Put a leash on the dog, but fold it into your hand until only a foot is left between your hand and the dog's neck. As the dog holds the dummy, command "fetch" and begin to draw the dog forward. If it tries to spit out the dummy, warn it to "hold it" or repeat the command "fetch." You probably will have to hold the dummy in the dog's mouth a few times. But a Brittany Spaniel will ordinarily get the idea very quickly.

Now lead it about, warning it to "fetch" and praising it. Once it will carry the dummy, begin to praise it continuously. Then have the dog sit and deliver the dummy to hand. Now praise and pet it with all the enthusiasm you can muster. In this way, the dog will become immensely proud to carry something for you, and it will do so with great style.

If the dog shows any tendency to chew on the dummy, drive some blunted nails through it in such a way that any attempt to clamp down on the dummy will bring pain, but will not puncture the mucous membranes of the mouth. The dog will quickly learn to carry gently, or as field people say, "with a tender mouth." Practice until the dog will carry for at least 100 yards.

The dog is now ready for actual retrieving lessons. Place the dog in a sitting position. Kneel beside it. Throw out the dummy and command "fetch." If the dog does not move, draw it to the dummy by the leash, pull its head down by force on the collar, and force the dummy into the mouth. Then, still commanding "fetch," return the dog to the spot from which you started. In most cases, the dog will carry the dummy, since it has already learned to carry. But, if it drops the dummy, scold it with a stern "no." Then again draw its head down, and force the dummy into the dog's mouth. Once you have returned the dog to the spot from which the dummy was thrown, make the dog deliver to hand, as in the carry exercise. Then praise it and give it much petting.

We have said that carrying and retrieving can be taught in the home or in the back yard. It is important that whatever spot you choose be one which is free of distraction. You want the absolute attention of the dog. No other dogs, nor any other people should be about. But once the lesson has been learned, then practice before other people, and in the presence of other dogs. Dogs enjoy showing off both for people and other dogs. But also, they learn to work under all conditions.

The last step in retrieving is to teach the dog to carry and retrieve all sorts of things. These should include your gloves, a small basket with a handle, a pigeon, pheasant, woodcock, or other upland game and ducks. Of course, you can teach the retrieving of game by using the wings of various game birds. These can be tied to rolled up newspaper, or nailed to a block of wood. But finally, the dog must retrieve live game unharmed. If you have followed this system carefully, the latter will be no problem.

Probably dogs like to retrieve pigeons least of all. So use a live pigeon for this. There are two methods to do this. One is to tape the wings to the body, and to tape the feet together. The latter is necessary to keep the pigeon from scratching tender mouth tissues. Taping the wings to the body also helps to protect the pigeon from injury. The second is to lock the pigeon's wings. This is done by folding the wings above the body. Then the left wing is crossed over the right, and the right is hooked over the left. The pigeon's wings are sufficiently loose to permit this without breaking them. But use care. Also, tape the legs together. The pigeon's body is now exposed, and a small, young dog will have an easier carry.

A final step in yard breaking is to teach the dog to beware of automobiles and trucks. Take the dog on leash along any highway. Walk along the shoulder, but do not have the dog at heel. That is, use a long leash or rope and let the dog wander onto the highway itself. Then, as a car or truck comes along, give the dog a tremendous jerk over to the shoulder. After a few such lessons, the noise of any approaching auto or truck will cause the dog to rush to the side of the road. This lesson could save your dog's life.

Some memorable dogs posed here at an early field trial are (l. to r.) Antonede Reservere, handler unidentified; Domino de Klemanor, handler Bill Kull; Ch. Loufel's Handsome Harry, handler Nicky Bissell and Ch. Ashurst Jerry, handler Buck Bissell.

# 36

# Final Field Training of the Brittany Spaniel

IT is beyond the scope of this book to try to tell the reader how to give the final lessons in field work. But there is one major lesson which every person who wants a field dog, or a field trial dog, must learn. Perhaps the following story will illustrate the point.

The author once interviewed the owner of a Coonhound which had just won the national championships in competition against some 500 dogs. This is his story.

"I had a pretty good bitch. She was a real cooner, and every hunter in Kentucky and West Virginia knew her, and knew how good she was. Well, sir, I bred her to the greatest dog any of us knew about.

"She had eight pups. And by golly I just made a vow to keep every darn one of those pups. I wanted to train them all until I made mighty certain which was the best one.

"But the boys from everywhere heard about those pups. So they would come around with a jug of hard cider, or maybe a bit of moonshine. And we'd sit under the old apple tree in the yard and talk about hounds and coons.

"And every one of those guys told me what a wonderful friend he had been to me. And every one of them told me about all the favors he had done for me. And how I really owed him one of those pups.

"And you know how it was. They got everyone of those pups away from me except an ugly marked kind of runty pup which nobody wanted. Well, sir, that's old Buckeye Joe. Yes sir, the same Buckeye Joe that just won the money.

"You ask me the secret of why he's the national champion. Heck, I don't know. Except this. He's been worked on coon 365 nights a year ever since he was old enough to run a trail."

The all-important ingredient in the making of a champion is experience. So you've got to get your dog out into the field, and into game fields, as often as possible. You can't take it out just two weeks before the hunting season and expect it to be a top grade performer.

Among other things, the dog must get toughened up for the work. It must get rid of excess fat, must strengthen muscles, must harden its foot pads, must tighten its toes. There is evidence, too, that the dog must sharpen its nose.

After a long layoff, or an illness, a dog may have to learn over again how to interpret the various wind-borne odors which come to him. Perhaps one can say that it must gain "re-experience."

Many dogs are trained on planted game. But there is vast difference between the planted pheasant and a wild one. The planted pheasant is less physically strong. Its odor may be different. It will lack experience in running, dodging, and hiding—those faculties which the wild pheasant has sharpened by a summer of escaping from predators. When working such game, the dog may make unproductive points and may be accused of being dishonest or of having a faulty nose. Yet the fault may be lack of experience. After being shot at for a couple of days, pheasants tend not to fly, but to run, dodge, and hide. It then takes a highly experienced dog finally to pin the bird.

Many dogs will have to learn to run on a drag line. Some will have to be broken of chasing rabbits. A brilliant young derby dog could never be broken of chasing deer. Every dog must be taught to back, that is, to honor the point made by another dog.

There are many books which cover all these subjects thoroughly. You should find them listed in libraries under the names of such authors as Henry P. Davis, William F. Brown, Er M. Shelley, and Richard A. Wolters. If you will be doing some woodcock shooting, then you ought to learn all you can about the famous "timberdoodle." Check your library for John Alden Knight's *Woodcock,* and Bennett's *Training Grouse and Woodcock Dogs.*

Dual Ch. Joel's Copper Jacques, owned by John G. and Ellyn Lee, holds an all-time record for the breed as winner of 16 open all age stakes. He is shown here with his handler, Lee Holman. *Brown photo.*

Fld. Ch. Miss Tammy III, owned by Dr. Herb Goldberg.

Swiss Ch. Qocarde de Rollix, owned by
Madame J. Genet.

Early in 1972, a training book designed especially for the Brittany Spaniel owner was published. It is: *Training and Hunting the Brittany Spaniel* by Ralph B. and Robert D. Hammond. The publisher is A. S. Barnes, and the price, $5.95.

Dog books, by the way, are usually kept in the technology division of the larger libraries. But, also, you should visit old, and rare book, stores. Many of the best books on bird dog training are now out of print. Do not confine yourself to one book. The best trainers are better in some phases than in others. Your problems will be partially unique. So study all the books you can, and choose the methods which seem to give the best solutions for your problems.

You ought also to seek help from thoroughly experienced Brittany field people. There are some great amateurs and some supremely competent professionals. Perhaps you can arrange to work out with a top amateur. Chances are he will know the best places in which to train.

This last is an extremely important point. You must not discourage a young dog by forcing it to work for hours in unproductive cover. You, yourself, should be on a constant search for birdy areas in which to train. And your training should include some use of planted, or at least released, pheasants.

You can space out the time between birds as the dog gains experience. As he gains experience in coming onto point over many birds, he will be less likely to become discouraged when working barren territory. And you need to give him some barren territory. If you give him too many birds in too short a time, he may then become a quitter if he has to hunt for half an hour without finding a bird.

Now there is a difference between a field dog and field trial dog. The difference is in competition. In a trial, you will need as much experience as will your dog. So you should plan to attend as many trials as you can. Follow every brace, and study the work of dogs and handlers, both on the back course, and in the bird field. Finally, enter your dog. Only in competition can you gain the experience which both you and your dog will need. Don't worry about losing. The best handlers and the best dogs lose at times.

Ask experienced handlers, including the professionals, to watch you and your dog. Then ask them to tell you what you did wrong. Most of them will tell you. The next time, you won't make that mistake. A mistake you should not make is to think your dog should be the winner. You are wrapped up in the performance of your dog. You'll give it every advantage in your own mind. So will other owners in assaying the performance of their dogs. But the judges see all the dogs. They take notes. They try to figure out the winners impartially. Sometimes they make mistakes too, since often they have to make instant judgments on controversial points. Forget all that. Just try to correct your dog's mistakes, and hope for better luck at the next trial.

Dual Ch. Lund's Trooper, owned by Ejner (handling) and Gilda Lund, has established a record as one of the leading sires of all breeds. He has fathered a total of 22 champions including six duals. This is truly a most outstanding accomplishment.

# 37

# A Great Amateur Writes About Field Training

by Ejner Lund

*(Author's Note: Because of his great record in training and handling his own dogs at field trials, we have asked Ejner Lund to give you his personal advice on field training. Mr. Lund is the owner of Dual Ch. Lund's Trooper, Dual Ch. Faulkner's Reddy, and Dual Ch. Black Butte Ricochet Trooper.)*

I HAVE been asked to put down a few notes on our experience in starting puppies. We have really started only a few, so perhaps I am not the greatest expert on this.

Our experience has been to get the pups out at the earliest opportunity. Eight to 10 weeks is not too early to begin letting the pup explore the wonders of nature, and to let it get used to the environments, strange noises, and excitement. Let it explore on its own. In other words, let it develop its natural instincts naturally. Don't be over-protective. The "college of hard knocks" can be a wonderful teacher.

Don't over-do the workout. If you are working an older dog along with the pup, be sure to pick up the pup as soon as it shows signs of tiring. Then carry it along. Something exciting often develops such as birds or rabbits flushing. This will help to stimulate the pup's interest. Soon it will show enthusiasm and start ranging out on its own.

If the pup is not starting to run as well as you might like, don't ever try to chase it out. This would only frighten the pup and cause it to quit running altogether. Be encouraging and run forward. Act excited and shout "atta boy," or "atta girl," as the case may be. The pup will see your excitement and try to beat you. If you get a few good casts, pick the pup up and show it that you are very pleased. Then call it a day.

If you are trying for a field trial dog, don't make your lessons too long. You don't want the pup to think it has all day to explore at its leisure. Ten or fifteen minutes is ample to start with. Later, as the dog develops you can lengthen your outings to a time similar to what is required in the appropriate stakes.

When the young dog really starts to run, the tendency of most novice handlers is to over-handle. They are afraid that the dog is not going to turn when it should. If a pup has been taken out regularly—several times a week, if possible—it will turn when it comes to a point where is has trouble keeping track of you. If you think it may be confused or be getting lost, let out a few good war whoops so it knows where you are. But don't call the dog. You will soon see it swinging in from somewhere. It will enjoy working for you when it finds you are not a killjoy. You will find it will not be a run-away dog, but a bold and enthusiastic explorer.

As it gains experience, you can guide it into running the type of ground heat you want by keeping close watch on the way it patterns. If it side casts too much, give it a war whoop or whistle to get its attention. Then start running to the front. It will swing forward on seeing you do it.

As soon as it is going in the right direction, slow down to your regular pace again. Watch it closely to see that it continues. If it is running well to the front, but onesided, right or left, again a whistle or loud war whoop should be given to get its attention. Then start running forward. Remember, this should be always forward, but to the opposite side, so that the dog will swing with you. When it responds,

Fld. Ch. Rufus Rastus Johnson Brown, a liver and white dog, bred by Mrs. Nicky Bissell, is shown on point at the 1971 National Open Championship, in which he placed fourth. Handler Lyle Johnson moves forward to flush the bird. The mounted observers are (l. to r.) Ronald Stevenson, owner; Ken Jacobsen, reporter; and Leslie Tichenor, judge.

Ch. Toffe Idoc de Basgard, owned by Dr. J. E. Talbott.

again slow down to your regular pace. Be ready to repeat as necessary. In most cases your dog will soon be running and quartering as you want him to do.

In getting the dog's attention, never call it. You do not want it to come in. This is not desirable, and it will cause your dog to be penalized in trials. Should it happen that it does come in, run toward your dog. Yell "no" when it gets close. It will soon realize that you don't appreciate its coming in to visit.

Also, it must be remembered that, if you run your dog where no game is to be found, it will not run with enthusiasm for very long. No good will come from this. Wild birds are far better than planted birds. Many bad habits are formed from too many planted birds. The puppies quickly learn that they can catch them. Some will quit pointing, or they may develop a habit of crowding their birds. This is because the dizzied birds won't flush naturally. A pup can seldom catch a wild bird since, if crowded, it will flush.

Don't worry if your dog isn't holding point. That will generally come naturally with experience. That is, unless the dog has been allowed to catch the birds. In that case, some training may be necessary. Do not be in too much of a hurry for finished training. A lot of good dogs have been ruined by an over anxious owner. Such training as "coming when called" and such other obedience as knowing that you mean "no" is good for the dog. Every pup is an individual, and should be trained as such. Give kindness and praise. Remember that being firm will accomplish a lot more than will roughness and harsh treatment.

When the dog approaches two years old, and you see that he is pointing staunchly, it is advisable to consult a good trainer. Breaking a dog is not difficult, if it has been brought along properly, and the person is experienced. But the age of two is a critical time. And since it is easy to ruin a dog by too much pressure, you should consult an expert.

Bringing along a young dog can be a wonderful and rewarding experience for anyone. You need only a reasonable amount of time and patience. And of course, the time to develop the "know how."

# 38

# The Obedience Winners

OBEDIENCE is the third branch of sport in which the Brittany Spaniel competes. Somewhat understandably, Brittany competition in obedience lags behind the other two. The greatest interest for Brittany Spaniel owners has been in hunting and field trial competition. Show competition has been second.

There are four titles which can be won in obedience competition. These are Companion Dog (C.D.), Companion Dog Excellent (C.D.X.), Utility Dog (U.D.), and Tracking Dog (T.D.). A dog could make a grand slam by winning a U.D.T. title. This is the highest title which a dog could win in obedience.

A Brittany Spaniel could, of course, win field and show championships as well. To the best of the writer's knowledge, only one dog in any breed has ever won a dual championship and a U.D. degree. The dog was an un-registered Cocker Spaniel, and it competed nearly 35 years ago.

It can be argued that, since a Brittany Spaniel is a bird dog, or one that uses wind scents to locate upland game, it would be unreasonable to expect it to pass a tracking test. Yet this should not be difficult for a dog which is experienced in tracking a wounded pheasant. All dogs have exceptional noses. And though they may, by instinct or aptitude, use them in certain ways, they can also be taught to use them in other types of work. Thus, Borzois, which are sight hounds, have won Tracking Dog titles. One Brittany Spaniel, the Canadian dog Speckles Dark Loon, has won the Canadian T.D. title.

At the time of writing, one Brittany Spaniel has a chance to win all the titles offered by the American Kennel Club. He is National Amateur Champion Gringo De Britt, owned by Dr. Tim Poling. In addition to his field championship, Gringo has won both majors in show competition, and has a C.D. degree.

Two Brittany Spaniel show champions have won U.D. titles. They are Ch. Diane De Beauch U.D., and Ch. Pete's Gimlet U.D. Two champions have won C.D.X. titles. They are Ch. Brentwood's Chere Regards C.D.X., and Ch. Penny Half Penny C.D.X. At least 17 other show champions have won C.D. degrees. Two U.D. winners—Fluvannas' Buck and Prince of Spots—have sired U.D. winners.

In summary, 14 have won U.D. titles, 54 gained the C.D.X. degree, and 164 have added C.D. to their official names. Listed below are the dogs, and their sires and dams, which have won U.D. degrees. Listed also are the show champions which have won the lower titles. In the summaries, it should be noted that higher degree winners are counted among those winning the lower titles.

## Utility Dog Title Holders

Ch. Diane De Beauch, by Potic De Beauch C.D.X. out of Bonnie Lassie

Ch. Pete's Gimlet, by Dual Ch. Tigar's Jocko x Pete's Daiquiri

Trixie of Edough, by Roger of Edough x Patsy of Edough

Fluvanna's Buck, by Pete's Tommy x Aotrou's Lady

My Boy Pepper, by Fluvanna's Buck x Lucky Sue

Fancy Stepper, by Patrice's Trojan Snowball x Christina of Blackmoor

Prince of Spots, by Prince of Preble x Renee Antoine

Dot of Belleau, by Prince of Spots x De Pere Belle

Star Omion (also Canadian C.D.) by Joli Tic x Trudy's April Lady C.D.

Yellow Hammer, by Taylor's Rusty Towsey x Taylor's Ginger Girl

George's Plain Jess, by Rancho Gabriel's Fessant x Loner Lyon

Penelope of Robin drive, by Ranger of Richmont x Imming's Taffy Candy

Ma-Petite Dor'ee, by Juchoir's Showman x Betty's Pride Freckles.

Gabrielle Du Blanc De Prix, by Barnaby Gaston De La Cartier x Gisele

## Champions with C.D.X. Degrees

Ch. Brentwood's Chere Regards
Ch. Penny Half Penny

## Champions with C.D. Titles

Ch. Chesru's Prince
Ch. Dana's Panduf Daisy of Sequani
Ch. Lund's Randy of Troy
Ch. Winnetka Calvie
Ch. Sun Tan's Happy Hy-Tone (also Canadian C.D.)
Ch. Nelson's Star of Tiny
Ch. Gaard's Sweet William
Ch. Greenfield Thunderbird
Ch. Gaard's Jubilee
Ch. Fenton's Goldilocks
Ch. Miss Sue's Gad-A-Bout
Ch. Ree's Cindy Bales
Ch. Brentwood's Jane of Hearts
Ch. Suzette De Brentwood
Ch. Sam's Son of Buckshot
Ch. Suzabob's Bobo
Ch. Baron of Brentwood

Ch. Miss Sue's Gad-A-Bout, C.D. was a winner on the bench and in obedience competition. The dog is shown winning the Sporting group under the author at the Oak Ridge Kennel Club.

# 39

# Obedience Trials and Training

A Brittany Spaniel should be owned first of all for companionship. But men and dogs have always happily expanded that companionship in sport. For an owner and a Brittany Spaniel there are three branches of sport in the dog game. These are dog shows, field trials, and obedience trials. In America, obedience trials were first organized by Doberman Pinscher and German Shepherd fanciers who were interested in attack training.

Then a new concept developed. It did so partly because many people condemned show dogs as being stupid. Many people claimed that mongrels were smarter than purebreds, and that purebred runts were smarter than their show dog litter mates.

But it was quickly realized that obedience trained dogs could compete against each other at dog shows. And so a fascinating new sport was developed. It became an instant crowd pleaser at the shows. But it did more than that. It became one of the greatest advertisements for purebred dogs. And perhaps more than any other single thing, it taught the public the value and pleasure of a well trained dog.

The Brittany Spaniel's destiny has always been the hunting fields, and secondly the field trials. But there are owners who, for one reason

264

or another, cannot take their dogs to the field. They may have the time to compete in the shows. But not every dog will be good enough to win a championship, or even championship points. For them, there is still the obedience trial.

A goal for all Brittany Spaniel owners should be a dual dog—bench and field, bench and obedience, or all three. Then the dog and owner will get the most out of their companionship. And they will always be presenting to the public a breed of dog which is worth owning. They will be advertising the breed by performance, and in ways which words cannot do as effectively.

For the most part, obedience trials are held in conjunction with dog shows. Thus, it is possible for a dog to compete in conformation classes and obedience trials at the same time. In England, both dog shows and obedience trials have grown so large that it is seldom possible to hold the two on the same grounds. This may happen in America. and it is already the case at many indoor shows in Canada. But where possible, Brittany owners should take advantage of the joint events.

One constantly hears show people say that obedience training ruins show dogs. This is absurd. The more training one gives to a dog, the better the dog becomes. Experience in the obedience ring gives the dog greater confidence in the conformation ring. Among reasons given for the "ruination" theory are that the obedience dog gaits too close to the handler, and therefore neither freely nor truly, and that when stopped, the dog automatically sits instead of standing.

But dogs quickly learn that the show ring is not the obedience test. They will have gained the courage in the obedience ring to gait gaily and correctly in the show ring. And obedience dogs are taught to stand for examination. Finally, the number of dogs which win championships and obedience titles is an obvious proof that obedience training does not hurt the show dog.

Here let us point out again that the well trained dog is a joy to own. And it will be the pride of every person in the neighborhood where it lives. Neighbors are often a little hostile toward the dogs on the street, and with good reason. But they love to brag about the well trained dog down the street, and about the responsible owner who has trained that dog. So obedience training and obedience trials can be a continuous source of joy.

In an earlier chapter, we have pointed out that yard breaking for the field dog is almost identical to obedience training for the show dog. In fact, obedience training developed in the 1930s out

Victoria At-A-Girl, owned and trained by Jewel Walton. This Brittany has the distinction of being the only living dog to hold three *Dog World* Awards of Canine Distinction. She made this record by winning her C.D., C.D.X. and U.D. degrees in consecutive shows with a composite score of 197. She was twice highest scoring dog in show.

of the centuries-old yard breaking procedures. If you have given your puppy any of the early training outlined in this book, obedience training for competition should be easy.

If, when you read this, your dog is an adult, do not make the excuse that it is too old to train. The old proverb, "You can't teach an old dog new tricks," doesn't apply to dogs. It was invented by men to excuse their own laziness. In the very early beginning of obedience trials, a 10-year old Dalmatian won all three obedience titles, C.D., C.D.X., and U.D., (Companion Dog, Companion Dog Excellent, and Utility Dog), in one year. Since a Brittany Spaniel is one of the most easily trained of all dogs, it follows that you can start it at any age. But the younger you start it, the longer you will enjoy its good manners.

There are many excellent books which teach obedience work, both for the home and for the show. One is the *Koehler Method of Dog Training* by W. R. Koehler. This is published by Howell Book House, as is this book. Mr. Koehler teaches far more than obedience, since he includes curing bad habits—dozens of them. At your book store or library you should also be able to find books by such authors as

Pearsall and Leedham, Blanche Saunders, Harriet Schact, and others. The great Saunders books are also published by Howell Book House.

You should also try to find a group training class in your neighborhood. Such classes are given all over the United States. Sometimes, the trainers should not be allowed to conduct classes. But the majority will give at least the minimum amount of training in preparation for the novice obedience classes. The value of such classes, aside from the ability and wisdom of the instructors, lies in the fact that your dog must learn to be obedient in the presence of a dozen other dogs, and under other distractions.

If such classes are not available, you can train your dog alone. But you must practice in the presence of neighborhood dogs, at shopping centers where many people are passing by, and even when people are tempting the dog in some way—for instance, tempting the dog to get up when you have ordered it to lie down and stay put.

If you train at home, you will need something more than just a book on obedience training. You will need the latest copy of the American Kennel Club's booklet *Obedience Regulations*. Single copies of this can be obtained without charge by writing to the American Kennel Club, 51 Madison Ave., New York, N.Y., 10010. Since, in a given week, the AKC gets as many as 50,000 letters, address yours to the "Publications Department," or to "Obedience Regulations."

This booklet gives the general regulations. And then it very carefully outlines each step of each exercise. It also explains scoring procedures and maximum scores allowed for each exercise or part of it. It also gives, by word and by drawing, specifications for building your own bar, high jump, and broad jump standards. The dumbbells which are used are not easily made at home. But you can purchase these at all dog shows, and at some pet shops.

There is some danger in obedience training. This is that you will train so severely as to bore your dog. Or, too much competition may bore the dog which must repeat the same exercises over and over. Competition in the show ring helps to avoid this. But you must always be careful not to over-train your dog. This is less of a problem in field work because conditions are always different—different wind conditions, different cover, etc. But in obedience competition, the tests are always the same, and every effort is made to keep them identical, not only for each dog, but at trial after trial.

There are some slight differences in procedures in Canada, Mexico, and Bermuda. So sometimes it helps if you take your dog to one of these countries. Many people do this by arranging to attend the foreign shows while on vacation. In Canada, a club can give two shows in the same building on a weekend. In some cases, three shows are given. So your dog has a chance to complete a title in a single three day weekend. And, of course, it can win a bench championship at the same show. Bermuda offers four shows in one week during early November. Mexico City has four shows on the same grounds over two successive weekends the last of November and early December.

These shows offer sufficient differences to keep your dog excited and interested. They offer you a chance to win foreign titles. And you have unusual opportunities for vacation fun and sight seeing at the same time.

In closing this chapter, we are quoting the purpose of obedience trials, as given in the AKC booklet *Obedience Regulations.*

"Obedience trials are a sport and all participants should be guided by the principles of good sportsmanship both in and outside of the ring. The purpose of obedience trials is to demonstrate the usefulness of the purebred dog as a companion of man, not merely the dog's ability to follow specified routines in the obedience ring. While all contestants in a class are required to perform the same exercises in substantially the same way so that relative quality of the various performances may be compared and scored, the basic objective of obedience trials is to produce dogs that have been trained and conditioned always to behave in the home, in public places, and in the presence of other dogs, in a manner that will reflect credit on the sport of obedience. The performances of dog and handler in the ring must be accurate and correct and must conform to the requirements of these regulations. However, it is also essential that the dog demonstrate willingness and enjoyment of its work, and smoothness and naturalness on the part of the handler are to be preferred to a performance based on military precision and peremptory commands."

To this, we can only add that when you get into the obedience ring for the first time, the chances are the dog will make fewer mistakes than will you. So don't expect to make winning performances until you have gained plenty of experience yourself.

# 40

# Some Thoughts on Color

IN Chapter 4, we wrote about the tail-less Brittany Spaniel. At one time, a controversy raged in France on this subject. The argument even spread to the United States and Canada. Many people thought that a dog born with a tail should not be registered as a Brittany Spaniel. A tail-less dog to be forever a mark of the purity of the breed, as well as a distinctive feature of the breed.

Had such a provision been kept in the standard, all other features, including hunting desire, nose, pointing instinct, stamina, and coat would have been sacrificed for a feature which has nothing to do with hunting ability.

Eventually, good sense won out and the argument was dropped. As an aside, in the early days in the United States, some "converts" from Pointer and Setter ranks, wanted a long tailed Brittany. This idea, too, was finally dropped, though not until after long and sometimes bitter arguments.

Now a somewhat similar situation exists as to color. Recently, a Brittany old-timer said to the author: "Juan Pugibet had those awful liver and white dogs." Well, there was nothing wrong with them. And in any case, Pugibet had both colors.

The early Brittanies in the American Kennel Club records were listed as being of various colors. Among them one finds orange and white, white and orange, liver and white, white and liver, red and white, white and red, lemon and white, and mahogany and white. There were dogs spotted with these colors, ticked with them, and there were roans.

All of these dogs had one ability in common. They could hunt. The original prejudice against any but orange and white—or white and orange—seems to have come from Alan Stuyvesant. And because he was the greatest of all importers, orange and white came to dominate the American sporting scene. These dogs simply were numerically superior.

The great performances of Gwennec de l'Argoat, under the handling of "Hall of Famer" René Joubert, quite naturally focused the attention of Midwest sportsmen on orange and white dogs. Howard Clements and Allamuchy Valley Luke had a similar influence in the Chicago area. Fenntus, Gwennec's Pascey II, and others of that day also tilted sportsmen in favor of the orange and whites.

Still, the other colors were fairly well represented. John C. Weiler was a pioneer breeder who seems to be nearly forgotten today. On Dec. 8, 1935, his Franche's Smarty (a daughter of Franche du Cosquerou), whelped a litter which included Margot De Basgard, a mahogany and white bitch. The sire was Keryvon de Basgard. Weiler had both colors, and Franche's Smarty produced both. When bred to Gwennec de l'Argoat, she produced Dr. Chester Keough's noted Mirabile Dictu, an orange and white. Weiler sold the mahogany and white, Spring Hill Sandy to Julien Clark of Natchez, Miss.

Louis de la Fleche, one of the early importers and pioneers, bought dogs from l'Abbe Feurgard. And from them he got both orange and white and liver and white. Basgard got both colors because l'Abbe Feurgard bred for performance, and without regard to color. Keryvon de Basgard was orange and white, Keryvette, liver and white.

Juan Pugibet and Dr. Keough had the same philosophy. Thus, Dr. Keough imported the liver and white Leltic de Pradalan from Jean Quemener. Leltic (often misspelled Lettic) was by Fanch de Pradalan out of Follette II de Pradalan.

Weiler's Pouponne du Stormally was also mahogany and white. Pouponne was whelped Jan. 19, 1936, by Franche du Cosquerou out of Hase de la Casa Blanca. Thus, Pouponne represents a crossing of the best blood of the dogs imported by Thebaud and Pugibet.

Howard P. Cline's Ch. Benedictine MacEochaidh was the first liver and white to win a bench championship. The sire was Idoc de Cornouaille, the dam, Leltic de Pradalan, whelped Sept. 9, 1941. Benedictine was the 10th dog to win a show championship.

Fld. Ch. Fisty
Miss Kaer, owned
by Nathan
Butchard.

An early liver and white, Gar Roux, bred by Donald L. Benjamin.

Here, perhaps, there should be a word of explanation. Dual Champion Britt of Bellows Falls, bred by Edgar Lutz of Montrose, Pa., and owned by Lucien Ufford of Bellows Falls, Vt. was the first dog to win an American Kennel Club field championship and the first to win a dual title. He was whelped July 15, 1941.

There is an old saying that "records live, opinions die." But in the case of Britt of Bellows Falls, all the records seem to be wrong. The American Kennel Club stud book, which is the official breeding record, lists Britt as having been white with liver markings. Neither the author nor anyone else who personally remembers Britt, considers this to be correct. Moreover, Britt was by Kaer de Cornouaille out of Oged of Casa Blanca. Both were orange and white. It would be impossible to get liver and white from such a breeding.

Earlier records have listed Kaymore's Megs as having been the first liver and white dual champion. If Britt of Bellows Falls was truly white and liver, then he would rank as both the first liver and white field champion and the first liver and white dual champion.

However, the earlier records are wrong in another respect. Dr. R. C. Busteed's Broad Archer of Richmont is listed as a dual champion. This is an error. He was a field champion only. He was also liver and white, and he was certainly one of the great field dogs of his day.

To return from this rather lengthy aside, there have been—and are—some very great liver and white dogs. And we have shown that some of the very good producers yielded both colors. The rule must always be to breed for type and performance, and both come in both colors. Those, therefore, who hold a prejudice against one color may be limiting their breeding success, and may be harming the breed as well.

Earlier, we have mentioned Dr. R. C. Busteed. He is a professor of genetics at the West Texas State University at Canyon. He is surely one of the world's greatest geneticists, and he has been "practicing what he preaches" for 30 years. His success is legendary.

Dr. Busteed has bred brother and sister together for at least 15 generations. This is the closest possible inbreeding. Others who have tried this have generally failed. Often, they have lost size and breeding potency, and sometimes disposition or basic health. Dr. Busteed's dogs have lost none of these.

In this section, we are interested only in color. Since the early days enough liver and white Brittany Spaniels have performed brilliantly to prove that color is not truly a factor in field performance.

Ch. Ultra-Mend Jackie (Ch. Ultra-Mend Jacques ex Ch. Gold-stone Ultra-Mend Sioux), owned by Frank W. McHugh.

In the chapter on the Brittany Spaniel in France, a French breeder reported that orange and whites had died out in North Africa because they could not stand the intense heat. On the other hand, the liver and white dogs prospered.

It is difficult to believe this, except as it proves that the liver and whites have stamina and nose which are not affected by intense heat. Aside from this, behavior and performance are too complex to ascribe them to one factor, in this case—color. Orange and white dogs taken to North Africa may have come from a strain which carried factors for weak performance in heat, which other orange and whites would not have inherited.

In the United States and Canada, black is a disqualifying color in Brittany Spaniels. But this offers no problem. American and Canadian dogs are totally free, hereditarily, of any gene for black. Unless someone should import a French Brittany which carries a black gene, there can never be a black Brittany in either country. As Dr. Busteed has pointed out, any Brittany in America which shows up with black is a mongrel. Should this happen, the situation should be reported to the American Kernel Club, and an investigation made so that the dog's registration papers can be destroyed.

The current policy of the American Kennel Club is to register any dogs whose papers seem to be in order regardless of disqualifying factors. Thus the AKC will register a white Boxer even though such a dog would be disqualified in the show ring. This permits unscrupulous breeders to cut the throats of legitimate breeders by advertising—and selling—"rare white Boxers" at prices which cannot be obtained for properly colored dogs.

But, since black cannot occur in pure bred Brittany Spaniels in North America, the presence of black would indicate a mis-mating. If, then, the matter were to be brought to the attention of the American Kennel Club, it is possible that the registration of that liter, and its puppies, would be cancelled.

Liver is the result of a gene which is dominant over one for orange, so that a dog with both genes will invariably be liver. If two liver dogs, both of which contain hidden genes for orange, are mated, some orange pups may result. Such pups are pure for orange, and can only produce orange. Factors for roan and ticking appear to be different, that is, to differ from each other.

This chapter is not meant to be a treatise on genetics. Its purpose is only to try to place the question of color in its proper perspective. There are far more important matters for breeders of Brittany Spaniels to consider. These are stamina, nose, pointing instinct, intelligence, and shyness, to name but a few.

# 41

# The American Brittany Club

THE American Brittany Club is a member club of the American Kennel Club. It is also recognized by the American Field as the official breed sponsor. The American Brittany club is composed of many regional or local clubs, located from coast to coast, and from north to south.

Brittany Spaniel owners will find a breed club reasonably close. These clubs hold regular meetings to discuss breed problems. They conduct training sessions, fun trials, and informal match shows. Each club also holds a licensed field trial in the spring and in the fall of each year. Many also hold licensed unbenched shows, either in conjunction with one of their field trials, or at other times of the year.

Membership in one of the regional clubs carries with it an automatic membership in the American Brittany Club. Cost is $10 a year. Memberships run from January 1st to December 31st. A half year membership is available after July 1st for $7. You can join a regional club in your area. Or, if no club is close, you can join the American Brittany Club as a member at large. Thus, Brittany Spaniel owners in Canada, Mexico, Alaska, Hawaii, or the Caribbean Islands can join.

If you elect to join a regional club, you make application to join directly to it. If you wish to join the parent club as a member at large, then make your application directly to it. The address is:

> The American Brittany Club
> 2515 Oakley
> Kansas City, Missouri 64127

The parent club publishes a monthly magazine *The American Brittany*. Either type of membership entitles you to receive the magazine without cost to you. This magazine is sent to members only, although single copies can be bought for $1 each. The magazine is one of the most distinguished breed publications in America. It has repeatedly won national honors in the annual competitions sponsored by the Dog Writers Association of America.

In 1958, more then 50 breed magazines were submitted in the awards competitions of this organization. At that time, Dr. S. Allen Truex was editor. The judges gave the magazine first place. This is extraordinary, if one considers that Dr. Truex had to put the magazine together during whatever time a dog fancier and a doctor has to spare.

Twice since, under Dr. Fred Z. White as editor, the magazine won either first or honorable mention. Again publishing and editing the magazine had to be done in Dr. White's spare time. Dr. White also won honors for special articles contributed to the magazine. Mrs. Nicky Bissell has continued the high quality of the magazine. She is one of the greatest statisticians in the history of any breed.

Yet the magazine—and the American Brittany Club—have now grown until being executive secretary and editor at the same time have become too great for one person. Now Mrs. LaReine Pittman of the Missouri Club will take over the statistical work. Mrs. Pittman is adequately qualified to do this, being a statistical expert in her own right. In recent years, as art editor, George Giesler has done an exceptional job, so that the magazine is tastefully arranged and produced.

The magazine was first founded in 1942 by Dr. David Ruskin and Jack L. Whitworth. Edgar Averill then became editor and A. H. Ady business manager. It was called the *Brittany Field and Bench*. However, there were not enough members to sustain such a magazine. So for a time it was published as a bulletin.

Jack Whitworth operated the print shop of what was then Hotel

Cleveland. Eventually, he took over as publisher and editor. In 1949, Ed McKernan and Evelyn Monte became editors. Mrs. Monte wrote a dog column for a Newark, N.J. newspaper, and later joined Harry Miller in the Gaines Dog Research Center. She also served for a time as president of the Dog Writers Association of America. She, therefore, did a great deal to help the breed quite apart from her editorship of the magazine.

When the American Brittany Club was incorporated—under Ohio law—the name of the magazine was changed to the *American Brittany*. Hugo Blasberg joined Mrs. Monte as an editor. Then George Monk and later R. R. Machlett Jr. joined her.

In 1957, Dr. S. Allen Truex became secretary of the American Brittany Club, and also editor of the magazine. At that time, Dr. Fred Z. White became advertising manager. Later, Dr. White took over the editorship until, in 1964, Mrs. Bissel became the editor. It should be noted also that Dr. White's wife, Ann, played a major role in getting out the magazine. You will recognize them in their kennel name, Fredan.

When the American Brittany Club was first formed, it named two people honorary members. These were René Joubert who, after the closing of the French Line office in Detroit during the war years, had moved to Houston, Tex., and Dr. Chester Keough. Both had played a great part in popularizing the Brittany Spaniel.

Honorary members have to be elected by the Board of Directors. Over the years, the following people have been so honored.

**E. W. "Bill" Averill** (now Edgar W. Averill, Ph.D.) is still active as a show and obedience judge.

**Howard P. Clements.** His Allamuchy Valley Luke brought the breed to the attention of Chicago area sportsmen. He served as club president, and helped to organize the national trials. He was national trials chairman for some years.

**Coy Conwell.** His greatest contribution to the breed came in the organization of the regional clubs. This was a highly complex problem, and his success became a major factor in the growth of the breed.

**Paul Dawson.** He judged one of the earliest trials, and became so fascinated with the Brittany that, for a time, he trained some. He was one of the breed's most respected early judges.

**Jerome N. Halle.** Mr. Halle judged the first licensed bench show and a number of specialty shows after that time. He helped to write the American standard, and he campaigned Brittanies on the bench and in the field. He had the unique experience of winning a Brittany and a Beagle field championship and a Brittany show championship on the same weekend.

**René Joubert.** He took over the dogs of Louis A. Thebaud and competed with them in Michigan bird dog trials. The performances of those dogs made the Michigan and Ohio area the American capital of Brittanydom for a time. One can credit his work for the election of the Brittany Spaniel as the Michigan State Dog.

**Dr. Chester H. Keough.** Dr. Keough, as mentioned earlier, was one of the true founders of the breed. He brought in some of the earliest liver and white dogs. And he and Juan Pugibet used the breeding stock of each other with great success.

**Walter B. Kleeman.** The name of Walter Kleeman appears throughout this book. He served as president of the club, and he helped to finance it in its dark periods. Klemanor became a great name in Brittany history. But it was the time and intelligent efforts Mr. Kleeman gave to the club and breed which make him an immortal.

**Jack T. Mayer.** Jack Mayer was—and is—a bird dog trainer. He brought the Brittany Spaniel to the great woodcock and grouse areas of New Brunswick. His success with Britts assured the breed's success in Canada. He has judged the nationals.

**Laurence E. Richardson.** A pioneer importer and breeder who helped to organize the Brittany Spaniel Club of North America. Later, he participated in the merging of that club with the American Brittany Club. His genuine sportsmanship was a major factor in the merger.

**Maxwell Riddle.** He is credited with being a leader in drawing up the breed standard. He also went to New York to plead the cause of the American Brittany Club in its fight for recognition.

**Alan Stuyvesant.** He was the breed's greatest importer. He also placed great dogs in various parts of the United States and Canada with sportsmen who would keep the breed before the public. Stuyvesant also went personally to France to select dogs for other American breeders and sportsmen. He was president of the ABC for a time.

**Lucien Ufford.** He owned the first field champion, the first dual champion, and the first futurity winner. Ufford also campaigned his dogs against the best Pointers and English Setters in Canada. In doing so, he helped to establish the breed in Eastern Canada, and particularly in the Maritime Provinces.

**Dr. Fred Z. White.** Dr. White edited the magazine for some years, and he also served as secretary of the American Brittany Club. Without his genius for administration, the ABC could hardly be the strong club it now is. The magazine is still published under the policies Dr. White established. He bred two dual champions, Saxon of Fredann and Fredan's Buddy. Probably his election should have included his wife, Ann.

**James Bell, Jr.** He and his wife Marcelle campaigned a great many dogs, and produced three dual champions—Belloaks Ibby, Belloaks High Flyer, and their son, Belloaks King. All were at one time campaigning together. The Bells won the national amateur championship twice, with Marcelle handling. James Bell gave the American Brittany Club a great deal of financial support.

**W. E. Stevenson.** Mr. Stevenson trained and campaigned all his own dogs. Among his great Helgramite dogs were Howie D'Acajou, Shamandre, Tarquinius, Chip, and Howie. For years, he was the top amateur handler, and he was certainly one of the breed's greatest trainers. He used to campaign only two dogs at a time. They were always "house dogs" and he proved that a house dog could be a great field dog as well. Many have made such a claim. Mr. Stevenson proved it. His two sons are active in the breed; one as a vice president of the ABC, the other in setting eastern field trials dates.

**Robert Buick.** Among his great "Edough" dogs were Dual Ch. Patsy of Edough, Dual Ch. Mandy of Edough, and Dual Ch. Amos of Edough. The latter is the only dual champion of the breed to get a first in the sporting group at a dog show. Buick had a remarkably keen eye for field performance. He was successful in getting many to train and campaign the pups he sold them. He was a Chicago contractor. He died in California totally blind.

**Howard Crippen.** Mr. Crippen owned the immortal Pontac's Dingo. His Hero's Master Spot was a great field dog which suddenly dropped dead while still a young, hard-going field dog. He was a master handler, and handled many dogs for others though himself an amateur.

**Thurmond MacWhorter, Sr.** Mr. MacWhorter lived at Bakersfield, Cal. He and his son, a veterinarian crippled by polio, formed the California Club and kept it going until the '60s. Without him there would be no California club.

**Henry Holleyoak.** Henry Holleyoak lived at the time when the great center of Brittany activity was in Michigan, Ohio, and Illinois. Therefore, he had to buck the best of the breed. Yet he became an oustanding breeder, particularly of bench dogs. He owned the dual champions, Holley Haven Duchess and Holley Haven Casey. His Ch. Holley Haven Sugar is the all-time winner among bitches.

He was a gentleman who never spoke against other people's dogs, and he always strived to produce dual purpose dogs.

**Dr. R. C. Busteed.** Dr. Busteed is a professor of genetics at West Texas State University at Canyon, but he began breeding Brittany Spaniels in 1941 while living in North Carolina. He bred the first liver and white field champion, Broad Archer of Richmond. His inbreeding program has produced one of the world's purest strains in any breed. One of his great dogs was Dual Ch. Tex of Richmont.

**John W. Lee.** The Leeway dogs have been prominent for many years. Mr. Lee has been president of the American Brittany Club, has been chairman of the Futurity, and has headed the legal division. But his devotion to the cause has made him a willing helper in all departments of the club.

**Jack L. Whitworth.** Mr. Whitworth was one of the organizers of the American Brittany Club. During the early years, he kept the magazine going even when it was losing money. He was prominent at both trials and shows. His great dog was Dual Ch. Avono Happy.

**Gerald Price.** Mr. Price founded his Way Kan Kennels in 1951. He quickly became one of the best known breeder-trainer-handlers in America. Two of his bitches—Price's Sunflower Gal and Way Kan Jill—are in the Brittany Spaniel Hall of Fame. *Sports Afield* named three of his breeding—Way Kan Mandy, Way Kan Jill, and Way Kan Jeff—"Brittany of the year." He has been a member of the Midwest Club for many years.

## Member Clubs

At the present time there are many functioning regional specialty clubs in the United States that are also member clubs of the American Brittany Club. As in the parent organization, officers change frequently. Anyone interested in contacting a member Brittany Club should contact the Secretary of the American Brittany Club (through the American Kennel Club, 51 Madison Avenue, New York, N.Y. 10010) who will have the names of all current member club Secretaries.

**East Coast**

Central New England
Del-Val
Eastern New England
Edisto

Greater Atlanta
Hudson Valley
Maryland
North Jersey
Southeastern

Southern New England
Susquehanna
Upper New York

**East Central**

Buckeye
Greater Indianapolis
Hoosier
Kentucky
Michigan
Michigan-Saginaw
Ohio
Pennsylvania
Western Michigan

**Central**

Badger
Greater Milwaukee
Greater St. Louis
Illinois
Iowa
LaSalle
Minnesota
Missouri
Volunteer

**Midwest**

Alamo
Fort Worth

Hawkeye
Lone Star
Midwest
Missouri Valley
Nebraska
North Oklahoma
Ringneck
Skyline
Sooner
Southern Kansas
Stillwater
Sunland
Texas Coastal
Top O' Texas
West Texas

**West Coast**

California
Central California
Golden Empire
Greater Phoenix
Idaho
Northern California
Oregon
Sahuaro
San Diego
South San Joaquin
Washington

# Appendix

The material which follows is taken directly from the files of the American Kennel Club. It is presented here through the courtesy of A. Hamilton Rowan Jr., former secretary of the American Kennel Club. These records give the organization date of the Brittany Spaniel Club, and the later change in its officers.

In a letter dated May 1, 1944, Laurence Richardson reported to Jack Whitworth that Miss Clara Perry had escaped from France on the last ship to leave before France fell to the Germans.

Mr. Richardson, an army officer, had just been placed on inactive duty for the duration of the war. Louis de la Fleche had returned to France. Apparently, he had taken the club's files with him, and he could not be reached by mail. We quote here from Mr. Richardson's letter.

> "I have no list of the old club members. I find a letter dated May 10, 1939, from Mr. Stuyvesant which says: 'Unfortunately we have not got M. de la Fleche's files. I don't know whether he took them away to Europe with him, but Mr. Thebaud, when he asked me to take over the reorganization of the club, was unable to find them.'"

Later, as will be seen, Mr. Whitworth was able to reach M. de la Fleche, and did get his approval for the merger of the two clubs.

## BRITTANY SPANIEL

Admitted to the American Kennel Club Stud Book at the Aug. 1934 Board Meeting. Standard of perfection received from the French Kennel Club in July 1934.

Translation of the Standard of Perfection sent in by Miss Clara G. Perry approved by the American Kennel Club—March 12, 1935.

Mr. Arthur F. Jones wrote the Article on the Brittany Spaniel which appeared in the 1935 edition of Pure-Bred Dogs.

Mr. Louis A. Thebaud was the person who brought up the question of recognizing this breed.

June 19, 1944.

Mr. Jack L. Whitworth, Sec'y,
American Brittany Club,
Nagel Road,
Avon, Ohio.

Dear Mr. Whitworth:

        I am in receipt of your letter of
June 6th, with its enclosures.

        I am certainly glad to learn that
you have finally been able to accomplish the amalga-
mation of the two Brittany Spaniel clubs. It is a
real job to do a thing of this kind and the documentary
evidence shows that a real job was done in this case.

        I will bring the merger before the
Directors of the Kennel Club at their July meeting and
I have no fear that it will not be approved; the name
of the member club being changed from the Brittany
Spaniel Club of North America to that of the American
Brittany Club.

                        Very truly yours,

                        H. D. Bixby,
                        Executive Vice-President.

hdb:jb

July 14, 1944.

Mr. Jack L. Whitworth, Secretary,
American Brittany Club,
Nagel Road,
Avon, Ohio.

Dear Mr. Whitworth:

        The Board of Directors of the American
Kennel Club at their meeting on July 11 approved the change
in name of our member club from that of the Brittany Spaniel
Club of North America to the "American Brittany Club".

        There was no occasion for them to formally
approve the merger, but they asked me to write you and the
officials who had charge of working out the merger, complimenting
them on the very efficient and complete way in which the matter
was accomplished. It is a pleasure to see such careful work
done as was evident in this case, and I wish to compliment you
upon finally effecting the change, which I sincerely believe
will be for the betterment of the Brittany Spaniel.

                        Very truly yours,

                        H.D. Bixby,
                        Executive Vice-President.

HDB:PBE.

**These letters from the American Kennel Club are part of the correspondence
concerning the merger of the Brittany Spaniel Club of North America and
the American Brittany Club.**

American Brittany Club

CLUB NAME — LICENSED — MEMBER ✓ — LOCATION

| SHOW DATES | JUDGES APPROVED | PROOFS RETURNED | PREMIUM LIST CHECKED | FEE RECEIVED | DEPOSIT RETURNED | SUPT. | O.T. | REMARKS |
|---|---|---|---|---|---|---|---|---|
| Nov. 27, 1943 | 11-4 | 11-9 | ✓ | $25   11-8-43. | | Riddle | | |
| " 11, 1944 | 8-15 | 10-4 | | | | | | |
| " 20, 1945 | 8-20 | 10-5 | ✓ | | | | | Embreached Fried $10. Fined $10. |
| " 8, 1946 | 9-6 | 10-3 | ✓ | | | S.S. | | |
| " 28, 1947 | 10-29 | 10-29 | ✓ | | | S.S. | | |
| " 19, 1948 | 9-20 | 9-20 | ✓ | | | | | |
| May 16, 1949 | 3-1 | 3-29 | | $15  4-1-49? | | | | Ravenna, Ohio. |
| Nov. 11, 1949 | 9-1 | 9-22 | | $25 dep. ⟩ 9-25 | | S.S. | | Carbondale, Ill. |
| " 3, 1950 | | | | $25 dep ⟩ 9-25 $15 fee | | S.S. | | |
| Dec. 1, 1950 | 8-16 | 8 | | $25 dep. 1/10 fee'd | $50 ret'd 3-15-51 | | | |
| Nov. 26, 1951 | 9-21 | 10/8 | | $25  dep 9-22 | | | | |
| " 30, 1952 | 7-30 | | | $15   8-13   1-28-53 | | | | |
| " 8, 1952 | | 10-7 | | | | | | |

SEE NEW CARD

11C-1M 6-49

# JOINT RESOLUTION BY

The Board of Directors of the American Brittany Club, hereinafter referred to as the ABC, and the Board of Directors and/or properly authorized agents and/or highest available ranking officers of the Brittany Spaniel Club of North America, hereinafter referred to as the BSC of NA.

Whereas, the ABC and the BSC of NA have each held a meeting according to the constitution of their respective clubs, and

Whereas, the ABC and the BSC of NA have each independently considered their activities affecting themselves, their members, the other Brittany spaniel clubs and all other organizations having an interest in the Brittany spaniel, and

Whereas, the BSC of NA, a member club of the American Kennel Club, has not been active for several years and has not shown any interest in the promotion of Brittany spaniels, bench shows or field trials, and

Whereas, the BSC of NA is not in a position to fully discharge its duties to the Brittany spaniel breed, its members, owners and breeders, and

Whereas, the ABC, an active club of Brittany spaniel owners and breeders, and recognized by the American Field (F. D. S. B.), has been active and is able to continue to be actively helpful to owners and breeders of Brittany spaniels, its members and non-members; and

Whereas, the ABC is unable otherwise, at the present time, to obtain free action as the parent club, and fully discharge its duties to breeders and owners of Brittany spaniels and its members, and

Whereas, at the present time, neither the BSC of NA or the ABC are able to obtain complete recognition and become the approved authority of the breed in this country;

## Be it Hereby Resolved, that

1. The ABC and BSC of NA are separately and jointly in favor of a merger of the two clubs.

2. Such merger should be dependent upon a majority vote of each qualified member of each club.

3. For the purpose of convenience, the vote shall be taken by closed ballot, jointly, for each club.

4. Each club shall count the ballots from their members independently from those of the other club.

5. A majority shall be required by each club to enable the ABC and BSC of NA to effect a merger.

6. A majority shall mean a majority of ballots returned, except when, due to conditions of war, a ballot unreturned from a member in the armed forces, if entitled to a vote, shall be construed to mean a vote against the merger.

7. Should the members of each club indicate, as above, that a merger is favored, such merger shall take effect not more than 60 days following the announcement to all voting members of the results.

8. Not less than 10 or more than 14 days shall be allowed from the time the ballots are mailed to the time the ballots are counted.

9. Ballots shall be numbered and each eligible voter assigned a number, a complete list of voters with their addresses and numbers shall be supplied to Mr. Frank L. Grant, 145 E. 209th St., Euclid, Ohio, who shall have the duty of checking and mailing the ballots and to whom the ballots must be returned. A notarized statement of the results shall be furnished the secretaries of each club by Mr. Grant, but the actual ballots shall be sealed and remain in his possession.

10. Ballots should be clearly printed to indicate their purpose, identical ballots being supplied to all eligible voters, by mail, of both clubs.

11. All records of above action are to be kept in a safety deposit box for a period of 7 years under the name of ballot supervisor, the expenses of which are to be carried by the ABC.

12. There shall be no contest of the ballots after 60 days following the merger.

## Be it Further Resolved, that

1. The two clubs will become one.

2. The revised organization shall be known as the American Brittany Club and shall operate under the Constitution of the original American Brittany Club as of January 1, 1944.

3. No changes in the constitution, mentioned above, be made until after the next annual election, which shall be postponed to such date as to make it possible to hold a general meeting at the same time as the Bench Show and Field Trial of 1944 sponsored by the original American Brittany Club.

4. All offices of the revised American Brittany Club be held by the present officers of the original American Brittany Club as of this date until the 1944 general election.

5. All active members of the Brittany Spaniel Club of North America be automatically admitted to paid up membership of the revised ABC for the year, and entitled to all rights and privileges equal to those of the members of the original ABC.

6. All officers now holding office with the BSC of NA shall be considered as still holding such office jointly until next election with the present officers of the ABC, wherever there are similar offices in both organizations.

7. The function of the officers, until next election, shall be as follows:

   (a) President: The officer holding this office in the original ABC shall continue to retain all former duties and functions, and shall in all cases be the presiding officer. In case the president's power to vote is ever called upon, it shall be paired with that of his jointly holding officer from the BSC of NA before it is counted.

   (b) All other officers representing the two clubs hold the same relationship to each other as the two presidents.

   (c) The officers from the original ABC shall, in all cases, until election, be the functioning officers.

   (d) The officers from the BSC of NA shall hold what amounts to honorary office, whose assistance may be called upon by his ABC counterpart, but whose policy forming duties and powers, until next election, are purely veto in character, in which case they may pair off their votes against those of their ABC counterparts.

8. The new American Brittany Club shall apply for, and be empowered to transfer, with the approval of the American Kennel Club, all parent membership rights and privileges of the AKC to itself from the Brittany Spaniel Club of North America.

9. Such AKC membership transfer shall not involve any transfer of funds, the AKC being empowered to credit the new ABC with the membership funds now held by AKC.

10. No act or action by any member or officer shall be construed as obligating or cancelling or transferring of obligations or funds of any member, officer or club to any other member, officer or club, except as mentioned above.

11. The transfer of ownership of the membership fee deposited with the AKC shall have no effect, past, present or future upon obligations to or by members of, officers of or the organizations of the ABC or the BSC of NA.

12. As soon as merger is effected, a commission of not more than 3 men be appointed by the original ABC president, and approved by the highest available ranking officer of the original BSC of NA, and instructed to clarify the standards of the Brittany spaniel, with explanatory notes, for adoption by the new ABC and the American Kennel Club, such work to be completed and ready for submission to the club one month before the next annual meeting.

NOTE: Original, used above, applies to status immediately before merger of either club.

*Signed by*

*Jack L. Whitworth, Secretary*
**American Brittany Club**

*Louis N. de la Fleche, Secretary*
**Brittany Spaniel Club of N. America**

Revised List of Members of the Brittany Spaniel Club of
North America and the American Brittany Club Now Merged
and Known as the

## American Brittany Club
### (January 1, 1944)

Adams, Mrs. Katherine
Ady, A. H.
Ady, Mildred
Alford, Mrs. S. E.
Ashworth, R. D.
Averill, Edgar W.
Baldridge, Raymond H.
Barcroft, Gladys
Barcroft, W. H.*
Batson, Dr. G. C.
Becht, William J.
Becker, Dr. R.
Benjamin, Donald L.
Blohm, Wallace
Bray, Dr. Harry A.
Britton, E. D.
Brown, Thomas M.
Burnham, Mike
Burnside D. R.
Busteed, Dr. Robert
Clements, Howard P.
Cline, Hal P.
Conover, H. B.
Conwell, Coy M.
Cooley, Dr. R. M.
Corbin, George A.
Cox, Thomas W.
Cullen, Jack
Danforth, R. E.
Dasher, Don E.
Dell, Kenneth
Denne, Walter
Detmold, G. W.
Doerr, J. Paul
Elliot, Dr. E. S.
Erhardt, George*
Evans, Scott
Feeley, James
Feeley, Mrs. Mildred
Ferguson, Sen. Homer
Felt, Harold B.
de la Fleche, Louis
Frank, C. E.
French, Lee I.
Fisher, H. J.
Fitzpatrick, Thomas C.
Floyd, L. B.
Forthofer, Dr. C. H.
Galloway, Edgar B.

Gayek, Bill
Gee, Joseph Sr.
Germain, U. E.
Gillen, J. J.
Gillen, Tommy*
Hacquoil, James A.
Haehnle, Casper
Halle, Jerome N.*
Hamill, James L. III
Hamill, Dorothy B.
Hanlon, Miss Ainslee
Heffner, A. D.
Higbie, Western
Hostetter, Harry B.
Hughes, Ralph E.
Joubert, Réne
Katterheinrich, V. E.
Kerr, S. H.
Keil, William E.
Keogh, Dr. Chester H.
Kern, Fred
Kleeman, Walter B.
Lankester, Stephen
Larson, Wallace*
Larson, Mrs. May*
Laughter, John
Lucas, Paul A.
Lynch, Dr. Charles C.
MacMichaels, Jack
Martin, William K.
Maul, Carl
McCurdy, R. B.
McWhorter, Thrumond
Moulton, Dr. Allen
Mowbray, Frank W.
Nothstine, Lloyd
Nothstine, R. M.
Oberlin, W. S.
Olson, Thorwald
Patterson, L. D.
Pease, H. Randall
Perry, George B.
Perry, Miss Clara
Peterson, Hilmer
Plank, Edward
Plyler, C. P.
Plyler, Lena B.*
Powers, Jack
Pringnitz, Louis A.

Reed, Fred T.
Richardson, Laurence E.
Riddle, Maxwell
Ritts, Elias E.
Ruskin, Dr. D. B.
Roush, J. R.
Savage, Terry
Schaufelberger, Hugo S.
Schmidt, William T.*
Scoonover, H. M.
Shepard, Ernest E.
Smiley, R. Z.
Spangler, Robert M.
Sprague, L. M.
Smith, Howard M.
Stafford, T. C.
Starke, James*
Stinchcomb, Keith V.
Stobie, George J.
Strobel, Lester A.
Stout, Lee H.
Stuit, Melvin R.
Stuyvesant, Allan R.
Tasche, Dr. Leslie W.
Todd, William V.
Ufford, Laurence J.
Ufford, Mrs. Laurence J.*
Ufford, Lucien H.
Ufford, Mrs. L. H.*
Van Buren, Robert S.
Vietto, John
Waller, Don
Wassau, Herb
Warren, D. M.
Wheeler, George C.
White, J. G.
Whitin, Paul Jr.
Whitworth, Jack L.
Whitworth, Genevieve
Williams, Charles L.
Williams, Mrs. Charles L.
Williams, Walden J.*
Wittig, Dorothy
Wood, E. L.
Yant, Dr. J. R.
Yoder, Ivan
Yoder, Paul

* Denotes Associate Member

# BIBLIOGRAPHY

ALL OWNERS of pure-bred dogs will benefit themselves and their dogs by enriching their knowledge of breeds and of canine care, training, breeding, psychology and other important aspects of dog management. The following list of books covers further reading recommended by judges, veterinarians, breeders, trainers and other authorities. Books may be obtained at the finer book stores and pet shops, or through Howell Book House Inc., publishers, New York, N.Y.

## Breed Books

AFGHAN HOUND, Complete — *Miller & Gilbert*
AIREDALE, Complete — *Edwards*
ALASKAN MALAMUTE, Complete — *Riddle & Seeley*
BASSET HOUND, Complete — *Braun*
BEAGLE, Complete — *Noted Authorities*
BLOODHOUND, Complete — *Brey & Reed*
BOXER, Complete — *Denlinger*
BRITTANY SPANIEL, Complete — *Riddle*
BULLDOG, New Complete — *Hanes*
BULL TERRIER, New Complete — *Eberhard*
CAIRN TERRIER, Complete — *Marvin*
CHIHUAHUA, Complete — *Noted Authorities*
COLLIE, Complete — *Official Publication of the Collie Club of America*
DACHSHUND, The New — *Meistrell*
DOBERMAN PINSCHER, New — *Walker*
ENGLISH SETTER, New Complete — *Tuck & Howell*
ENGLISH SPRINGER SPANIEL, New — *Goodall & Gasow*
FOX TERRIER, New Complete — *Silvernail*
GERMAN SHEPHERD DOG, Complete — *Bennett*
GERMAN SHORTHAIRED POINTER, New — *Maxwell*
GOLDEN RETRIEVER, Complete — *Fischer*
GREAT DANE, New Complete — *Noted Authorities*
GREAT PYRENEES, Complete — *Strang & Giffin*
IRISH SETTER, New — *Thompson*
IRISH WOLFHOUND, Complete — *Starbuck*
KEESHOND, Complete — *Peterson*
LABRADOR RETRIEVER, Complete — *Warwick*
MINIATURE SCHNAUZER, Complete — *Eskrigge*
NEWFOUNDLAND, New Complete — *Chern*
NORWEGIAN ELKHOUND, New Complete — *Wallo*
OLD ENGLISH SHEEPDOG, Complete — *Mandeville*
PEKINGESE, Quigley Book of — *Quigley*
POMERANIAN, New Complete — *Ricketts*
POODLE, New Complete — *Hopkins & Irick*
POODLE CLIPPING AND GROOMING BOOK, Complete — *Kalstone*
PUG, Complete — *Trullinger*
PULI, Complete — *Owen*
ST. BERNARD, New Complete — *Noted Authorities, rev. Raulston*
SAMOYED, Complete — *Ward*
SCHIPPERKE, Official Book of — *Root, Martin, Kent*
SCOTTISH TERRIER, Complete — *Marvin*
SHETLAND SHEEPDOG, New — *Riddle*
SHIH TZU, The (English) — *Dadds*
SIBERIAN HUSKY, Complete — *Demidoff*
TERRIERS, The Book of All — *Marvin*
TOY DOGS, Kalstone Guide to Grooming All — *Kalstone*
TOY DOGS, All About — *Ricketts*
WEST HIGHLAND WHITE TERRIER, Complete — *Marvin*
WHIPPET, Complete — *Pegram*
YORKSHIRE TERRIER, Complete — *Gordon & Bennett*

## Care and Training

DOG OBEDIENCE, Complete Book of — *Saunders*
NOVICE, OPEN AND UTILITY COURSES — *Saunders*
DOG CARE AND TRAINING, Howell Book of — *Howell, Denlinger, Merrick*
DOG CARE AND TRAINING FOR BOYS AND GIRLS — *Saunders*
DOG TRAINING FOR KIDS — *Benjamin*
DOG TRAINING, Koehler Method of — *Koehler*
GO FIND! Training Your Dog to Track — *Davis*
GUARD DOG TRAINING, Koehler Method of — *Koehler*
OPEN OBEDIENCE FOR RING, HOME AND FIELD, Koehler Method of — *Koehler*
SPANIELS FOR SPORT (English) — *Radcliffe*
SUCCESSFUL DOG TRAINING, The Pearsall Guide to — *Pearsall*
TRAIN YOUR OWN GUN DOG, How to — *Goodall*
TRAINING THE RETRIEVER — *Kersley*
TRAINING YOUR DOG TO WIN OBEDIENCE TITLES — *Morsell*
UTILITY DOG TRAINING, Koehler Method of — *Koehler*

## Breeding

ART OF BREEDING BETTER DOGS, New — *Onstott*
HOW TO BREED DOGS — *Whitney*
HOW PUPPIES ARE BORN — *Prine*
INHERITANCE OF COAT COLOR IN DOGS — *Little*

## General

COMPLETE DOG BOOK, The — *Official Pub. of American Kennel Club*
DOG IN ACTION, The — *Lyon*
DOG BEHAVIOR, New Knowledge of — *Pfaffenberger*
DOG JUDGING, Nicholas Guide to — *Nicholas*
DOG NUTRITION, Collins Guide to — *Collins*
DOG PSYCHOLOGY — *Whitney*
DOG STANDARDS ILLUSTRATED
DOGSTEPS, Illustrated Gait at a Glance — *Elliott*
ENCYCLOPEDIA OF DOGS, International — *Dangerfield, Howell & Riddle*
JUNIOR SHOWMANSHIP HANDBOOK — *Brown & Mason*
SUCCESSFUL DOG SHOWING, Forsyth Guide to — *Forsyth*
TRIM, GROOM AND SHOW YOUR DOG, How to — *Saunders*
WHY DOES YOUR DOG DO THAT? — *Bergman*
WORLD OF SLED DOGS, From Siberia to Sport Racing — *Coppinger*
OUR PUPPY'S BABY BOOK (blue or pink)